The American
Political Party System

THE AMERICAN POLITICAL PARTY SYSTEM

CONTINUITY AND CHANGE OVER TEN PRESIDENTIAL ELECTIONS

JOHN S. JACKSON

BROOKINGS INSTITUTION PRESS
Washington, D.C.

Copyright © 2015
THE BROOKINGS INSTITUTION
1775 Massachusetts Avenue, N.W., Washington, D.C. 20036
www.brookings.edu

The Brookings Institution is a private nonprofit organization devoted to research,
education, and publication on important issues of domestic and foreign policy. Its
principal purpose is to bring the highest quality independent research and analysis
to bear on current and emerging policy problems. Interpretations or conclusions in
Brookings publications should be understood to be solely those of the authors.

Library of Congress Cataloging-in-Publication data

Jackson, John S., 1940–
    The transformation of the American political party system : continuity and change
over ten presidential elections / John S. Jackson.
        pages   cm
    Includes bibliographical references.
    ISBN 978-0-8157-2637-1 (pbk. : alk. paper)—ISBN 978-0-8157-2638-8 (e-book)
1. Political parties—United States—History. 2. Two party systems—United
States—History. 3. Political conventions—United States—History. 4. Presidents—
United States—Nomination—History. 5. Presidents—United States—Election—
History. 6. Political culture—United States—History. I. Title.

JK2261.J34 2014
324.273—dc23   2014022511

9 8 7 6 5 4 3 2 1

Printed on acid-free paper

Typeset in Adobe Garamond

Composition by Cynthia Stock
Silver Spring, Maryland

To my wife, Nancy W. Jackson,
for unending love and support that has lasted over half a century

and

To our grandson, Caleb Samuel Jackson,
who I hope grows up in a more rational political world
than the one I have lived in for more than seven decades.

Contents

Preface

Any author of a book that spans over four decades of empirical research and is based on literally thousands of surveys necessarily incurs a multitude of thank-you notes. My obligations are due to a wide variety of people, including scholars, former students, journalists, and staff members at the Paul Simon Institute at Southern Illinois University Carbondale and at the Ray C. Bliss Institute at the University of Akron.

Let me start with John C. Green at the Bliss Institute at the University of Akron. In 1992, after I had been surveying convention delegates since 1976, often working with limited resources, my attention divided by my administrative duties at SIUC, John agreed to become a cosponsor of the surveys. We combined forces and funding, and between 1992 and 2008 we designed the questionnaires and took the surveys together. The joint efforts of the Bliss Institute at Akron and the Simon Institute at SIUC gave the studies a solid grounding and the value of bipartisanship. John and I also co-authored several chapters in the State of the Parties series, which John has edited with several of his colleagues.

I want to offer a special note of thanks to Denise Baer, John C. Green, and Jerome Mileur, who read all or parts of this manuscript and offered very constructive comments and criticisms. The book benefited in many ways from their counsel, although I made the final judgment calls.

Earlier in my career William Crotty, originally at Northwestern University in Chicago and then at Northeastern University in Boston, and I coauthored two books on presidential nominations and elections. Writing and working with Bill, who is widely known and recognized in our discipline, was a pivotal experience in my professional development. I learned much from his storehouse of knowledge about American politics and parties, and I still value his friendship.

My first survey was conducted among delegates to the Democratic Party's midterm convention in Kansas City in December 1974; it was this conference that adopted the party's charter, or constitution. I followed with a survey of the Democratic Party's National Convention in 1976. I did these surveys because I was interested in party change and reform and especially in the impact of the McGovern-Fraser Commission on the parties and on the way we nominate presidents. I was assisted in both of these initial studies by SIU students, who helped take the surveys, code the questionnaires, and turn the questionnaires into punch cards, which was the technology then. We have come a long way in the way we gather and process data now, but the whole enterprise is still very labor intensive. I have had the good fortune to work with many very dedicated students, some of whom wrote research papers, theses, and dissertations based on a secondary analysis of the data.

Some, and surely not all, of these students include, in alphabetical order: Denise Baer, David Bositis, Barbara Brown, Jesse Cecil Brown, Nancy Clayton, Charles Dewitt Dunn, Mark Ellickson, Jane McBride Gates, Paul Glover, Perry Knop, Alan McBride, Tim Millmore, and Bob Slaghter. These former students have gone on to productive and distinguished careers in political science and other fields, and I like to believe that they got a good start here at SIUC working on one of my surveys. Also a note of appreciation to Brad Cole, who along with Denise Baer and Barbara Brown helped obtain the official party lists of delegate names and addresses during the conventions every four years. Of course, thousands of delegates were also crucial to the writing of this book by taking the time to fill out and return my questionnaires.

I also want to recognize the excellent help we received from faculty, students, and staff at the University of Akron, especially John C. Green, Dan Shea, Nathan Bigelow, and Rick Farmer.

The people of the Paul Simon Public Policy Institute deserve my deepest appreciation. I pursued this study through the tenure of four directors: our founder, Senator Paul Simon; his successor, Mike Lawrence; interim director Matt Baughman; and our current director, David Yepsen. Each encouraged and assisted the empirical research and the writing of this book, and I salute them for that help. In addition, staff people have been generous with their time. Earlier, Pam Gwaltney and Chris Rich and, most recently, Vanessa

Sneed and Cary Day provided essential help. Carol Greenlee made especially invaluable contributions.

Many people, at both SIUC and Akron, helped collect and process the data. Most recently, and over the past several years, however, Paul Gottemoller has been my right-hand man on doing the data processing, and I literally could not have done this book without his essential and constant good work.

The party elite data gathered under my direction are supplemented by longitudinal studies done by *CBS News* and the *New York Times*. Their data are used by permission. The party identifiers data were taken from the American National Election Studies conducted every four years by the Center for Political Studies at the University of Michigan and obtained through the Inter-university Consortium for Political and Social Research. Their help is gratefully noted.

My editors at the Brookings Institution Press provided invaluable assistance. Chris Kelaher initially encouraged this project and helped launch it. Later Janet Walker stepped in at a crucial juncture and put the book on track, and her good work ensured its publication. Copy editor Diane Hammond took my sometimes meandering prose and made it much more focused and cogent. I thank them all.

Finally, a special note and tribute to my family and their assistance and support. My children, Jeffrey C. Jackson and Jill Elise Jackson, were barely toddlers when I started this research. They are now adults, grown and gone from Carbondale, but certainly still much loved and appreciated. The book is dedicated to my wife, Nancy, who has given me love and unconditional support for a very long time, and to our new grandson, Caleb, who arrived just as the book was completed. The dedication says it all.

1

The Evolving American Political Party System

Documenting and explaining continuity and change is a crucial challenge in the study of American political parties and politics (Schattschneider, 1960; Campbell and others, 1960). This work takes up that challenge with respect to the party system over the last quarter of the twentieth century. The chapter also presents a stocktaking of the condition of the party system at the midpoint of the second decade of the twenty-first century.

Ideological Party Polarization

It is now commonplace to observe that the nation and the parties are deeply polarized, divided into ideologically different and warring camps. That polarization happened over the four decades covered in this study. This book analyzes how and why that polarization took place among party activists and among the mass public. Understanding our political parties is a big step toward understanding where we are and how we got here. Complex organizations, like the two major American political parties, can attempt to preserve the status quo and survive in their traditional patterns, or they can change in the face of new demands. Any complex organization faces the challenge of deciding how much of its public identity, core values, and established patterns to preserve and how much to change in order to survive (Zald, 1970; Zald and Denton, 1963). American political parties and their leadership are no exception to this rule. The basic premise of this book is that political parties—that is, the organizations, the activists who run them, and the party in government—will do what they deem to be necessary to adapt and survive. This organizational imperative animates and disciplines them.

American political parties were confronted with tremendous challenges during the last quarter of the twentieth century and through the first decade of the twenty-first century. The ways the parties adapted and changed and the people who led the changes to meet those challenges are the focus of this book. The first three chapters provide a description and analysis of the recent history of the American party system and the major trends in American politics especially regarding presidential elections. The basic proposition explored here is that changing the way we nominate and elect presidents will have a significant impact on political parties and on the entire political system.

The subjects of the empirical analysis are delegates to their political party's national convention. National convention delegates include all elements of the party—national, state, and local officials elected to public office in the name of the party (the people who have the responsibility of governing the nation and its component parts, or the party in government); official members of the national, state, and local party committees, their officers, and staffs (who oversee the day-to-day affairs of the party as an organization); and political consultants, fund-raisers, pollsters, and the leaders of interest groups and social movements (who assist the party in both campaigns and governance).

National convention delegates are empowered to act on behalf of the national, state, and local parties in naming the party nominees to be president, the most important political position in the land. They are also empowered to define the public policy positions of the national parties in the adoption of the party platform and to establish the rules that govern the national parties and the rules by which the next presidential candidates will be nominated. In these capacities, they also face a myriad of challenges and pressures to speak for the party, represent its values, and make the crucial decisions that will chart the future course of their respective parties. They embody those signature values of the parties and thus help to create the images of the parties held by the mass public (Bartels, 2000; Hetherington, 2001; Aldrich, 1995). In addition, national convention delegates provide a window on local and state party organizations (Miller and Jennings, 1986; Miller, 1988; Maggiotto and Wekkin, 2000). There also is a symbiotic relationship between these party activists and the presidential candidates they choose. This broad definition and interaction is captured by John Aldrich (1995, 20–21):

Party activists shade from those powerful figures with concentrations of, or access to, money and information . . . to the legions of volunteer campaign activists who ring doorbells and stuff envelopes and are, individually and collectively, critical to the first level of the party—its office seekers. All are critical because they command the resources, whether money, expertise, and information or merely time and labor, that office seekers need to realize their ambitions. As a result, activists' motivations shape and constrain the behavior of office seekers, as their own roles are, in turn, shaped and constrained by the office seekers.

The activists that are the subjects of this study are the people Jeane Kirkpatrick (1976, 22) calls "the new presidential elite" in her monumental study, in which she provides the rationale for focusing on convention delegates.

Delegates to national conventions are interesting to students of politics because, for the period that they serve as delegates, they are members of *the elite political class,* persons whose decisions are felt throughout the political system. . . . The political elite is that political class that has more influence than others in the shaping of specified values through political processes. Collectively, they embody the human, social, and political characteristics of a national party. Collectively the delegates constitute a slice of American political life broad enough to include persons from every state and thick enough to include representatives of all political levels. (italics in the original)

Although some scholars have studied state party organizations and county party organizations at one point in time with great profit and have produced important empirical and theoretical results (Eldersveld, 1964; Eldersveld and Walton, 2000; Gibson and others, 1985), others (Kirkpartick, 1976; Miller and Jennings, 1986) use the national conventions, as I do. The present study is also about the political reforms that have transformed the way we nominate presidential candidates, how the rules of the game have changed, and what that has meant in the candidates the parties nominate, the polarization of the parties led by the party elites, and the impact on the ability of the president to govern. If we change the rules, we are very likely to change the game, and this is what happened during the era studied here.

The 1972 election was the first held after the reforms instituted by the McGovern-Fraser rules were promulgated. The bulk of this study is devoted to what has happened since these reforms and how the party activists who nominate national candidates changed during this era. This study extends from 1976 through 2008 (indirectly, as a point of comparison, the data taken from other studies extend backward to 1968 and even earlier, where the data are available, before the reforms were instituted). The comparisons amount to a before and after and pre-reform versus post-reform study of the era. The reforms constitute what is now a mature rules regime, which has changed incrementally but which has been basically stable for ten presidential election cycles.

This study documents the longitudinal changes in the major players and in the way we nominate and elect presidents. These changes are fundamental to the way the parties changed at the organizational level, which in turn changed the way we nominate and elect presidents. The changes of this era also helped lead to the much-discussed polarization of the two major parties. That polarization has made it much more difficult for presidents to govern and indeed for the government to perform some of its basic and essential functions, like nominating key officials, implementing new laws, adopting a budget, and raising the debt ceiling. The resulting political stalemate and legislative gridlock are critical to explaining how the party system operates—and often does not operate—in today's America.

The government was shut down in the fall of 2013. Economic disaster loomed because of the failure to increase the national debt ceiling. The president finds it almost impossible to lead the fractured government. These are all important markers of the kind of government produced by ideological and partisan polarization.

Presidential Elections and Presidential Government

In a fundamental sense, this book is also a story of presidential politics. The presidency came to dominate American government thoroughly in the twentieth century. Thus the ways in which we choose the president are crucial to understanding how presidential government works. Originally, the federal government was not supposed to be a system with a dominant executive, and the framers of the Constitution were for the most part people who believed in and supported legislative power first and foremost. They wanted an independent executive, but they also actively feared executive power, believing that a chief executive might become too powerful and destroy liberty. They were all too familiar with this pattern from their experience and from their reading of history, and they were determined to avoid it in America. Madison's model of separated powers with checks and balances was designed to ensure that no branch of government had the power and authority to dominate the other branches and that the different centers of power established by the Constitution could serve as counterweights to each other, thereby keeping the entire system in the sort of equilibrium that would secure liberty. This balancing of power was particularly designed to rein in the power of the president. The list of delegated powers given to Congress in article I of the Constitution is much more lengthy and impressive than the powers provided to the president listed in article II. Madison and most of his colleagues at the Philadelphia Constitutional Convention clearly thought the legislative branch should be the first among equals.

All of this changed, however, in the twentieth century, as the national government became more important and the president became the spokesman for the American people. The twentieth century has been called the "era of the executive," since it was a time of expansive growth in the real political power of the president (Rossiter, 1960). This expansion of the presidency into a dominant role in the national government was led by two cousins, Theodore Roosevelt and Franklin Roosevelt (Savage, 1991). It was initiated at the start of the twentieth century, when Theodore Roosevelt assumed the presidency. He was a strong and activist president and he led the expansion of the power and scope of the federal government and the role of the presidency on both the international front and the home front. Increases in the power of the president dramatically expanded even more during the New Deal and World War II, when Franklin Roosevelt won an unprecedented four terms in the White House and the role of the federal government expanded first to fight the economic ravages of the Great Depression and then to mobilize the nation successfully for World War II.

This trend accelerated in the 1950s and 1960s under the impetus and logic of a massive cold war against the Soviet Union and then under the impetus of the civil rights revolution, which required the federal government to address state-supported segregation and to erase the last de jure remains of the Civil War. After World War II the president also became the keeper and guarantor of our economic prosperity, at least in popular opinion and expectations, if not always in economic fact. Together, the two Roosevelts, reacting to the crises and challenges of their times, remade the job of president, changed public perceptions of the office, and expanded the size and scope of the executive branch far beyond that originally envisioned in article II. Presidential power now drives our form of government, and presidential politics dominates our national political dialogue and our daily conversations. These foreign and domestic challenges led to the expansion of the legal powers of the presidency as well as to the expansion of the public's expectations and, thereby, the informal power of the president.

We expect the president to keep the nation peaceful and prosperous, and all the candidates who seek that office essentially promise that both objectives will be met if they are elected. However, if war comes it is likely to be primarily a presidential war, with a decidedly secondary role played by Congress. The president's power to make war without a formal declaration of war from Congress was proved again and again by the significant wars waged in Korea, Vietnam, Kuwait, Iraq, and Afghanistan and by numerous smaller deployments of American troops to fight in places as diverse as Somalia, Bosnia, Kosovo, Grenada, Panama, and Haiti. No other augmentation of presidential power has been more important than the growth of the role of commander in chief and all that title entails regarding the president's power and authority to raise and commit the military force of the one remaining superpower in the world. The American military is unchallenged and unequaled in modern warfare, and as that military has been deployed repeatedly around the world, the role and reach of the commander in chief have also grown. The fact that this role also augments the image and authority of the president in domestic settings helped the president to dominate the political discourse and politics of the late twentieth and early twenty-first centuries.

The growth of presidential power has led not only to debates about the nature of the office but also to questions about the proper method for selecting its occupant. The Constitution is almost silent on this question. Originally, the Electoral College was expected to be adequate for both the nomination and the election of a president, and it worked that way for the nomination of George Washington. However, the elections of 1796 and 1800 showed the inadequacies of the Electoral College as a nominations device, and something else was needed. Starting in 1804 the congressional caucus was the method employed. It consisted of the party's representatives in the U.S. Congress getting together and deciding on who they would support for the presidential nomination. This method worked reasonably well until the election of 1824, when that system broke down in chaos and the House selected John Quincy Adams over Andrew Jackson, thanks to a bargain Adams's supporters struck with Henry Clay's supporters. Jackson came back to defeat Adams in 1828, and subsequently Jackson and his followers profoundly changed the American party system, effectively turning it into the modern mass-based system that still survives today (Crotty and Jackson, 1985, chap. 1).

In 1832 Andrew Jackson's supporters introduced the national party convention as a more democratic way to choose presidential candidates. Through the remainder of the nineteenth century political party organizations dominated the process, picking delegates as well as choosing the nominee. In the early years of the twentieth century, direct primaries were introduced, with their proponents arguing that they were more democratic by giving individual party members a stronger voice in the picking of the nominees. The primaries were important in some years, but most years between 1912 and 1968 they were secondary to the main show, which was the national conventions. Following the McGovern-Fraser reforms, first applied in 1972, presidential primaries came to dominate the process by which delegates to national conventions and presidential nominees were chosen (Ceaser, 1979; Shafer, 1988). This book looks at presidential nominations and elections since those reforms were instituted in order to provide a context for understanding the contemporary system.

The Continuing Role of Political Parties

Most scholars believe that political parties are essential to the operation of a modern mass democracy. It is ironic that many of the founders of the republic decried the "baneful effects" of party while at the same time taking steps to gain the advantage in the political conflicts of the day, thus ensuring the birth and growth of the first mass parties in the world. Today, scholars believe in and articulate a strong case in favor of the essential role of political parties no matter how skeptical the public and the mass media are about them. E. E. Schattschneider (1942, 1) asserts that "political parties created democracy and . . . democracy is unthinkable save in terms of parties." A more contemporary scholar, Larry Sabato (2009, 138), echoes this sentiment: "Once avoided in their entirety by the Founders and the Constitution, political parties have become the sine qua non of American democracy." Despite all the change in the nation and the republic since 1789, the parties, most notably the two major political parties as we know them today, continue as essential as ever to the operation of a democratic republic.

Whatever the institutional changes in the balance of power among the three branches since the 1790s, the political parties have been responsible for organizing the elections and structuring the choices placed before the voting public. The nation has changed dramatically, and the structure and scope of the national government have grown, but the role of the parties continues. In national elections for both president and Congress, it is party organizations that select candidates and organize the contest. The choices made periodically by the American people are more stable and more predictable each election because of their foundation in the partisanship of the American electorate (Green, Palmquist, and Schickler, 2002; Campbell and others, 1960). The electoral connection provided by the parties is at the heart of America's representative democracy and is the major purpose of political parties. Despite much talk and speculation in the 1970s and 1980s about the decline of political parties, the fact is that, for all of the twentieth century, only two major political parties, the Democrats and the Republicans, dominated American politics. The dominance of these two parties extends backward through the first half of the nineteenth century, with the founding of the Republican Party in the mid-1850s and the modern Democratic Party in the early 1830s. The parties will always try to ensure their own continuity, and thus it is that duopoly that extends forward well into the twenty-first century. The longevity and scope of this two-party system are unparalleled in the rest of the world.

Parties as Linkage Mechanisms

Political scientists have long recognized that one of the major functions of the political parties in a mass democracy is to link groups and individual voters to the decisionmakers who have control of the levers of public power (Leiserson, 1958). The parties' continued success, and even their basic survival, depends to an important extent on how well they perform that linkage function and represent their people. The holders of national and state offices achieve their control over public power by being nominated and elected, and the parties are key intermediaries in this exchange. Moreover, the vast majority of all of these public officials at the federal and state levels are nominated and elected under the aegis of either the Democratic Party or the Republican Party. Only at the local level are there many officially nonpartisan office holders, and many of these are really associated with one of the major parties even though they may run without benefit of the party label. Very few minor, or third-party, candidates run for and are elected to office in the United States. Such challengers simply do not find a following stable enough to ensure their long-term survival. Since 1856 the Republicans and the Democrats have dominated the American presidency. No other party has won the presidency since that year, and most years no third-party candidate has even scored in the double digits in terms of percentage of popular votes won.

On occasion, candidates of other parties have won election to Congress. Progressives, Populists, Farmer Labor, Socialists, and a few others have come and gone in popularity; however, none has ever commanded a substantial block of votes in either house of Congress for any extended period. In the current Congress there are only two members of the Senate who are officially independents—Bernard Sanders of Vermont and Angus King of Maine, but both vote with the Democrats at least for organizational purposes. In the previous Congress there were only Sanders and Joseph Lieberman of Connecticut (who also caucused with the Democrats). While there are often one or two governors of the states who are independents, the vast majority are either Democrat or Republican. The same is true of the state legislatures. Although Nebraska's unicameral legislature is officially nonpartisan, almost all of the other state legislators are either Democrat or Republican.

It should be noted that this party dominance has been achieved in spite of some major third-party challenges (Rapoport and Stone, 2005). In the 1912 presidential race, Theodore Roosevelt, a former Republican president, ran on the Progressive (Bull Moose) ticket. He came in second to the Democrat, Woodrow Wilson, beating the Republican incumbent, William Howard Taft, who ran an abysmal third. That was the only time in the twentieth century when a third party even managed to run second in the presidential sweepstakes. There have been other notable third-party challengers, including J. Strom Thurmond and Henry Wallace in 1948, George Wallace in 1968, John Anderson in 1980, Ross Perot in 1992 and 1996, and Ralph Nader in 2000. In 2000 Ralph Nader ran on the Green Party ticket, and Nader certainly helped throw the race to George W. Bush and had a major impact on the outcome; however, he received only 3 percent of the popular vote. Nader tried again in 2004, but his vote total fell below 1 percent, and his impact was minimal that year. Nader ran again in 2008, and this time he garnered even fewer votes and less support than he had achieved in 2004. His experience illustrates the overall pattern in American history: that the more times a third-party candidate runs, the lower his or her percentage of the vote. None of these challengers has received as much as one-fifth of the popular vote. Perot's 19 percent in 1992 was the high-water mark for third-party presidential challengers, after Roosevelt's runner-up finish in 1912. No third party has shown the ability to move up to the size and status of the Liberal Party in Great Britain, which is now a part of the coalition government, and none has made it to the status of second party, or governing party, since the Republicans achieved that feat in 1854–60.

Many explanations have been given for the dominance of two major parties in American politics. The French scholar Maurice Duverger (1967) offers perhaps the most persuasive, arguing that an electoral system of single-member districts with plurality elections will produce a two-party system, whereas multimember districts with proportional representation will produce a multiple-party system. Leon Epstein (1979) and others point to the influence of the British political culture inherited by Americans. Our culture and history condition most of us to think of the political choices we are offered in terms of Republicans and Democrats and to expect only their candidates to win. Whatever the root causes, American politics for a century and a half has been dominated by two major parties, the parties that perform the linkage function for the mass of voters and function as gatekeepers to public power.

The Crucial Role of Party Elites

The stable electoral system and the staying power of the inherited political culture are undoubtedly two important explanations for the stability and continuity of the two-party system in the United States, in the face of enormous social and economic changes. This book, however, takes a somewhat different tack and suggests that the political elites and activists who lead the two major parties and who staff the organizations also explain this continuity. The continuity and adaptability of the two major parties did not just happen; someone had to make it happen. The adaptability of the parties has been due in part to rational strategic decisionmaking by the people who make up the activist echelons of the two parties. Rational minds had to struggle with the external environment, understand the important trends and pressures, and devise a strategy to cope with what was happening in the world that would impinge on the way the two parties did business.

The road to adaptation and survival was not always marked with good decisions. The decisionmakers were not always prescient enough to avoid major conflict and dislocations. They made inadequate decisions at some turns. They lost large blocks of their former voters to the opposition. They sometimes squandered the opportunity to mobilize significant blocs of new voters. For a while both parties also lost adherents at the grass roots, as more people identified as independents.

The continuing loss of the parties' base and the popular distrust of the two parties led many in the 1970s and 1980s to predict the imminent "dealignment" of the public and the decline of the two-party system as we had known it (Wattenberg, 1991; Crotty, 1984; Kirkpatrick, 1978; Broder, 1972). More recently, both of these trends seem to have been arrested, and the level of partisan identification with the two parties has stabilized. Indeed, those who identify with one or the other of the parties now are more firmly committed to their party and less likely to defect to the other party, or even to vote a split ticket, than was the case in earlier decades, when some were writing the obituary of the two-party system.

We live in an era of remarkable polarization, and this polarized polity guarantees a firm and dedicated core of supporters for each of the parties. That core starts with the party activists and then radiates out from them to the base of party identifiers, especially the strong partisans. In addition, the party organizations themselves not only have survived but have been renewed and strengthened, particularly at the state and national levels. During the era of this study, party leaders continued to work at defining their party's role, mission, policies, and ideological positions in ways that would appeal to enough voters for their candidates for president, Congress, and state offices to often win—and for the future of their parties to be ensured. In short, party elites behave strategically, calculating the costs and the potential benefits of the policies they pursue in ways consistent with rational choice theory. This book adopts the perspective of Anthony Downs (1957, 2), who argues that public officials act "in the most efficient manner possible given their limited capabilities and the cost of information."

In synoptic form this assumption means that party elites have goals; they pursue these goals using the options relevant to realizing these goals. In the more technical language of economic theory, decisionmakers act to "maximize their utilities." In economic theory, this means that they will study the products available, decide what qualities they want in the product they seek, and then find the lowest price available for the product that meets their basic specifications. In the commonsense language of politics, this means that the party elites have definite political preferences and usually take actions that are consistent with realizing those preferences. In this study these preferences include the short-term goal of electing their candidates to office, the adoption of policies and programs most favored by their party, and the implementation of those policies and programs in ways that benefit the party's constituents. In the long term these preferences include an emphasis on the health and survival of the political party. Analysis at the individual level is complemented by the potential for rational behavior also occurring at the group or aggregate level, as for example in mass voting behavior (Popkin, 1991).

Of course, these political elites, and people in general, are not automatons, and they are not always completely and coldly rational. They are all too human at times. Their strategic vision is not always clear, and their level of rationality is sometimes suspect. They make mistakes and let biases, human frailties, and shortcomings cloud their vision and hamper their decisionmaking. They yield to the impulse of the instant or let slip an ill-chosen word or phrase in an unguarded moment in the heat of political battle, when reporters or an unsuspected live microphone are present. Yet they do make decisions and move the organization forward. In the words of Herbert Simon and Charles E. Lindbloom, they make "satisficing decisions" (Simon, 1957, xxiv) and muddle through (Lindbloom, 1959). People take the accumulated knowledge and information they have at that point and weigh the options as they understand them and make the best decision they can under the circumstances.

In short, the theoretical position called *bounded rationality* is the overarching theoretical position of this book (Simon, 1982, vol. 1; Simon, 2000). Bounded rationality holds that humans strive to approximate the pure rational model to the extent possible; however, it also recognizes that decisionmakers suffer from a variety of shortages, which must be dealt with as the decision is being made. They may have inadequate information, they may not have considered all the options, and they may be limited in their ability to sort out all of the rewards or payoffs. They may be tired, angry, prejudiced, sleepy, jet lagged, or all stressed out at the time of the decision. These shortcomings notwithstanding, human beings in complex organizations cope. They make decisions, and they—and the organizations they direct—move on to another day and another set of challenges.

Kristen Renwick Monroe (1991, 78) summarizes the concepts of rational actor theory and bounded rationality in the following list of assumptions central to the theory:

—Actors pursue goals.

—These goals reflect the actor's perceived self-interest.

—Behavior results from conscious choice.

—The individual is the basic actor in society.

—Actors have preference orderings that are consistent and stable.

—If given options, actors choose the alternative with the highest expected utility.

—Actors possess extensive information on both the available alternatives and the likely consequences of their choices.

Monroe points out that "bounded rationality relaxes the assumptions" in the last three statements, "to accommodate a large body of research which recognizes that most humans most of the time are not necessarily capable of ordering their preference, choosing the option most likely to lead to success and possessing the information levels necessary to make the optimum choice" (79–80). I agree; the concept of rational choice modified with the corrections afforded by bounded rationality is the overall perspective adopted in this book. It seems to be the most relevant way of looking at the political elites who are the focus of this study.

External Challenges to the Parties

The two major U.S. parties have a record of adapting to the challenges produced by the environment or the opposition. This record of successful adaptation is the major story line for the modern Democratic and Republican Parties in late twentieth-century and early twenty-first-century America. It is a record of remarkable overall success although one that has not been achieved easily. The successes have been achieved in a political environment fairly hostile to parties in general and to the two dominant American parties in particular. Throughout American history the two major parties have been beset by critics both inside and outside of their organizations.

The mass media have been especially important in providing a constant critique of the major parties and their leadership during the era studied here. The culture of the mass media is heavily influenced by the progressive and muckraking traditions of the early twentieth century and is deeply suspicious of political power in general and political parties in particular. The progressives were essentially nonpartisan or even anti-partisan, and they were especially critical of party bosses, who wielded political power, especially in the cities, at the turn of twentieth-century America. There were, to be sure, many abuses, and crusading journalists did a great service by uncovering and publicizing many of them. There is a straight-line progression from the crusading journalists of the 1920s and the investigative journalism of Carl Bernstein and Bob Woodard when they unraveled the intricacies of Watergate and became instrumental in the resignation of Richard Nixon in August 1974. Nixon's actions and the Watergate scandal and aftermath almost unraveled the Republican Party before it was able to redefine itself and get back on track after the 1976 elections. Watergate, and Nixon's resignation, was just one of the major crises faced and surmounted by the parties in this volatile era. The media have led the charge against the parties much of the time.

That investigative and adversarial journalist tradition of Watergate lives on today in the way the news media define the news, frame their stories, and pursue their jobs on a daily basis (Jamieson and Waldman, 2003). This media culture demands a form of constant assessment and stringent criticism that can lead to very harsh treatment of those officeholders currently in power and of the candidates who would like to gain power. American parties have always been subjected to a constant barrage of criticism and cynicism regarding their role in democracy. This distrust of political parties has deep roots and is a signature component of the American political culture (Ranney, 1975). Beginning with George Washington, Americans generally have not appreciated the vital role political parties play in the operation of a mass democracy. Mistrust of political parties goes back to the founders, and it is deeply engrained in the political culture of twentieth-century America. It is a theme widely purveyed via the mass media throughout popular culture. The increase in the power and intrusion of the media on American politics in general and on presidential nominations and elections in particular is one of the themes of this book.

As Austin Ranney (1975) shows, American parties have always occupied an ambiguous position in a political culture that does not understand their importance or support their role in the political system. Throughout American history the parties always have come in for more than their share of the blame. This skepticism and criticism toward the political parties have intensified recently in the national political dialogue and especially over the years covered by this study.

The media are only one, although one of the most powerful, critics of the American major parties. The dominant two-party system has borne the brunt of this criticism. Third-party candidates have certainly tried to make a case that it is time for a change and that the nation is being ill served by the hegemony of the two major parties, and they have urged the American people to end the dominance the Republicans and Democrats have enjoyed over the past 150 years. People like Ross Perot, George Wallace, John Anderson, Ralph Nader, Pat Buchanan, and Jesse Ventura have constantly criticized the Democrats and Republicans and urged the American people to break the two-party hold on power and vote for them instead. The Tea Party movement, which found its voice in 2009 and 2010, is but the latest in a long line of insurgencies that have railed against the dominance of the two major parties—or at least against the establishment wing of their own party.

Parties as Organizations and Their Leaders: Keys to Survival

Political parties are big, complex organizations that perform certain basic functions critical to the larger political system in which they are embedded. The modern Democratic and Republican Parties are, in many respects, bureaucratic organizations like other complex organizations in the private and the not-for-profit sectors. Of course, they also have particular functions and organizational features that give them a special role in the American polity. The parties focus on campaigns and elections in order to win control of public office and the exercise of public power. The parties recruit candidates and support their campaigns for public office when their candidates obtain control of the government. When the party wins, it tries to translate its ideology and policy preferences into law and to exercise whatever discipline is available to ensure that its officeholders accede to the party line. The parties thus have multiple political functions and organizational objectives, and those who operate the parties have complex incentives and objectives.

In his seminal work *Why Parties?*, John Aldrich (1995, 19) stresses the importance of viewing political parties as institutions populated by political elites who have complex incentives and objectives and who generally act rationally to achieve their primary objectives: "The public elects its political leaders, but it is that leadership that legislates, executes, and adjudicates policy. The parties are defined in relation to this republican democracy." Aldrich furthermore writes (23),

> "The policy formation and execution process. . . is highly partisan. The parties-in-government are more than mere coalitions of like-minded individuals, however; they are enduring institutions. . . . Thus, parties are institutions designed to promote the achievement of collective choices—choices on which the parties differ and choices reached by majority rule. . . . In a republican democracy politicians may turn to partisan institutions to solve the problem of collective choice. In the language of politics, parties may help achieve the goal of attaining policy majorities in the first place, as well as the often more difficult goal of maintaining such majorities.

Aldrich's theoretical position provides some of the fundamental undergirding for this book. The treatment of political parties here emphasizes the basic nature of the political party as a particular and even unusual type of institution seeking to serve multiple functions crucial to the democratic system, and it focuses on the people, especially the activists, who are the most deeply committed to, and have the largest stake in, the party organizations.

Most of the empirical research in political science has been devoted to the base of the political party, that is, "the party in the electorate" (Key, 1958). This is the area where we know the most, in an empirical-research-and-longitudinal-data sense of accumulated public knowledge. Much of the literature on the decline of the political parties focused on a weakening of voter identification with a party and the abysmal levels of voter participation in American campaigns. That focus led prominent observers to contend that the parties were in a state of dealignment, dysfunction, and decay. But many now argue that the party in the electorate should not be treated as a component of the political party in the same way as the party organization and the party in government are. Gerald Pomper (1996, 141) argues that "parties are not properly considered as collections of voters," agreeing with E. E. Schattschneider (1942, 35), who saw a party as "first of all an organized attempt to get power." In this view, Pomper continues, "voters are not members of the party organization, but rather its clientele, and it is confusing and inaccurate to think of them as the party." "We do better," he concludes," to think of the parties as seekers of voters, following Downs, Schumpeter, and Schlesinger."

Joseph Schlesinger (1991, 6) adopts from Anthony Down's seminal book his basic definition of what constitutes a political party and then builds on it an argument for the study of party organizations: "a party is 'a team seeking to control the governing apparatus by gaining office in a duly constituted election' . . . the definition directs us to rational choice explanations of party behavior. In so doing it reflects both the view that politics is goal oriented and the assumption that political actors are rational in the ways they seek to achieve their goals." Both the Schlesinger and the Downs themes are quite compatible with the basic theoretical position adopted in this book. The position taken here is that the life of the parties as organizations is dependent on how the people perceive them and react to them, especially in terms of how often they support the parties' candidates for office.

John Kenneth White and Daniel M. Shea (2001, 360) share this view, arguing that voters are like consumers that parties try to attract in each election. "The goal of the party organization," they write, "is to instill *brand loyalty* in order to expand their market share" (italics added). White and Shea see candidates as products offered by the parties to the mass voters in the hope of gaining control of public offices.

As noted, the major focus of this book is on party organization, particularly party elites. It is these elites who define the parties and determine what their brand means—that is, who influence public opinion and the mass public's conception of the identities of the two major parties and what they stand for (as a number of scholars demonstrate; see Aldrich, 1995; Bartels, 2000; Hetherington, 2001). If the party elites are now seriously polarized (as I demonstrate), then their polarization will help illuminate the issue polarization in the mass public and even explain its origins. The classic questions from representational theory are, How close to the base of the parties do the party elites stand? And which party better represents the views and values of the mass public? (McClosky, Hoffman, and O'Hara, 1960; Jackson, Brown, and Bositis, 1982). This study stresses the concept of representation and how well those holding official party office represent the views of those outside of the organization, that is, the voters.

Continuity and Change in the Role of the Political Parties

Electoral politics today is commonly described as candidate centered, meaning that to win a party nomination for office candidates put together their own organizations. But even in a system in which candidates may be self-starters, the party label remains the currency of the realm in electoral politics. A candidate ambitious for success cannot afford to run outside the party system (Schlesinger, 1966). Almost all candidates at the state and federal levels ultimately seek the imprimatur, and run under the label, of one of the major parties.

Once elected, public officials are highly dependent on their party organizations and leadership, especially in the legislative branch, where they are encouraged by a variety of institutional constraints and incentives to behave as partisans. The parties have always been important in the legislative branch, and that importance has increased in the era studied here. The level of partisan polarization in Congress and in many state legislatures has increased markedly in the past two decades. The two major parties organize and structure campaigns and elections for almost all of the offices above the local level. They then act as partisans in the legislative process. This partisanship reinforces the views the public holds of the parties.

Candidates wear the party label as they compete for office and in so doing help to define the two parties for the mass public. A substantial part of the mass public relates to the political world through partisan eyes (Green, Palmquist, and Schickler, 2002; Aldrich, 1995; Campbell and others, 1960). Even the parts of the mass public who reject party labels are aided in their decisions by the party identification of candidates, which provides cues as to how candidates are likely to act in the political drama. Tens of millions of Americans use the party name to make sense of issues, ideologies, and personalities in this age of cable television, twenty-four-hour news cycles, and the Internet. Thus even in a candidate-centered system, the political party plays a critical role.

This study presents the political parties as both dependent on the external political, social, and economic environment in which they are embedded and at the same time independent, as they make strategic decisions to appeal to new constituencies, emphasize new themes and issues, present new programs and policies, and offer new faces to the American public. Their brand name has a factual history, a cultural heritage, an issue and ideological agenda, and a set of heroes and villains, all of which are an essential part of the party's image and identity. There are signature stories that have become defining narratives of the parties. To be a Republican or a Democrat in twenty-first-century America is to accept as a part of one's own personal identity the baggage of one's party. It involves a form of brand name loyalty, which evokes a whole gestalt of political and personal characteristics. The political parties' maintenance of brand name control calls to mind the concept found in the literature associated with American marketing. The Nike swoosh on shoes, the golden arches of McDonalds, and the distinctive script of a Ford or Coke sign are much like the Democrats' donkey and the Republicans' elephant or the blue state and red state logos.

Democrats and the Republicans long ago became highly recognizable in the cognitive framework of the American public. Those are hard-won names.

They are also not easily matched by a new party. This is one of the obstacles to third-party prospects (Rapoport and Stone, 2005). These name brands are most prominently worn and advertised by the political elites, who identify strongly with one or the other major party. This book empirically identifies the ideological and issue-oriented commitments that result from the adoption of these name brands.

The more things change the more they remain the same is a cliché, but it is also an accurate description of America's two major political parties at least since the 1850s. The decades between 1970 and 2000 were turbulent indeed in American politics, perhaps exceeded only by the disruptions of the 1960s. During these decades the two major parties were faced with relentless pressures for change. They were challenged on every side from the external environment. They also challenged each other as each party tried desperately to gain the upper hand in the competition for office and even to put the other out of business—or at least to deny the other party access to the levers of political power. The political precinct is a tough neighborhood; the political game rewards competitive, confident, intelligent, and aggressive behavior. In the context of such a challenging environment, the two major political parties have survived, transformed themselves, and emerged as newly reconstructed but with still recognizable ideologies, traditions, programs, missions, activist bases, and interest groups. In short, these four decades provide evidence of both continuity and change in the sweeping history of party evolution and development in America.

Plan of the Book

This chapter provides the historical and the theoretical underpinnings of the book. It discusses the basic functions of the political parties, especially as they include recruiting candidates and mobilizing support for them in contesting the elections. It emphasizes how crucial the candidates are in attracting political activists and in defining the parties for the voters. It emphasizes the parties as organizations, discusses the importance of the political elites who lead them, and explores the importance and limits of rational behavior by the elites. It posits the central concept of rational decisionmaking as the basic model underlying the fundamental premises regarding how party leaders behave. That model is tempered by the related concept of bounded rationality.

Chapter 2 provides the historic context by detailing the macro, or mass-level, political trends in American politics, which have so significantly altered the political landscape in the last three decades of the twentieth century and the first decade of the twenty-first. This chapter provides a synoptic account of major national campaigns, particularly recent campaigns for the presidency, which are the driving force in American politics. The focus is particularly on the importance of the candidates nominated and on the way they and their campaigns define the parties and the political and policy-based choices offered to the American people. The last half of the twentieth century saw a major realignment of the two major parties, and chapter 2 describes the significant contours of that realignment. The realignment of the American South and, to a lesser extent, the Northeast and Midwest is a crucial geographic component of that change. In addition, the electoral behavior of women, African Americans, and white voters, especially in the South, has provided the group basis of this realignment. The realignment has produced an ideological and issues-based polarization of the two major parties and of the mass public, which is the most important feature of the political landscape at the close of the first decade of the twenty-first century.

Chapter 3 provides the historic context by presenting the major party changes and the reforms initiated by party leaders as they attempted to cope with their strategic challenges. This chapter is particularly focused on the McGovern-Fraser reforms of 1970, which helped usher in the whole reform era, profoundly shaping our presidential nominations and elections ever since. It also covers all of the subsequent reform commissions and rules changes in both parties during that transformational era. The rules of the game are important, and this chapter highlights those most relevant to changes within the parties and to the fortunes of the presidential candidates. Today's conflicts within both parties are rooted in and conditioned by the events covered in this chapter.

Chapter 4 is grounded in the theory of representation, guided particularly by the seminal work of Hannah Pitkin (1987) focusing on what the theory of representation has to do with the characteristics of the political elites who make up the convention delegations. The chapter sets the reforms into the context of how markedly the use of the presidential primaries has increased for both parties. While it may not have been the intended consequence of the reform movement, highlighting and increasing the stakes involved in the presidential primaries has certainly been one of the most important unintended consequences. This chapter also focuses on the impact of the reforms on the demographic composition of the conventions, which was one of the most tangible intents of the early reformers.

Chapter 5 continues that discussion with a thorough exploration of the most prominent political values of the presidential elites. We look at the self-identified ideological positions of the elites of the two major parties from 1976 through 2008. In addition, elite positions on a wide range of domestic and foreign policy items are documented, using one of the largest longitudinal data collections on party elites available.

Chapter 6 compares the values and political views of the political elites to those of the mass party base. Following Pitkin, if representation is to have any real meaning in the political world, it must be that governors in some measure reflect the views and values of the governed and that leaders act in a way that is broadly acceptable to the governed. The chapter examines the important question of how well the two parties reflect the values of party identifiers.

Chapter 7 examines the backgrounds, political socialization, and political recruitment experiences of the political elites. How did these political activists first become interested in politics, and who recruited them for the positions they hold? Are they the representatives of a self-perpetuating elite group, or is there an open and porous party structure that encourages and welcomes the "circulation of elites," which can bring new views and new blood into the parties (Miller and Jennings, 1986, chap. 1)?

Chapter 8 adds an emphasis on party factions and explores the candidate coalitions that make up the political parties. The composition of these coalitions and the factional wing of the party that prevailed in the nominations contest are critical components of the polarization of the two parties.

Finally, chapter 9 provides a summary of the findings and a prediction of what these findings mean for the future of the American political party system in the coming decades. This chapter closes with recommendations for how we might change the system to provide more rational and user-friendly choices for the American people. These changes would produce a system that would acknowledge the president as the true driving force in the American system but that would allow the people to make more informed choices. Such a system would lead to a coherent form of majority rule.

2

Party Politics in the Reform Era

The research in this book began in the early 1970s during the era of the McGovern-Fraser reforms and the writing of the first-ever national charter, or constitution, for the Democratic Party. These changes were initiated by the disruptions of the highly contentious 1968 Democratic National Convention in Chicago and continued after the disastrously divided convention in 1972 in Miami. This was an era in which the basic concept of what a political party should be, who it should serve, and how a party should be organized to respond to external forces and demands was being debated and was very much up for grabs within and across the two major parties.

It was also an era in which there was a shift from one type of political party to another. There was significant support in some quarters among the party elites, especially within the Democratic Party, for this change, which was a shift from the older, more venerable, more pragmatic party model, with its emphasis on control of public power and whose primary reason for being was to win elections. Reformers wanted a change to a more open and participatory party, one that provides an opportunity for grassroots activists and mass voters to have a greater say in party affairs and especially in the selection of the party's presidential nominee. Whether by conscious design or not, these reform impulses led in the direction of the responsible party model, with an emphasis on issues and ideology and a goal of offering a coherent, policy-oriented program to the public (Committee on Political Parties of the American Political Science Association, 1950; White and Mileur, 1992; Green and Herrnson, 2002). While many who sought party reform in that era would not have articulated their advocacy in the theoretical terms of the responsible party model, the practical steps they took led both parties in that general direction. The consequent reforms, coupled with other political changes taking place in the political environment to which the parties were trying to respond, produced the party system we have today.

The realignment of the two parties into distinctive conservative and liberal camps was a parallel development. This realignment produced the familiar polarization of the two parties into competing ideological movements, with their accompanying "culture wars," which are one of the markers of the last three decades of the twentieth century and the first decade of the twenty-first. Adherents of the two major parties have sorted themselves into two warring camps, with the Republicans distinctively conservative and the Democrats ranging from moderate to liberal but with the center of gravity tilted significantly toward the left or liberal side of the continuum (Levendusky, 2009). This chapter offers an overview of that era, when the parties were undergoing that transition. It also offers an analysis of the most important and most hotly contested elections for president and for control of Congress, which have been driving forces in that transition over the past forty years.

One of the important questions in this transition has been what value or importance the parties, especially the Democrats, should place on internal party democracy. Should the party open up its insider and elite-dominant procedures to more groups and individuals? Should it give them the opportunity to participate in all of the party's decisions, most notably the decision about the nominee for president? The alternative—the elite-dominant party model—already existed; and both parties had operated under it since the 1800s. Under the elite-dominant model, party leaders (party bosses) had the most clout, and they were understandably loath to allow outsiders a voice and a role in the party's affairs, and especially its nominations decisions. Some of the party leaders simply wanted the old party system to continue as it had since well before the turn of the twentieth century.

That original debate began in earnest at the 1968 Democratic National Convention in Chicago. After 1968 the debate over the rules continued, rising to prominence every four years, as the nation tried to select its presidential nominees. The first act in that selection process was party primaries and caucuses, followed by the national conventions. The spotlight of reform was directed at the entire process. The 1968 Democratic convention had many ripple effects but none as lasting as the transformation of the presidential nomination process in the early years of the 1970s, which we now refer to as the reform era.

This chapter recounts the story of the ideological and geographic realignment of the two major parties. One must understand this history in order to understand the party system of today and how its roots extend back to the immediate post–World War II era in American history and arguably even back to the founding of the New Deal coalition of the 1930s. This chapter provides a synoptic account of the ebb and flow of presidential elections, and to a lesser extent congressional elections, from the mid-twentieth century through the first decade of the twenty-first century, with projections toward the 2016 elections. This story most notably covers the entire post-reform party era, which started in 1968–72 and extends through the presidential election of 2012. This chapter concentrates on the general elections because they are the most high-profile events in the whole American political process, and they help shape the major perceptions of politics and political leaders for the mass public.

The primaries and the general elections provide the context and the driving force for most of the changes in the American parties. Those primaries and elections—and the candidates the two parties nominate—define for most Americans the important differences between the two major parties and the directions they offer for the public to choose from in each election cycle. Candidates for president are the highest-profile players in the American political system. They dominate our civic discourse and our political perceptions and imaginations. They tend also to epitomize for much of the American public the parties and what they stand for (Hetherington, 2001; Bartels, 2000). To a somewhat lesser extent, congressional elections provide the same function in the formation of mass opinion. For much of the public, political parties are known by the candidates they keep.

Traditionally, as has been noted, over most of their history American parties have been first and foremost electoral machines. This is the basic definition of what is called the pragmatic party era. That emphasis on winning elections remains their central role in the first decade of the twenty-first century. At the same time, they are now composed of many individuals active in the organizational precincts of the party who are also intensely interested in issues, ideologies, programs, and platforms. This interest in issues is a marker of the responsible party model (Committee on Political Parties of the American Political Science Association, 1950). The insurgents who came to command much attention in the debates over party reform in the late 1960s and 1970s, especially within the Democratic Party, embraced this view of the party's role. Many of the liberal activists in the Democratic Party rejected the pragmatic party approach as a failure, since it had gotten the Democrats into difficulties in the wake of Lyndon Johnson and Vietnam. These activists objected to a party bereft of ideological commitment, where issues took a backseat to electoral needs. They especially objected to a party dominated by governors and big-city mayors, who managed the selection of national convention delegates and, ultimately, presidential nominees, as being inappropriate in a genuine democracy, where power should belong to the people.

The displacement of these party insiders, the "regulars" as they were often called at that time, was the goal of the reformers, who advocated the transfer of power to the voters at the base of the party and, especially, to activists like themselves, who were dedicated to a cause or to a set of issues they wanted to advance through the nomination and election of candidates favorable to their cause. In the Vietnam War era the antiwar crusade drove the party's reform efforts, although the civil rights revolution was always in the background. These activists focused on the national conventions and the presidential nominations process, especially the national conventions of 1968 and 1972. The antiwar activists became the leading voices, advocating a change in the way the parties, especially the Democratic Party, did business. This movement gained enormous strength and thousands of adherents and threatened to sweep away the long-established moorings of the traditional two-party system.

These divisions played themselves out for the public primarily in the electoral arena and especially in the race for the presidential nomination and then for the presidency. Since the decade of the 1960s the important issues increasingly have come to be marked by greater distinctions between the two major parties and by a realignment of the two-party system. Eventually, all the deeply divisive issues on the public agenda become important partisan issues, which have to be addressed by the candidates for major public office and especially by those running for president. The candidates must discuss these salient issues and stake out a position on them and expect to be grilled by their opponents in the presidential debates and by the mass media. The race for the presidency is the premier arena for the playing out of these issues. Whether issues are a means to an end, as pragmatic party advocates would argue, or whether they have intrinsic importance, as responsible party model adherents would contend, is hotly debated. What is not debatable is the fact that one must first win control of political power—that is, win public office—to have any chance of translating issue positions into policy. So in that sense, both the responsible party model and the pragmatic party model have relevance in the eclectic American party politics of today.

Control of the presidency is the key to the shaping of a party's image and electoral fortunes. The president is clearly the "chief of party," in Clinton Rossiter's (1960) terminology, and leadership of his party is one of the most important roles he plays. He is also chief of the federal bureaucracy, which is a source of patronage jobs, lucrative contracts, and power over the tax code and law enforcement. In addition, the presidency is the bully pulpit, with all of its powers to shape the party's image. President George W. Bush took his duty to the Republican Party and to shaping its future more seriously than perhaps any other modern president (Skinner, 2008–09; Edwards, 2007; Jacobsen, 2004). Bush's major political operative, Karl Rove, sought to coalesce a "new Republican majority" using all the tools of the presidency. Parties tend to prosper when they are led by presidents who, like Bush, want to build the party as well as advance their own policies.

The Shift of the South and Party Realignment

Nothing is as important to the story of political party development and realignment as the shift of the South from the Democratic Party to the Republican Party. Over the span of just two decades, what had once been the base of one of the major parties shifted to become the base of the other. Like much else in American politics, this momentous change in the morphology of the two parties was driven by race. At the 1948 Democratic National Convention, Hubert Humphrey, who was then the liberal mayor of Minneapolis, Minnesota, led a drive to insert a progressive civil rights plank into the party platform. Humphrey and others also wanted to eliminate a rule requiring that the nominee receive at least two-thirds of delegate votes, since this rule had always provided the South with veto power over Democratic nominees.

The 1948 national convention nominated the incumbent, Harry Truman. Truman was personally and politically a product of his time, getting his start in the Pendergast machine of Kansas City, and initially he was regarded as a machine politician. Truman had certain prejudices and racial biases, as two of his distinguished biographers make plain (Hamby, 1995; McCullough, 1992). Nevertheless, he openly embraced the term *liberal* for himself and his party, and he adopted increased civil rights for minorities as an important liberal objective for his administration. He also favored fair housing laws to ensure equal treatment for minorities in real estate transactions. He was an advocate of antilynching laws, which supporters thought would put the federal government's protective cloak around minorities, who clearly needed protection against mob violence in the South. Truman also desegregated the U.S. military when he signed an executive order in 1948 dismantling the prevalent system of segregation in the nation's armed forces, a system that had existed up through World War II. Whatever his own personal prejudices may have been,

Harry Truman's policies were at the leading edge of the drive for civil rights in the last half of the 1940s (Neal, 2002). Humphrey and his liberal allies were determined to push the Truman administration and the Democratic Party even farther along that path by means of the Democratic platform. This determination sparked a bitter convention fight within the party, and especially with the southern wing of the Democratic Party, which was at that time the bedrock of the party's presidential coalition.

The election of 1948 saw race and civil rights play a crucial role in who the nominated candidates were and in the final results of the general election. When Humphrey and his allies pushed hard for the pro-civil-rights plank in the platform, a contingent of the southern state delegations walked out of the convention. They were led by Strom Thurmond, governor of South Carolina and a staunch segregationist, and by Fielding Wright, governor of Mississippi. Thurmond and Wright ran as presidential and vice presidential candidates on the States' Rights Democratic Party label and were popularly referred to as Dixiecrats. The party carried only four Deep South states (Louisiana, Mississippi, Alabama, and South Carolina), with thirty-nine electoral votes. Nonetheless, the Dixiecrats were the harbingers of an extraordinarily important electoral shift in American presidential politics.

Truman survived the challenge from the right by the Dixiecrats and also from the left by former vice president Henry Wallace, who ran for president under the Progressive Party banner. Truman narrowly won the election over these and also the Republican candidate, Thomas Dewey. The year 1948 was, however, the beginning of the end of the New Deal coalition that Franklin Roosevelt had assembled and that had dominated American politics for a generation by that time. It took years, even decades, for the New Deal coalition to completely unravel, but unravel it did, finally, in the 1960s and 1970s, hastened by the party reform movement: 1948 is as good a date as any to denote the beginning of that transition. The parties of the twenty-first century are still trying to build a permanent governing coalition, one that will allow them to hold power for several decades and, potentially, control American politics for as long as the New Deal coalition. So far neither party has been able to duplicate Roosevelt and Truman's New Deal coalition, although both parties continue to try.

Effect of Presidential Elections on Parties

The election of 1948 was the last time the Democrats could afford to be deeply divided internally and still have any realistic chance of winning the presidency.

Roosevelt's New Deal coalition was beginning to come apart at the seams; from a narrow victory under Truman, the Democrats went on to suffer landslide defeats with their nominee, Adlai Stevenson, in both 1952 and 1956. General Dwight Eisenhower, the Allied commander on D-Day and one of the major architects of the Allies' victory in World War II, became the Republican nominee in 1952, after a close and contentious struggle with Senator Robert Taft of Ohio. Taft represented the conservative bedrock of the Republican Party in the Midwest; Eisenhower represented a more moderate strain of the party, which he called the New Republicans. In essence, Taft wanted to repeal the New Deal and roll back the scope and power of the national government, while Eisenhower only wanted to contain the power of the national government and bend it to Republican objectives. Eisenhower won the nomination at the Republican National Convention in July 1952 and went on to defeat Adlai Stevenson of Illinois quite handily in the general election. With California senator Richard Nixon as his running mate, Eisenhower garnered over 33 million popular votes, to approximately 27 million for Stevenson. Eisenhower received 442 Electoral College votes to only 89 for Stevenson. Even with Senator John Sparkman of Alabama as his running mate, Adlai Stevenson lost three of the Old Confederacy states (Tennessee, Texas, and Florida) to Eisenhower, in what was a harbinger of electoral results to come.

In fact, Stevenson carried only nine states in 1952, all of them southern or border states: Arkansas, Louisiana, Mississippi, Alabama, Georgia, South Carolina, North Carolina, Kentucky, and West Virginia. These are now among the most dependably Republican states in presidential politics. In the 1956 landslide, Stevenson carried only six southern states plus the border state of Missouri, for 73 electoral votes, against 457 amassed by Eisenhower (CQ, 1975, 255–56).

In 1960 John Kennedy carried six southern states, plus he split the vote in Alabama (CQ, 1975, 257). In 1964 Lyndon Johnson, who was from Texas and who had always been close to the southern senators and power brokers, carried only six southern states and lost five to Barry Goldwater (CQ, 1975, 258). In 1968 Hubert Humphrey carried only Texas in the South, losing the rest of the South to Richard Nixon or George Wallace (CQ, 1975, 259). By then the march of the South out of the national Democratic Party was picking up speed. In 1972 Richard Nixon carried the entire South, as he did the rest of the nation (except for Massachusetts and the District of Columbia). During that period the "solid" South was effectively becoming a competitive region, where the right Republican could win the presidential vote, despite the fact that most elected state and local officials in the South were still Democrats and most southerners still identified themselves as Democrats. But a new alignment of the two parties was well under way, and the South as well as border states like Missouri and Kentucky were the lynchpins of that realignment.

Since the 1970s the South has given any Republican presidential candidate a significant strategic advantage in planning their Electoral College strategy. Between 1972 and 2008 the only way the Democrats could win any presidential electoral votes from the South was to have a southern presidential candidate on the ticket, and even then their success has been limited. Jimmy Carter of Georgia carried ten southern states in his successful race for the presidency in 1976, losing only Virginia of the eleven traditional southern states. He also carried the border states of Missouri and Kentucky. That was the last time a Democratic presidential candidate has won a majority of the southern states or carried either Missouri or Kentucky. Other than Clinton in 1992 and 1996 and Barack Obama in 2008 and 2012, the Democrats lost all of the southern states to the Republican presidential candidates during this era.

In 1980 against Republican Ronald Reagan of California, out of the entire South plus the border states, Carter carried only his native state of Georgia. In 1984 Walter Mondale lost the entire South to Reagan. In 1988 Michael Dukakis lost all of the southern states to George H. W. Bush. In 1992 the Democrats made something of a comeback with Bill Clinton of Arkansas and Al Gore of Tennessee at the top of the ticket, but 1992 was the last echo of the old New Deal coalition, which Franklin Roosevelt had assembled and which the loss of the solid South had destroyed. Even then, with two moderate southern candidates at the top of the ticket, the Democrats lost seven of the eleven southern states to incumbent George H. W. Bush. In 1996 Clinton and Gore again carried four southern states: Arkansas, Tennessee, Louisiana, and Florida. In 2000 Gore lost the entire South in his excruciatingly close race against George W. Bush. Even laying aside the extremely controversial loss that Gore sustained in Florida, if he had carried either his home state of Tennessee or Bill Clinton's home state of Arkansas, Gore would have been elected president, not only by the popular vote, which he carried by more than half a million votes, but also by the Electoral College vote, which he lost by five votes in the wake of the Supreme Court's controversial 5-4 decision in the case of *Bush* v. *Gore*.

In 2004 John Kerry lost every southern and border state, and despite running a close race against George W. Bush, he was unable to put together an electoral coalition of states outside the South that would add up to the required 270 Electoral College votes. The Democrats simply were not able to build a winning coalition. The Republicans hoped that their Electoral College advantage, especially in the South, would carry them to victory in 2008 in what appeared to be a very challenging political environment. Of course, they were destined to have those hopes dashed, as Barack Obama won the popular vote by 52 to 48 percent and the Electoral College vote by 365 to 173.

Obama fashioned a popular vote majority and an even bigger electoral vote majority in 2008 partially on the strength of the nation's reactions against the administration of George W. Bush. Based on the economic dislocations on the domestic front, and popular reaction against the increasingly unpopular war in Iraq on the international front, Barack Obama became the nation's forty-fourth president and its first African American president on January 20, 2009. Obama was the first nonsouthern and clearly liberal candidate to win for the Democrats since John F. Kennedy in 1960. He even managed to win three southern states—Virginia, North Carolina, and Florida—the first Democrat to win any state in the South since Bill Clinton was able to do so, and he won all the states carried by John Kerry in 2004. Obama also won nine states that had been carried by George W. Bush in 2004. Obama thus won the right to govern for the next four years. Those four years proved to be controversial and challenging for Obama and the Democrats as the nation struggled to dig its way out of the economic hole created by the Great Recession of 2007–09.

In the 2010 midterm elections, congressional gains made by the Democrats in 2006 and 2008 were largely erased in a Republican wave, which was widely interpreted as a repudiation of some of Obama's policies, especially the Affordable Care Act, his landmark health care legislation. It was also a reaction to the slow recovery of the economy and especially the high unemployment rates resulting from the Great Recession. These new Republican victories, especially the gain of sixty-three new seats in the House and the resulting divided government, raised new questions about the future of the Democratic Party and more generally about the future of the nation's politics (Theiss-Morse and others, 2011).

This divided government and the conflicts it engendered became the backdrop for the very volatile run-up to the presidential election of 2012. The two parties appeared to be very close to evenly divided going into 2012, and the partisan polarization that had been evident for several years only seemed to be intensified and solidified by the rhetoric of the political campaign and the actions of the two opposing camps. In 2012 Obama lost North Carolina, which he had carried in 2008; however, he hung onto both Florida and Virginia. The vote of white southerners was overwhelmingly for the Republican, Mitt Romney. The vote of African Americans was even more overwhelmingly for Obama, thus continuing and exacerbating the polarization of the nation along racial lines.

The Ideological Basis for Realignment

What happened in the last four decades of the twentieth century to bring about the electoral realignment in American presidential politics? There are many good academic and popular treatments of this story, and especially of the role of the South in the realignment, and it need not be the major focus here (Black and Black, 1987, 1992). Edward Carmines and James Stimson (1989) write persuasively about the crucial role of race in American politics and in this transition. Race has always divided the United States and created conflict within national, state, and local politics, but it is only in the recent era that racial divisions have overlapped the cleavages between the two major parties and become coterminous with their identities. Formerly race and partisanship were on crosscutting cleavages in American society, but more recently the two fault lines have become aligned. Thus partisan sorting and ideological polarization have deepened and become more permanent (Levendusky, 2009).

This polarization is particularly true of race in the South. Racial politics is not the only factor in the transformation of the white American South out of the Democratic Party and into the Republican Party, but it is the most central factor. In addition, a predominantly conservative political culture in the South, reinforced by evangelical and fundamentalist churches, added impetus to racial divisions (Silk and Walsh, 2008). Even those explanations, however, fail to account for the precipitous decline of a strong strand of progressive politics that had been part of the southern political tradition for generations. Progressive southerners like Jimmy Carter, Bill Clinton, Dale Bumpers, David Pryor, Albert Gore Sr. and Jr., Estes Kefauver, Ralph Yarborough, Lawton Childs, Bob Graham, Lister Hill, John Sparkman, and J. W. Fulbright, to name just a few, were elected either governor or senator, or both, in the era of 1950 through 2000. It is doubtful any of them could be elected as a Democrat in the South of today. Also, a penchant for supporting a strong military, often identified in the popular mind as more of a Republican than a Democratic position, is a part of the explanation for the partisan changes in the South.

Opposition to gun control, and its identification as a Republican-favoring issue, is also a part of the story. In the South and some other rural areas of the nation, guns and any threat to their continued easy availability is a compelling issue, and it is one that works mostly for Republicans, along with a few NRA-aligned Blue Dog, or moderate, Democrats in Congress. In addition, the whole morality and "family values" movement, skillfully exploited by the Republican Party and extremely popular in the South, is a part of the story. Included in that mixture is opposition to abortion and advocacy of so-called right to life positions. And opposition to some forms of gay rights, especially gay marriage, proved to be a compelling issue in all recent presidential contests. All of these specific issues are undergirded by a religious framework and become a part of the religious right's appeal to evangelical and fundamentalist Protestants (Silk and Walsh, 2008; Putnam and Campbell, 2010). These positions are particularly salient in the white South, and the South is consistently more conservative on these social issues than most of the rest of the nation. These same dynamics also hold in many rural areas and small towns in the rest of the nation. Thus what has happened in the South is a metaphor for the rural versus urban realignments that have taken place in many other sections of the nation, with perhaps a somewhat reduced emphasis on the politics of race in those other sections.

Politics, history, culture, region, race, and religion have thus become a part of a coherent and holistic way of looking at the world for many in the South (and outside as well). Taken together, these issues form a matrix of public policy measures that Republicans have exploited successfully, especially in presidential politics and especially among white and working-class and less-educated voters in the South and elsewhere. All of these issues provide the Republican Party with direct access to the conservative and fundamentalist churches of the South and their national organizations, especially the Southern Baptists and various Pentecostals and other nondenominational evangelicals who are the backbone of much of the culture of the South. Appreciating the crucial and particular role of religion in the South is pivotal in understanding the South, and the Republican Party has utilized this insight into the white South very effectively.

The Democrats have benefited from the unstinting support of the black churches in the South; however, that advantage has not come close to offsetting their losses in the churches of the white South. No single issue is as important as race in the politics of the South. It now has a direct overlay of religion and politics, where racial and religious cleavages in society directly overlap and reinforce partisan divisions. All of these trends have worked to the distinct disadvantage of the Democratic Party in national politics over the past four decades. What the Democrats have lost in the South and in other rural areas they have attempted to make up for in urban and suburban areas of the nation. So far, they have enjoyed only sporadic success, particularly in the presidential contests and in many of the once solidly Democratic congressional districts. These were formerly represented by moderate-to-conservative Democrats but are now solidly Republican, especially since the congressional elections of 2010.

The Republican Transition

The Republicans experienced their own, more limited, version of this same internal debate over their party's future that the Democrats struggle with, asking such questions as where power should reside in the party and who should control the levers of power and what is the chief reason for the party's existence. Much of the Republican debate has been propelled by ideology and geography rather than by party procedures and rules.

This loss of the moderates among Democrats and Republicans is a crucial component of the Republican dominance in the House of Representatives since the 2010 midterm elections. In 2012 the GOP won a thirty-three-seat majority in the House in spite of losing the aggregate national popular vote by 1.7 million total votes. The factionalism of the Republican Party, especially evident in the House, has led to endless speculation about the future of the party. The tactics associated with the government shutdown of October 2013 and the potential for default on the national debt took a toll on the Republican Party's image and support. This debate over the future of the party was stimulated by the movement that conservatives associate with the Barry Goldwater era of 1964, as they tried to wrest power away from the more moderate and liberal elements of the Republican Party, epitomized by Dwight Eisenhower and Richard Nixon. Conservatives wanted control of the party and often mounted grassroots challenges to established party leaders as a way of taking party organizational power. This was also a geographic battle, with the more traditional Republicans anchored in the Northeast and Midwest, while the challengers supporting Goldwater were mostly from the West and the South.

The transition that the Republicans went through after Barry Goldwater's nomination and the triumph of the conservatives is still the defining epoch for the contemporary Republican Party. There is no doubt that the appeal of the programmatic party approach has grown, particularly in this polarized era. The Republicans have become the conservative alternative and the Democrats the liberal alternative in the programs and policies they offer, in the views and values of the party elites, and in the minds of the voting public. Many people are deeply divided over basic values and economic and foreign policy issues, such as the wars in Iraq and Afghanistan, health insurance, abortion, gay rights, stem cell research, prayer in public schools, gun control, affirmative action, the environment, and immigration reform (Green and Herrnson, 2002; Levendusky, 2009). The debate that started in earnest in the 1960s continues today.

The intramural debates over the future of the Republican Party initially were focused on the candidacy of Barry Goldwater in 1964. Typically, those debates involved both ideology and geography, and they separated the more conservative wing of the party from the more traditional moderate-to-liberal wing. They also separated the South, the Southwest, and the Mountain West from the Northeast and the urban areas of the Midwest. Barry Goldwater represented a very conservative and very ideological approach to politics, and he mobilized a whole new generation of conservative party activists (Kessel, 1968). In the battle for the Republican nomination in 1964, Goldwater was challenged by William Scranton, the governor of Pennsylvania, and Nelson Rockefeller, the governor of New York, both of whom represented the moderate eastern establishment wing, which had dominated the Republican Party since Eisenhower's victory over Taft in 1952.

Goldwater was not the favorite of the party's leadership, which was based largely on the East Coast and in the Midwest. He had a loyal following, but it was not clearly a majority of the party. Indeed, until Goldwater won the California primary on June 5, the last primary of the 1964 season, he had not won a clear victory in a single primary that year (Kessel, 1968). It is a mark of just how little used the primaries were at that time as a route to the nomination that Goldwater cinched the Republican nomination in 1964 based on a single narrow primary victory. Instead, it was the party leaders, the party elites, who made the nomination in 1964, as they had always done in both parties since the advent of the national convention system (1832 for the Democrats and 1856 for the Republicans). When Goldwater beat Rockefeller in the California primary and won the nomination, power started its inexorable shift from the liberal and moderate wing to the conservative wing of the party. It also started a geographical power shift for the Republicans from the Northeast and the Midwest to the Southwest, the West, and later the South. In 1964 in the wake of Goldwater's landslide loss to Lyndon Johnson, and the major gains the Democrats scored in Congress that year, many experts questioned whether the Republicans could ever emerge from their "permanent minority" status. Many Republicans worried about the same question. It was soon answered.

The Republicans recuperated very quickly with significant gains in the 1966 congressional elections, which presaged the Republican victory led by Richard Nixon in 1968. Each party enjoyed great victories and suffered significant defeats in the last quarter of the twentieth century, and that cyclic trend continues into the first two decades of the twenty-first century. Most of those victories and defeats were driven by the wins and losses of the presidency, which tends to drive the image of both parties. Those presidential box scores are supplemented or reinforced by the congressional election results, but those take second place in the minds of the voters to the more prominent presidential election results. There is an ebb and flow to all these contests and to their results, which helps to shape the popular images of the two parties and their potential for survival and expansion.

In the wake of the Bush victories of 2000 and 2004, his skillful political use of the 9/11 terrorists attacks, and the Republican congressional victories of 2002 and 2004, once again questions were being raised about the prospects for the Democrats to ever regain majority control in Congress or to win the White House again; even their long-term viability was questioned. George Bush and Karl Rove clearly planned to build a new Republican majority. During the six years between 2001 and 2007, Republicans were indeed successful in controlling the White House and, with the exception of a brief interlude in the Senate in 2001–02, Congress. But with the significant losses the Republicans suffered in the 2006 midterm elections, the deeply unpopular war in Iraq, and President Bush's extraordinarily low job approval ratings, by 2007 the Republicans, who once seemed on the verge of pulling together a new ruling coalition, were beset by fundamental questions about their party's future and whether they could regain any footing for the 2008 congressional and presidential elections.

Democrats were looking toward 2008 with a combination of hope and dread as they sought organizational salvation in the prospects of nominating a new presidential candidate who could lead them back from the political wilderness. The Democrats also continued to tinker with the nominations process and its rules, especially the calendar. The calendar and rules arguments of 2007 and 2008 in the Democratic Party would not have been unfamiliar to a national convention delegate to the 1968 Democratic National Convention, where the modern reform era could be said to have begun. The Republicans showed an interest in the same issues, especially the establishment of the window within which the primaries and caucuses had to be held; they were especially interested in the front-loading of the calendar. Republicans also increasingly acted as an unmovable block of opposition votes against the Democratic Party's policy agenda, starting with the Affordable Care Act but extending to virtually all other major domestic policies Obama advocated. Both parties were increasingly approximating the responsible party model.

After their loss of the presidential election in 2008 and their continuation as the minority party in Congress, the Republicans again were soul searching as they tried to define the party and chart its course. They chose the course of just saying no to almost any Obama initiative. They were internally united and disciplined in their opposition to virtually all of Obama's legislation, and they provided almost unanimous opposition to the health care reform act and the president's 2009 financial stimulus package. They bet that the economy was not going to heal enough to stimulate jobs growth and that their opposition to Obama could yield them significant dividends in the 2010 elections. In late 2009 and early 2010 the Republicans seemed poised for a comeback, as they won elections for governor in Virginia and New Jersey and, unexpectedly, the Senate seat in Massachusetts that Edward Kennedy had filled for forty-eight years. At this point the Democrats' nominal control of a filibuster-proof majority of sixty votes, which had lasted only six months, came to a close, and Republican opposition to the Obama administration's major policy initiatives became even more effective. After the Massachusetts Senate vote, Republican prospects for victory in the 2010 midterm elections seemed to be much brighter, and the prospects for a quick return to divided government became much more immediate.

This promise of a Republican resurgence was realized in abundance in the midterm elections of 2010. It is widely recognized that the party that controls the White House will most likely lose seats in Congress in the subsequent midterm election. Since the end of World War II, this loss has averaged twenty-seven seats in the House and three or four seats in the Senate (Theiss-Morse and others, 2011, chap. 1). To take control of the House and Senate, Republicans needed to gain thirty-nine seats in the House and ten seats in the Senate.

Early polls and all the other markers of projected party success led most prognosticators to predict a Republican takeover of the House and the potential of taking control of the Senate (Abramowitz, 2010b). There were also many predictions of Republican gains at the state level, both governorships and state legislatures. President Obama's job approval ratings hovered between 45 and 50 percent, and the generic ballot of who the voter preferred for Congress consistently gave the Republicans a positive margin. The whole race centered on the economy, most notably job loss and job creation. The economy was clearly experiencing a comeback from the Great Recession, and the loss of jobs (which exceeded 300,000 a month when President Obama took office) had been reversed. Indeed, the rate of new job growth in the private sector was over 90,000 a month in October, the last full month before election day on November 2. However, the unemployment rate was stuck stubbornly at just under 10 percent, and each new jobs report was greeted with disappointment, as economists and the media pointed out that a growth rate of over 300,000 new jobs a month was needed to make a dent in unemployment.

The media were fixed on that one metric of economic success. The Republican Party fueled that fixation by talking about nothing else. A fair number of other economic indicators, like the stock market and retail sales and the savings rate, had all increased; however, none of that seemed to matter to Republicans or to the media. The Obama administration's argument that the stimulus package had indeed worked and had saved as many as 3 million jobs that would have been lost without it was lost in the cacophony and lamentations regarding job creation. That became the dominant narrative of the 2010 campaign. Once it was adopted by the mass media and reinforced repeatedly by the Republican Party and its allies, the die was cast, and the Democrats were destined for a major defeat. The question then became whether this was a dress rehearsal for the 2012 presidential campaign.

The size and depth of the Democratic defeat in the midterm elections were truly historic. The Republicans gained sixty-three seats in the House of Representatives. The Democrats lost everywhere outside of the major urban centers and were reduced to a bare handful of members who still represented the rural and small-town hinterland from New England across to the West Coast. A number of long-time and powerful Democrats, many of whom were chairs of major committees, went down to defeat. The Republicans also gained five seats in the Senate, although they failed to gain the fifty-one-seat majority they had hoped for. The Republicans won the largest number of House seats they had held since 1928. They immediately took control of the House and started selecting new chairs for all the committees.

Historically, this extraordinary takeover of Congress echoed the Republicans' midterm success in Bill Clinton's first term, when they gained fifty-four seats in the House and ten seats in the Senate. The post–World War II record had been the Republican gain of fifty-five seats in the House and twelve in the Senate in 1946, when Harry Truman was president (Stanley and Niemi, 2009–10, 42). The Republicans also held thirty governorships, a gain of ten. They also held the advantage in twenty-five states, where they controlled both houses of the state legislatures. This meant that, a year before national redistricting battles began, the Republicans were in a position to control the process in many states. That redistricting dominance holds the promise for GOP control of the House at least through 2016 and perhaps through 2020.

The Obama administration was rocked back on its heels by the 2010 midterm election debacle. The president conceded that his party had taken a "shellacking," and he was bombarded with questions from the media about how he would deal with the new Republican majority in the House and the new Speaker of the House, John Boehner. Internal bickering started immediately among the Democrats in the House as they contemplated their loss of the majority and the speakership and as they tried to choose a new leadership team. Many members of the House Blue Dog caucus lost their seats, and the remainder of that group was especially incensed when the Democratic Speaker, Nancy Pelosi, announced that she wanted to stay on as the Democratic minority leader. Pelosi ultimately won this vote, 153-47, an indicator of the liberal versus moderate divide in the Democratic Party's congressional delegation. The future of the Democratic Party was once again up for debate and media speculation. The ebb and flow of American politics continued, and once again the Democrats ebbed while the Republicans flowed. The parties were more polarized along ideological lines than ever. The people who had lost were the more moderate members of the two parties, mainline Republicans having lost to Tea Party–blessed candidates. This ideological realignment carried over into everything that happened (or did not happen) in Congress in its 2011–12 session and particularly colored the rocky relationship between Congress and the White House.

This cycle of victory and defeat, celebration and despair has marked both parties in their constant struggle for electoral dominance, and winning the presidency has been the most important priority. Each party geared up for the 2012 presidential and congressional elections as the next big test in the constant challenge to ensure the party's future as a party and as potentially the governing party in the next era.

Of course, Obama won reelection by a fairly handy margin of 51 to 47 percent in the popular vote and by 332 to 206 in the Electoral College vote. Democrats also continued to control the Senate by 55-45. However, the Republicans reaffirmed their grip on the House with a win of 233 seats to the Democrats' 200 (Stanley and Niemi, 2013–14, 201). Thus divided government continued. Indeed, the partisan polarization in the House and the Senate and the logic of a separation of powers system, coupled with a loss of ability to compromise, continued the legislative gridlock and deeply divisive government of the 2011–12 period into the 2013–14 period. The partisan, gridlock-driven government shutdown of October 2013 and the narrow brush with defaulting on the national debt were just the most obvious public manifestations of a separation of powers system overlayered by a polarized party system so divisive as to render the whole system dysfunctional.

While the institutional systems of separation of powers and checks and balances and federalism all contributed to an almost frozen political system, the deep divisions among various interest and demographic groups also contributed immeasurably to the problem.

Party Response to Gender and Race Inequality

A key part of building each party's winning coalition is the exploitation of that party's advantage in the voting behavior of major demographic groups. The Democrats took an early lead in the 1970s in opening their party to women and minorities. Access to the leadership echelon was particularly notable in the provision of seats to previously disadvantaged groups, the party assisting them in becoming national convention delegates. Other public policies, such as support for affirmative action for women and African Americans, also attracted large numbers of those groups to the Democratic banner.

In contrast, the Republicans subtly and effectively appealed to male voters and to those female voters opposed to the women's movement. This backlash reinforced the resistance already under way against the civil rights movement, especially affirmative action for members of marginalized groups applying for jobs, housing, public contracts, or admission to elite universities, medical schools, and law schools. Americans profess strong support for equality; however, conflict has developed over the definition of *equality*. The rationale is advanced that equality is equality of opportunity, which is an almost universally shared norm in the country, as opposed to equality of condition, which implies government action to change conditions.

Proponents of affirmative action argue that governments at both state and national levels have long practiced, or at least allowed, overt and covert discrimination against marginalized groups. Opponents of affirmative action insist that the government should be blind to past discrimination, arguing that two wrongs do not make a right. These two arguments hold sway over practical policies, with the Republicans believing in equality of opportunity and the Democrats favoring equality of outcome.

These policies resulted in strong election support of Democrats by women and minorities and of Republicans by men, a difference known in the political parlance as the gender gap and the racial gap. Democrats enjoy a voter advantage of up to 10 percent among women, and Republicans enjoy a similar advantage among men. In 2012 women voted for Obama over Romney by 55-44. Men voted for Romney over Obama by 52-45 (Stanley and Niemi, 2013–14, 116).

The racial gap in the presidential elections is approximately 90-10, in favor of the Democratic nominee. This has become one of the largest and most persistent group-based gaps in the history of voting behavior. Among white voters, the division is much closer; however, recent Republican presidential candidates have achieved a 3-to-10 percent advantage. The election of Barack

Obama in 2008 seemed to confirm and reinforce those trends, even though he ran somewhat better among white voters than either of his two Democratic predecessors. If the electorate had been all white, John McCain would have been elected president easily, since McCain took 53 percent of the white vote but only 5 percent of the black vote. By comparison, Obama took only 45 percent of the white vote in 2008 (winning 93 percent of the black vote; see Stanley and Niemi, 2009–10, 124–25).

In 2012 Obama won only 39 percent of the white vote, compared to 59 percent for Romney, the worst margin ever for a Democrat who won (Stanley and Niemi, 2013–14, 116). The only problem with this result for Romney was that the white vote constituted only 72 percent of the total electorate, which was an all-time low point for majority voters. Obama won 93 percent of the black vote, emphasizing the racial polarization that has marked our politics since the civil rights revolution of the 1960s, a polarization that has seemed to grow in recent years. An ominous portent for the future is the fact that Romney won only 27 percent of the Hispanic and Latino votes in 2012 (Stanley and Niemi, 2013–14, 116).

Among Hispanic voters George W. Bush did the best of any Republican candidate in history, garnering 44 percent of that bloc in 2004. Bush avidly courted their vote during both terms of his presidency. However, in 2008 this GOP advantage declined precipitously, when McCain only received 29 percent of the Hispanic vote, compared to over two-thirds for Obama (Stanley and Niemi, 2009–10, 124–25). By that standard, the Hispanic voting bloc, which was once courted by both sides, seems to be leaning markedly toward the Democrats. In such states as Arizona, South Carolina, and Alabama, the majority of white legislators have made their antipathy toward illegal immigrants abundantly clear by passing restrictive laws disadvantaging these people, echoing the kinds of backlash that used to be directed against blacks and women. The fact that those legislators are widely supported by the voters of their states indicates that the majority in many of those states will reward their legislators for taking punitive action against immigrant groups. Many Republican leaders have expressed grave concerns about the party's tendency to alienate Hispanic voters, noting what it can mean for the party's future since Hispanics are the fastest growing minority in the nation. Others feel that they will more than compensate for Hispanic losses with gains among white voters, at least in the immediate future. This division was evident in the run-up to the 2014 midterm elections. President Obama made a major point of pushing repeatedly for the House to pass the immigration bill that had already passed by a narrow margin in the Senate. However, Speaker Boehner made it plain that there would be no action in the House until the November 2014 elections were over.

The racial gap and the gender gap are now apparently rather dependable features of most elections in the United States, particularly presidential elections. Those who lead the parties, and those who form their activist base, largely realize that politics entails conflict, and very few of their actions are ever free of a down side. They understand that in politics there are trade-offs and that, in the language of game theory, there are a lot of zero-sum games they must play. They must learn to navigate these political waters and make the best choices they can, as strategic and tactical situations come at them with ever increasing velocity in a twenty-four-hour news cycle where the cable channels are filled with talking, and sometimes shouting, heads demanding responses.

Rational Action by Political Elites and New Party Models

The leaders of political parties are faced with the constant demand to make strategic choices about which policies to advocate and which issues to stress and especially which candidates to recruit and try to elect and which candidates to fund in the more marginal races. These choices are very important, as they can help or hurt the party in the long run. The way leaders present their messages, mobilize media outlets, choose spokespersons, and frame the party's message, both in style and content, are crucial. All of these decisions accrue to the benefit or to the detriment of the party's long-term adaptation and survival. But the first demand on their time and energy is usually winning the next election.

The Democrats early in this era struggled quite publicly with the question of how to respond to what appear to be the incompatible demands of their political environment. In the initial stages of the party reform era the Democrats invested a lot of energy and debate in trying to change the rules of the national party and setting up a rules regime to help shift power from the traditional party bosses to party activists and to the voters in the primaries. As we see in more detail in the next chapter, Democrats emphasized intraparty reforms and grassroots democracy as their primary response to the challenges of party renewal. They stressed the development of national party procedures and codified formal rules in their attempt to ensure that new groups would be empowered and that the party would be more open to newcomers and fair to all who want to participate. Empowering new groups and responding to the social movements already afoot among minorities and women have been high priorities for the Democrats. That is much of what the reform era of the 1970s and 1980s was all about for the Democrats, and those rules and procedures still control much of what the party does today, particularly in the selection of its presidential nominee and the organization of its national convention.

These steps toward inclusiveness have been controversial, however. During the last three decades of the twentieth century and the beginning of this century, Democrats had to juggle the demands of advocates for minorities, especially women and African Americans and, more recently, Hispanics, against the demands of those who feel threatened by the gains of these groups. Contentious issues include desegregation of the schools and busing versus neighborhood schools, fair or open housing laws, affirmative action in government jobs and contracts, preferences in university admissions, depiction of the confederate battle flag on state buildings and in state flags, and the display of the Ten Commandments in public buildings.

At the same time, the Democratic Party had to deal with reaction from some who were offended by both the tactics and the objectives of the feminist and civil rights movements. Social movements demand a change in the status quo, and their advocates are not content with the incremental change that the American political system usually provides. Both the civil rights movement and the women's movement took their demands for a share of political power to the Democratic Party. The party responded by opening up their ranks to not only women and ethnic minorities but, to a lesser extent, young people. The party was aware of the pitfalls of responding to these demands: that is, the potential for the loss of some of the party's traditional base in the white South as well as among male and more traditional female voters. Those conflicts were not always limited to the South either. Nevertheless, the Democrats responded to these social movements both by altering the internal rules that govern the party and by advocating public policies that address some of the demands.

The leadership echelons of the parties are people capable of acting rationally, defined as having definite goals and seeing objectively the various alternatives for reaching those goals and evaluating the alternatives in light of the immediate and long-term goals and the costs of reaching those goals—and then choosing the route most likely to reach the goals. This is one of the most important theoretical perspectives of this book; that is, the positing of rational action by political elites. Political elites are capable of and accustomed to making hard strategic calculations about complex political questions. The fact that they manage bounded rationality in only some instances and in dealing with only some issues does not necessarily weaken the axiom that they constantly seek power and seek to preserve their parties through the strategic choices they make (Simon, 1989; Monroe, 1991). The assumption that political elites act on that axiom explains most of the strategic decisions made by both parties over the past four decades.

Republicans are no less capable than Democrats in this regard, although they use different strategies for reaching their goal of party building. In essence, Republicans choose the route of ideological appeals to conservatives and to the groups that would benefit from their policies when they are in office. They also choose to increase the services the national party provides to state and local parties and to its constituents. Republicans do not usually follow Democrats in emphasizing due process, although they occasionally have followed the Democrats' lead in this area and have provided some leadership of their own in addressing the front-loading problem.

This approach has served Republicans well. In both presidential and congressional politics, they have fared very well indeed over the past four decades. They undoubtedly recognized that in the throes of the disruption and conflict of the mid-1960s the future of their party was at risk. After the 1964 Goldwater electoral debacle Republicans were faced with charges that they had grown irrelevant. Yet from a landslide loss of the presidency in 1964, and despite minority status in the 1965–66 Congress, Republicans came back, after their 1966 midterm victories, to stop Lyndon Johnson's Great Society initiatives cold. In only four years after the Johnson landslide of 1964, Richard Nixon and the Republicans were able to win the presidency, albeit by only a narrow margin, over Hubert Humphrey. Nixon and Lee Atwater fashioned the "southern strategy" in order to appeal to the white South and to start building a new Republican majority. Nixon made a lot of other smart tactical moves in dealing with the electoral challenge of 1972, and in so doing he achieved a landslide over George McGovern that year.

Obviously, Nixon also made some very serious mistakes: overreaching, trying to build a massive reelection victory, and then eventually Watergate. In the wake of Watergate, the future of the Republican Party was once again questioned, just as it had been ten years earlier in the wake of Goldwater's massive loss. Fearing for their future, political party elites, especially centered at the Republican National Committee (RNC), first under the leadership of Ray Bliss of Ohio and later under the leadership of Bill Brock of Tennessee, fashioned a strategic plan for the revival of the Republican Party. This plan became a whole new party model, which transformed the Republican Party at the national committee level. (Later the Democrats would follow suit.)

The Republicans thus originated the modern service party, which emphasizes strengthening the party organization and making it combat ready for the electoral wars. That is, it emphasizes the raising and distribution of large amounts of funds and the targeting of those funds to the most crucial races for Congress and to the states where they will do the most good. The national party hires marketing and mass media experts and makes them available to Republican candidates. It hires pollsters and puts them to work for the party's presidential and congressional candidates, making the poll results available to Republican candidates far down the ballot. Bill Brock and the RNC used the power of the national party and its fund-raising ability to build the party through grassroots organizing, especially at the state and local level. They also built on the interest groups that supported Republicans and created a robust interest group coalition with deep allegiance to the Republican Party—and often with deep pockets, too. They created a massive fund-raising operation, which encouraged large gifts but which also depended on small donations via the massive database that Brock and the RNC assembled.

The Republican Party's transformation into a modern service party put in place the expertise necessary to raise and distribute multiple millions of dollars each election cycle. These funds were targeted so as to have maximum impact, usually in the marginal races where the party had a real opportunity to win competitive seats. The Republicans took early initiatives and an early lead in these strategic calculations regarding marginal districts (Herrnson, 1988). With the requisite level of campaign finance, they were able to put together a network of campaign management experts, the people trained in the arts and sciences of mass marketing, and the people who knew how to use public opinion polling and television, all for the purpose of advancing a message and selling a candidate (McGinniss, 1969).

The Republicans thus took the lead in developing the new model of national party; Democrats followed suit a bit later (Herrnson, 1988; Green and Coffey, 2007; White and Shea, 2001). The Republicans created a powerful party organization in each of the southern states, where almost none had existed before, and they mounted an extraordinarily successful appeal to white southerners (Maggiotto and Wekkin, 2000). The Republican response to party building following the Watergate disaster was a model of rational decisionmaking, in which they developed a clear-eyed goal of winning elections. They correctly calculated their strengths and weaknesses, as well as those of the Democrats, and developed a plan to increase their organizational capacity to help their candidates and adopted a political strategy, with ideological and geographic components, that built upon and expanded the party's base of voters and brought many voters into the party who had not traditionally supported Republican candidates. The result was that the Republicans won five of the seven presidential elections from 1980 through 2004. They also controlled the majority in Congress, almost uninterrupted, between 1995 and 2007. They lost their majority in the house in the 2006 elections but regained it, with a large margin to spare, in the 2010 midterms and reaffirmed that majority in the presidential election year of 2012. The service party model has been a crucial component of these electoral successes. The Republicans did so well with the service party model that the Democrats built their own organizational model based on the Republican model. It was especially necessary for the Democrats to build up their organizational and fund-raising strength, as labor unions declined in power and numbers due to changes in the economy. With the exception of the white collar unions, especially those in the public sector, labor unions have been losing strength and clout for decades in the United States. This undermining of the Democrats went largely unnoticed outside party circles. The Democrats compensated for the loss of union support by building up the Democratic National Committee, Capitol Hill committees, and state party organizations. They also built a network of sympathetic political action committees to provide deep-pocket funding.

As both parties were trying to build organizational strength, they were simultaneously emphasizing their ideological issues and becoming ideologically polarized. The Republicans increasingly branded themselves as the conservative party, offering a variety of conservative issue positions that virtually all of their top candidates espoused. The opposite reaction of the Democrats at that time constituted a liberal agenda that was also reasonably coherent and that provided an alternative to the Republicans. Each move by one party provoked an equal and opposite reaction by the other party. Both parties thus moved in concert while developing an ideological, issue-oriented, and policy-driven realignment—and the concomitant increase in ideological cleavages that heretofore had not existed so clearly in American party politics (Fleisher and Bond, 2001; Green and Herrnson, 2002).

While the parties' shifting did not reach the level of the ideological coherence of many European parliamentary parties, it certainly constituted "a choice not an echo," to borrow a phrase from Barry Goldwater's 1964 campaign. In the twenty-first century, the American voters are still being offered a fairly clear version of that choice in the campaign rhetoric, party platforms, and issue advocacy of the two major parties and their candidates. This constitutes, as noted earlier, a truly American version of the familiar responsible parties model, which was developed in European party systems (Pomper and Lederman, 1980; Pomper, 2001; Crotty, 2001). Both parties made then, and reaffirm with every subsequent election, the basic strategic decision to try to solidify the party's ideological and issue-oriented base first and foremost, as they build their campaign plans. Of course, the rational campaign planner then very quickly attempts to add to the party's base, by appealing as aggressively as possible to the true independents and to the middle of the American political spectrum. In fact, most pundits give Bill Clinton, and then George W. Bush, credit for appealing to the large and active middle while holding onto their traditional party base as the key component of their presidential election success in 1992, 1996, 2000, and 2004. In 2004 Bush depended most heavily on mobilization of the party's base, which he and Karl Rove did brilliantly with their "72-hour strategy," a plan that depended on a heavy turnout by Republican loyalists supplemented by a decent showing among independents.

Barack Obama, for his 2008 victory, replicated Bush's strategy of mobilizing and turning out the base first. His campaign replicated and perfected that strategy and extended it to a whole new plane in 2012. That election was marked by the most sophisticated get-out-the-vote campaign in presidential history. It depended on a unique combination of the old-fashioned ground game of getting volunteers out into the field and onto the front porches of their most likely voters—and more important, in front of those who were identified as being persuadable. For this, the campaign used modern data-mining techniques that would do NASA proud, using sophisticated laptop and mobile phone technology in ways that were unheard of up to that point. The campaign's use of social media, begun in 2008, was taken to an unprecedented new level in 2012, thus changing the way American presidential campaigns were conceived of strategically and then implemented in the field (Simon 2013; Balz and Johnson, 2009; Balz and Silberman, 2013). Throughout it all the campaign depended on a cadre of dedicated political activists who were committed to Obama personally and also to the ideologies and issue positions that the Democratic Party had come to embody. Republican activists were just as dedicated and committed to their ideals and value positions. They just did not have quite the strategic plan that the Obama campaign had, nor the grasp of conditions in the field.

Conclusion

While the two parties have their challenges and their internal weaknesses and divisions, and they certainly have their share of external critics, they continue to dominate the elections of federal and most state offices, as they have since their foundational era (the 1850s for the Republicans and the 1820s and 1830s for the Democrats). Whether the parties have been strengthened or weakened overall by the events and decisions of the 1970–2012 era is a matter of debate and controversy; however, on balance this book asserts that the two parties have been strengthened by these developments and that they seem positioned to continue their electoral dominance well into the twenty-first century.

3

The Era of Party Reform

The empirical research project that undergirds this book grew out of a specific interest in documenting the important changes taking place in the parties during the early stages of the reform movement. This movement was stimulated by an urge for survival and a commitment to being relevant to the political conflicts of the day on the part of both parties, but especially the Democrats, who had the most internal problems at the time. This movement wound up profoundly transforming the way presidential nominations were made and, in the end, also played a major role in transforming the parties themselves (Shafer, 1988; Ceaser, 1979; Crotty and Jackson, 1985; Jackson and Crotty, 2001). All these changes helped create the current polarized parties, a condition that resembles party government and the responsible party model but with a unique American twist to accommodate the constitutionally imposed separation of powers and the federal system.

These party changes initially were driven by the recommendations of the Democratic Party's Commission on Party Structure and Delegate Selection (1970), popularly called the McGovern-Fraser Commission. The McGovern-Fraser Commission was appointed as a response to the major dislocations and conflict in the Democratic National Convention held in Chicago in 1968. This is the convention that nominated Hubert Humphrey for president but that was so conflict ridden that it became almost impossible for Humphrey to win in the general election against Richard Nixon. One of the rules of survival for political parties is that they must respond to the deep-seated conflicts faced by the society and polity, especially at times of great stress. If they do not, they will sink into irrelevance and disappear, as the once powerful Whig Party did in the 1850s when faced with the challenges of slavery that led to the Civil War.

In the 1960s the nation was deeply divided over the Vietnam War, and dissidents and critics held President Lyndon Johnson, and indirectly his vice president, Hubert Humphrey, responsible for the war. Senator Eugene McCarthy was the political leader of the antiwar movement, and he challenged Johnson in the New Hampshire primary early in 1968. Johnson won the New Hampshire primary—but not as convincingly as he had hoped—and on the last day of March Johnson announced that he would not seek a second full term. Senator Robert Kennedy of New York had announced his candidacy for the presidency in early March, and he quickly became the front-runner after Johnson withdrew. Trench warfare then developed among Humphrey, McCarthy, and Kennedy. In early June, on the night of the California primary, Kennedy was assassinated. He had won that primary, which probably would have catapulted him into the lead for the nomination.

Vice President Humphrey had not contested any primaries; however, he was the clear favorite of party organization leaders such as Carmine DeSapio of New York and John Bailey of Connecticut; Democratic governors like David Lawrence of Pennsylvania; and big city mayors such as Richard J. Daley of Chicago. These are the groups that, up to that point, dominated American presidential nominations. The critics were incensed that Humphrey had not been forced to face the voters in a single state primary before the convention opened. In August the antiwar movement and representatives of a variety of other causes came to Chicago determined to protest against the war in Vietnam, against the Johnson administration and the nation's direction in general, and against the nomination of Humphrey. Hubert Humphrey was caught in the backlash against the war; he and his campaign became the target of the wrath of many of the dissidents, most of them young. (Think of a combination of Occupy Wall Street and the demonstrators who routinely protest G-7 conferences.)

The leaders of the Democratic Party, especially Democratic National Committee chair Senator Fred Harris of Oklahoma, realized that their party was in deep trouble and that its brand name had been severely damaged by the Johnson administration and the war. The party was deeply factionalized along an antiwar versus pro-Johnson administration fault line. Party leaders determined that they had to do something to quell the popular uprising that was taking place both inside the convention hall and on the streets of Chicago. This external and internal conflict provided the backdrop for the appointment of the McGovern-Fraser Commission at the 1968 Democratic National Convention.

The McGovern-Fraser Commission issued its report in April 1970 (Commission on Party Structure and Delegate Selection, 1970). That report and the recommendations it contained became the legal framework within which nomination contests were to be conducted and specified how the delegates were to be selected for the 1972 Democratic National Convention. These rules became party law when the Democratic National Committee adopted them in the spring of 1970, and they controlled the 1972 convention and the selection of delegates for it. The convention then elected Senator George McGovern to be the Democratic nominee. This period marked the transition from one type of party leader to another and from one type of selection process to another. Relying mostly on primaries and mass party voters and mostly shutting the traditional party leaders out have made the nominations system more participatory and increased the importance of party activists. This change has also created much more ideologically coherent parties, which have realigned into conservative and liberal blocs, making compromise much more difficult to attain.

The shorthand term is *polarized*. This condition has made the job of the president even harder, as he confronts and has been confronted by these newly engaged and polarized parties at the organizational level and in government. Government and policymaking are now mobilized by and responsible to the core of both major parties, and the opportunity for compromise has become increasingly difficult on any of the major issues facing the nation.

These changes transformed the Republican Party as well. A leading authority on presidential selection, William Mayer (2009, 87), quoting Byron Shafer, said of the McGovern-Fraser Commission, "The result has been justly described as 'the greatest systematic change in presidential nominating procedures in all of American history.'" I agree; and these changes have contributed to the transformation of American government and politics in the modern era. These reforms led to more openness and more participatory democracy at the party's grassroots level and to increased access and clout for party activists, who are more ideological and issue driven than the old party bosses. The activists then helped lead the core of the two parties to be more consistently liberal or conservative—thus the ideological realignment that has taken place at both mass and elite levels. All of these factors, combined, produced the polarized party system of today, and it all reached takeoff speed in the late 1960s and early 1970s, with deeper roots in the New Deal's fatal fault lines.

The McGovern-Fraser Commission Reforms

The McGovern-Fraser Commission report reviewed the past practices and rules that had controlled the delegate selection process and pronounced them to be outdated, subject to abuse, and unacceptable in the new political environment. In essence the commission found that most delegations were selected under arcane and obscure rules and informal traditions that allowed the insiders in the state and local party organizations to dominate the selection process and to exclude anyone else. The party organizational leaders used the delegate slots as rewards for past party service and enticements to support specific candidates. They bargained with other organizational leaders either before or at the convention to determine who the party nominee would be, which resolutions would pass, and what the platforms would be. The thrust of the commission's report was to ensure that all Democrats had what the commission called "a full, meaningful and timely opportunity to participate in the delegate selection process" (Commission on Party Structure and Delegate Selection, 1970, 34). In short, the old system was too dominated by party insiders and too opaque. It was time for reform of the party and of the nominations process, and the report was to serve as the blueprint for that reform.

The report divided its guidelines into two major categories, those that were required to be adopted and implemented by the states in time for the 1972 convention and those that were merely advisory. Required guidelines were as follows (Commission on Party Structure and Delegate Selection, 1970, 34–35):

—Adopt the explicit written party rules governing delegate selection. . . .

—Adopt procedural rules and safeguards for the delegate selection process that would forbid proxy; forbid the use of the unit rule and related practices, like instructing delegations; require a quorum of not less than 40 percent at all party committee meetings; remove all monetary assessments of delegates to the national convention; limit participation fees to no more than $10; limit petition requirements to no more than 1 percent of the standard used to measure Democratic strength; ensure that in all but rural areas party meetings are held on uniform dates, at uniform times, and in public places of easy access; and ensure adequate public notice of all party meetings involved in the delegate selection process. . . .

—Seek a broad base of support for the party in the following manner: add to the party rules and implement the six anti-racial-discrimination standards adopted by the Democratic National Committee; overcome the effects of past discrimination by affirmative steps to encourage representation in the national convention delegation of minority groups, young people, and women in reasonable relationship to their presence in the population of the state; allow and encourage any Democrat of eighteen years of age or older to participate in all party affairs. . . .

—Make, where applicable, the following changes in the delegate selection process: select alternates in the same manner as prescribed for the selection of delegates; prohibit ex-officio designation of delegates to the national convention; conduct the entire process of delegate selection in a timely manner (within the calendar year of the convention); in convention systems, select no less than 75 percent of the total delegation at a level no higher than the congressional district and adopt an apportionment formula based on population or some standard measure of Democratic strength; apportion all delegates to national conventions not selected at large on a basis of representation that gives equal weight to population and Democratic voting strength based on the previous presidential election; designate the procedures by which slates are prepared and challenged; and select no more than 10 percent of the delegation by the state committee.

Although some of these terms and references may seem arcane and even quaint today (such as the unit rule, which allowed the majority of the state delegation to control the votes of the entire delegation), every single one of these rules makes reference to a procedure or informal practice that the McGovern-Fraser Commission found to be in place at the time of the selection of the delegates to the 1968 convention, and most of these had been in place for generations. According to the commission's views, these practices make internal party democracy difficult or impossible to achieve, because party organizational leaders and those who support them were given unfair access to the conventions and to the appointment or selection of delegates. This in turn allowed the party bosses to control the levers of power, to dictate to rank-and-file delegates who they should support in the nominations fights and which platform and issue positions they should advance or oppose. In the eyes of the commission, a process that should be open and participatory had become closed and even dictatorial. Also, these rules and informal practices were systemically related to the dominance that certain party elites, particularly white males from upper-level and midlevel status, had used for generations to restrict the access of other groups, particularly minorities and women, to the party's inner councils and thus to the levers of power in the party.

The McGovern-Fraser Commission wanted to ensure representation for these previously excluded groups, notably women, African Americans, and young people. The new rules demanded such representation in "reasonable relationship to their presence in the population of the State" (Commission on Party Structure and Delegate Selection, 1970, 34). This somewhat inexact requirement set off a lot of debate as to just what that would mean in the real world of delegate selection rules. Ultimately, the commission's original report and the implementation of its requirements provided the quotas and the affirmative action efforts that resulted in far more women and minorities and young people having an opportunity to gain delegate status. From this report also flowed a whole new rules regime, becoming the basis for subsequent rules that are still very much in effect today. Generally stated, the major rules that national parties impose on state parties regarding the selection of presidential nominees include the following:

—The national parties fix the numbers of seats at the national conventions and then allocate to each state its share of the delegates. The formula is a complex one for both parties, but it includes a consideration of the size of the state based on the state's share of the Electoral College vote plus extra delegates given to each state based on the party's recent successes in electing major statewide officeholders, such as governors, senators. This tends to exacerbate the polarization between the parties overall, since the formula favors larger Democratic delegations for the states that are more urban and more liberal and favors larger Republican delegations for the states that are more rural and more conservative.

—The national parties fix the time frame within which the states must select their delegates. This is the so-called window within which the states can schedule their primaries or caucuses, while a few states, notably Iowa and New Hampshire, are traditionally given exceptions. Challenges to this window by Florida and Michigan in 2008 and 2012 promise another fight over this rule. The calendar is, of course, directly related to the front-loading issue.

—The national parties determine the formula by which the candidates are awarded delegates. This is based on the number of popular votes won in primaries or caucuses. The two generic options are the winner-take-all rule, which awards all of the delegates to the winner of the most votes, and proportional representation, which awards delegates according to percent of votes won. The Democrats instituted proportional representation in 1972 and made it mandatory in 1992. The Republicans used the winner-take-all rule in most of the states until 2012, when they adopted proportional representation for most states holding elections up through April 1, after which they allowed the winner-take-all method, too.

—The national parties stage and, with the active cooperation of the party's presumptive nominee, control the national conventions. They pick the major speakers, set the calendar, control access to the platform, set rules for demonstrations, choose the hotels where state delegations stay, designate where delegates sit on the convention floor, and determine what happens and when during convention week. The conventions officially nominate the candidate, but the real selection is done now through primaries and caucuses. The conventions continue to play an important role, though, by attempting to heal party factionalism, showcasing the candidates, celebrating the party and reinforcing its brand name, and getting the party ready for the fall general election.

Later Reforms

The Campaign Finance Acts of 1971 and 1974 and subsequent amendments effectively leveled the campaign finance playing field, starting in 1976, forcing both candidates and parties to spend the same amounts on their campaigns. However, since 2000 federal financing of nominations and campaigns has almost disappeared except for the federal subsidy of the national conventions. Since 2008 it has been possible for one party and campaign to vastly outraise and outspend the opposition. (Financing is a complex story and is not covered in any detail in this book; for good authorities on this matter, see Frank Sorauf, 1992, and Michael Malbin, 2006.)

For several subsequent electoral cycles a new party reform commission was appointed every four years: the Mikulski Commission (1972–76), the Winograd Commission (1976–80), the Hunt Commission (1980–84), and the Fowler Commission (1984–88) (Jackson and Crotty, 2001, 61). Each of these commissions examined the rules to see how well they were working and what changes should be instituted for the next electoral cycle. Studying the rules and recommending changes became something of a cottage industry for the Democrats during this era, and the commissions engendered considerable controversy inside the party and much criticism from outside, especially among Republicans. After 1988 the Democrats quit appointing commissions routinely and decided to stand on what they had already achieved and leave marginal rules changes up to the Democratic National Committee.

More recently, the Democratic Party returned, in a limited fashion, to the commissions approach. The party had a new commission in 2004, officially termed the Commission on Presidential Nomination Timing and Scheduling. It was chaired by Representative David Price, a political scientist from North Carolina who had been in Congress many years and is a political parties scholar, and Alexis Herman, secretary of labor in the Clinton administration (Kamarck, 2009, 75). For the 2012 election the Democrats appointed still another rules study commission, officially known as the Democratic Change Commission, chaired by Senator Claire McCaskill of Missouri and Representative Jim Clyburn of South Carolina. The Price-Herman Commission made some incremental changes in the 2008 rules with respect to the window and to the penalties for holding early contests. The McCaskill-Clyburn Commission made more recommendations, especially regarding the front-loading problem and reductions in the role of the superdelegates.

Overall, the original McGovern-Fraser rules became the basic law for the national party; whatever procedural changes came later built on the foundation of the McGovern-Fraser rules and on the provisions of the party charter adopted in a midterm national convention held in Kansas City in December 1974. All the additional procedural changes were simply tweaking the basic rules to meet a perceived problem at the time or to respond to the needs of a particular candidate (Kamarck, 2009). For example, the rules required that all delegates had to be selected in the year of the presidential election, which had not always been the case. This rule helped set off the rush to the early parts of the calendar (front-loading), after many states changed to presidential primaries. States wanted to hold their contests as early as possible in the election year to get the benefit of the national attention early contests engendered and to enhance their clout. Candidates who won the early states, and especially those who won more than one, developed momentum, were significantly advantaged in the nominations contest, and often went on to win.

Starting in 1980 the rules required a window during which delegates could be selected, with Iowa and New Hampshire consistently allowed to remain outside that window in deference to their traditions. From 1980 forward the dates for the window were specified, usually running from February or March through early June. Starting in 2004 the Price-Herman Commission took up the troublesome issue of why New Hampshire and Iowa should always be the first in the nation, and they were challenged by the desire of other states, particularly Florida and Michigan, to move to the front of the line. To mollify some of the critics and to introduce more diversity among the early states, the commission approved South Carolina (more African Americans) and Nevada (more Hispanics and union members) for early contests. In 2008 that rule then led to the controversial use of national party rules to disallow the results of the unsanctioned early Florida and Michigan primaries. From the McGovern-Fraser Commission's work and subsequent commissions' decisions flowed the several changes in the rules surrounding what later came to be called super-delegates. Starting in 1972 these ex-officio delegates (governors and senators and other party bosses) were outlawed explicitly by the McGovern-Fraser rules (Commission on Party Structure and Delegate Selection, 1970, 35). The ban led many of these public officials to skip the convention altogether or to attend as spectators only (Reiter, 1985, 66). From 1976 through 1984 Democrats struggled with defining what the role of party and elected officials should be in the convention. Party regulars contended that separation of the party leaders from the nominations process reduced the role of peer review in the nominations process and hampered the party in the general election. Further, it had allowed an "outsider" like Jimmy Carter to win in 1976.

The Carter administration's relations with Congress were often rocky, and Carter often had great difficulty even with the Democrats in Congress. They had had very little to do with his nomination, since he had proudly run as an outsider. Carter never did win over Democratic legislative leaders, and they felt little obligation to him (Polsby, 1983). This persistent conflict broke into the open during the fall of 1979 and spring of 1980 with Senator Edward Kennedy's challenge to Carter's renomination. Carter's loss to Ronald Reagan in the 1980 elections led to intraparty conflict and recrimination and to a demand to fix some of the nominations problems, that is, to reestablish peer review in order to ensure that outsiders like Carter would have a high hurdle to leap over to achieve the nomination.

In 1984, in recognition of this criticism, the Hunt Commission guaranteed a certain percent of seats to party leaders and elected officials (Ceaser, Busch, and Pitney, 2009, 93; Mayer, 2009, 91); these particular delegates were, for the first time, called superdelegates. Superdelegates that year numbered 566 (or 14 percent of delegate slots), had full voting rights, and were uncommitted (Kamarck, 2009, 156–57). They were immediately important in 1984 by lopsidedly favoring Walter Mondale over Gary Hart (Kamarck, 2009, 158-60; Mayer, 2009, 85–108). Hart created a controversy about this; however, the issue did not have much staying power, and he let it drop. In addition, he wanted their support in 1988.

Superdelegates thus became an integral part of the process and created no real conflict for the next twenty-four years. They did not reemerge as important or controversial until they helped decide the selection of Barack Obama over Hillary Clinton in 2008. During the intense conflict between Obama and Clinton, when both candidates claimed the momentum and scrambled for every delegate, the superdelegates were rediscovered by the media, because it appeared that neither Obama nor Clinton could win the 2,025 committed delegates necessary without being pushed over the top by the votes of the superdelegates, who constituted almost 20 percent of the total. At first the superdelegates who announced early public positions favored Clinton, and since she was the early front-runner, they acted as had been expected in earlier years. Then slowly but surely, as Obama won more and more primaries and caucuses, the tide turned, and in late May the superdelegates came to favor Obama, helping to put him over the top at the very end of the primary season (Southwell, 2012).

In effect, the superdelegates apparently followed the election returns and went with the candidate that appeared to offer the highest probability for winning in the fall. This was highly rational strategic behavior from their perspective, and what we would expect from such professional politicians. This outcome ensured that the superdelegates were here to stay.

Reform and the Republican Party

The Republicans have not been nearly as active in promoting a reform agenda as the Democrats; however, they were inevitably drawn into the conflicts engendered by the Democrats, especially as state laws regarding the dates for holding primaries and for control over delegate selection were components of the changes. For example, the drive to switch from presidential caucuses to primaries was led by Democrats in the state legislatures; however, state legislatures generally decreed that the two parties hold their primaries on the same date. Indeed, in the twenty-first century front-loading has been more of a problem for the Republican Party than for the Democratic Party, and starting in 2000 Republicans began devising ways to address front-loading.

The provision of party and public officials with automatic delegate status (the superdelegate question) has not been as controversial in the Republican Party as in the Democratic Party. In fact, the Republicans explicitly banned ex officio delegates between 1976 and 2000; however, they then added back the state party chair and two Republican National Committee members from each state as delegates in 2000 (Mayer, 2009). They also provide for Republican governors, senators, and some representatives to have seats at the convention. Often these slots are filled by state conventions held after the party primary or caucus has been completed. While these delegates ordinarily were not called superdelegates until 2012, they are the functional equivalent for the Republicans. Early in 2012 there was speculation that Republican party and public officials could be crucial in deciding the nomination when it looked like a very close contest between Romney and his challengers. Most observers thought the Republican superdelegates would favor Romney as the more establishment candidate, and when it looked like the contest could be close there was speculation that those officials could made a crucial difference. The issue became moot when Rick Santorum dropped out.

On balance, the question of superdelegates continues to be important for both parties, because it goes to the heart of who will play a role in nominating U.S. presidents: political insiders of the pre-reform era or the state and local activists who have come to the forefront since the McGovern-Fraser reforms.

In addition, the requirement for proportional representation is a critical feature of present-day rules. Proportional representation in its pure form is an attempt to have the number and percent of representatives from a district be a faithful reflection of the number and percent of that district's popular vote in the previous election.

Proportional Representation and Other Rules

At first the McGovern-Fraser Commission did not explicitly require proportional representation, but it was an underlying value for the reformers on the panel (Kamarck, 2009). The report did require that the convention "adopt procedures which will provide for fair representation of minority views on presidential candidates" (Commission on Party Structure and Delegate Selection, 1970, 36, 44). How to attain that fair representation has proved to be a challenge. To some commission members this meant the institution of proportional representation immediately, and the reformers on the McGovern-Fraser Commission had a strong bias in favor of proportional representation as opposed to winner take all. To some extent this was simply a philosophical commitment (Kamarck, 2009, chap. 4). Proportional representation was simply their operational definition of what "fair representation of minority views on presidential candidates" meant (Commission on Party Structure and Delegate Selection, 1970, 36).

Democratic Party regulars at first resisted this formula because they believed that winner-take-all rules would assist the party in reaching an earlier decision and would also probably guarantee the nomination of a stronger candidate, one more acceptable from their viewpoint (that is, not an outsider like Jimmy Carter). From 1972 through 1988 there was uneven application of proportional representation and an internal party struggle over it, as opposed to other forms of representation, most notably variations on the winner-take-all theme. But beginning in 1992 proportional representation became the requirement at all levels of the delegate selection process (Kamarck, 2009, 82–83; Nelson, 2011, chap. 8). The use of that system has had a profound impact on the party and its ability to choose its candidates early as well as on which candidates have the ability to envision the sequence of state primaries and caucuses and to plan strategy successfully. Elaine Kamarck (2009) cogently demonstrates that Democratic rules place a premium on understanding the calendar and sequencing events. The imperative is to strategically select the states to contest and employ resources rationally. The competitive candidate must win real votes early to make the top tier and develop momentum to stay in the top tier, which quickly comes to mean that the top two or maybe three candidates, and then one, must win an ever-increasing delegate count as the contest wears on and the focus shifts from popular votes won to delegates won.

Closely related is the question of what threshold to use in the allocation of delegates to second- and third-place finishers. What percent of votes must a candidate get in order to be awarded at least one delegate at the congressional district level, for example? The answer has a big impact on likely second- or third-place candidates, like Jesse Jackson, who, in 1984 and 1988, wanted a low threshold, whereas the front-runners in those cases, Walter Mondale and Michael Dukakis, wanted the thresholds to be as high as possible, thus allowing the front-runners to amass more delegates faster. This threshold has varied from 15 percent to 20 percent; however, after 1988, as a result of a compromise between Jesse Jackson and Michael Dukakis, it was fixed at the 15 percent level for representing second- and third-place finishers.

The Republicans have left the selection methods decisions up to the states by and large; however, they have allowed both winner take all and proportional representation at the state level, and most states traditionally utilized winner-take-all rules in the Republican primaries. The Republican winner-take-all bias in their rules has significantly contributed to their ability to reach an early decision on their standard-bearer, which they have consistently done every year since Reagan challenged Ford in 1976. That changed again in 2012.

As noted, the Democratic rules changes had a spillover effect in the Republican Party as well. Even when the Republicans did not fully embrace the specific rules adopted by the Democrats, they felt the unintended consequences. The number of states using primaries has escalated, and the two national parties have worked together closely on the calendar window, since the scheduling of primaries and caucuses usually involves state legislatures and governors. The DNC and the RNC have generally cooperated in the definition of the window and the threat of sanctions for those states violating the agreed-upon window. In fact, Republicans have been as aggressive as Democrats, and perhaps more so, in trying to control the calendar and to prevent front-loading. This newly aggressive stance started in 2000 and continued through the 2008 convention. In order to discourage front-loading, the Republicans changed their rules and decided to use proportional representation more extensively for their 2012 convention, linking it to front-loading.

The Republican rules for 2012 required that the early states—that is, those holding primaries in January through March—were required to use proportional representation (with limited exceptions, such as in Florida). Only those holding primaries later—that is, after April 1—could use the traditional winner-take-all plan. This change threatened to prolong the contest over the Republican nomination in 2012, just as it did for the Democrats in 2008. Many observers thought this new requirement could help whoever was the alternative to the early front-runner, Mitt Romney, by allowing each alternative candidate to pick up delegates in the early contests. Some even suggested that it could be the key to denying Romney the nomination and lead to a brokered convention. This did not happen ultimately, but it was often claimed that the new rules adopted by the Republicans in 2012 had contributed to the temporary success of whoever happened to be the flavor of the week/month in the "anybody but Romney" sweepstakes.

Given how long it took Republicans to settle on Romney in 2012, there was a new debate within the Republican Party about the need to return to pure winner-take-all rules for 2016. However, for 2016 the Republicans decided to continue to allow Iowa, New Hampshire, Nevada, and South Carolina to hold their primaries in February. Other states holding contests before March 1, 2016, would incur a loss of delegate seats. States that hold contests between March 1 and March 15 would be required to use proportional representation. (After March 15 the remaining states could use winner take all.) In this manner, the Republican Party's Rules Committee hoped to contain the process within a narrow time period, reduce the impact of the outlier earliest states, and get it over with sooner than in 2012 (Dupree, 2014; Barabak, 2014). Thus the rules continue to roil in both parties.

The conflict over rules—proportional representation or winner-take-all systems, affirmative action, the threshold for awarding delegates, the calendar, and the window—is ongoing, and the rules continue to change with political circumstances and the changing interests of the candidates. The most consistent theme, however, has been to make the rules more friendly to party activists and to enhance the role of the public, especially in the primaries. Many of these rules—for example, requiring adequate public notice, removing monetary assessments on delegates, forbidding use of the unit rule, requiring a quorum to conduct business—have been accepted with little controversy, were quickly institutionalized, and have been reaffirmed by subsequent party commissions. No one in either party would even think of going back to some of the more egregious rules that existed before 1972. Few states would consider giving up primaries; if they did, it would be for only one year in order to save money or because an incumbent renomination was inevitable. The basic premise is that primary voters and caucus goers, instead of the party leaders and officials, get to select the party nominees.

Consequences of the Reform Era

Political context was the significant impetus for changing the way presidential candidates are nominated. Those changes, in turn, helped transform the party systems, making them more ideologically coherent. This coherence—or polarization—has, for better or worse, made America more difficult to govern. Other factors also contributed to the polarization of the parties, such as the emergence of cable television news channels and talk radio, which provided polarized media to lead and reinforce the more ideological and polarized electorate. The greater polarization of campaign finance and of interest group alignments also contributed. But changes in presidential nominations are the crucial components in the ideological and issue-oriented realignment that occurred in this period.

The pivotal elections of 1968 and 1972 were very much the product of their times. The fundamental changes originated during the national debate over the war in Vietnam, the civil rights movement, and the women's movement. Established power centers were being challenged and in some cases overthrown. Established ways of doing politics and the business of the parties were being challenged. And the work of the McGovern-Fraser Commission ultimately undermined and transformed the old regime.

The two Democratic candidates that those two conventions produced, Humphrey in 1968 and McGovern in 1972, were also very much creatures of their time, but their routes to the nomination were very different. Humphrey, who had been the party maverick in 1948, was by then a long-time senator and then the vice president under Lyndon Johnson. In effect, Humphrey came to epitomize the party establishment, and he benefitted very much from party insider support to attain the 1968 nomination. McGovern, a progressive and populist senator from South Dakota, volunteered to become the leader of an outsider challenge to the party's power centers. He led the charge for a more open and participatory form of internal party democracy, which transformed the ways the party did business and in a real sense ultimately transformed both parties into the kinds of organizations they are today. McGovern came to symbolize egalitarianism and participatory democracy to such an extent that Republicans continued to run against him for thirty more years. Although he lost the presidential election in a landslide in 1972, lost his Senate seat in 1980, and never again won public office, he and the reforms that bear his name became a shorthand for a whole movement and even for the generation that embodied it (Smith and Springer, 2009, chap. 1).

The rules regime that the McGovern-Fraser Commission established—the shift from traditional centers of party power to the voters in the party primaries and to the activists mobilized during election year—fitted the tenor of the times and led to greater demand for popular participation. It also led to dominance by the mass media and the narrowing focus and resultant polarization of the parties. These forces then transformed the presidency, the way we are governed, and the ability of any president or any party to govern.

4

On Representation

This chapter explores the meaning of the term *representation* and how this theoretical concept has played out over the past four decades in real-world debates surrounding the selection of delegates to the two national political conventions. There is, of course, a commonsense understanding of what it means to be a representative. The major point of free elections is that some people are elected to go to Washington or to the state capital to represent the rest of us; it is the rationale for free elections. It is also the meaning of a republican form of government, the form set out in the U.S. Constitution. In addition, the states are guaranteed a republican form of government by the national government. In essence, representation is at the heart of mass democracy. Political parties, like legislatures, are essential components of this system of representative government and have become even more important in the modern era.

Nevertheless, in her definitive study of the concept of representation, its origins, meanings, and implications for democratic government, Hannah Pitkin (1987) shows that there are several dimensions to this seemingly simple concept. In that seminal work, Pitkin identifies "descriptive representation," by which she means that the representative body (a legislature or party convention) should reflect or mirror the nation's population on important demographic and social indicators like gender, race, and class. Pitkin terms this form of representation the "standing-for" dimension, since the representative body is supposed to stand for the total population. One can ascertain the level of descriptive representation in a fairly straightforward manner, that is, by asking whether the representative body includes members of the group in question in some proportion roughly equal to their presence in the population. Are they a representative sample of the whole? This question is where much of the conflict over group representation in real-world legislative and political bodies has been centered over the last four decades. The group theory of politics gives a premier place to groups, their members, and leaders as representing the whole population (Bentley, 1908; Truman, 1951; Cigler and Loomis, 2002). This concept of representation is a variant of the group theory approach to politics.

A closely related line of inquiry analyzes the role of demographic and membership groups in mass voting behavior. This is what is now often termed the sociological or social-psychological school of thought in voting behavior, and it is clearly linked to the issue of how class and interest group membership influence voting behavior (Berelson, Lazarsfeld, and McPhee, 1954; Campbell and others, 1960). In the legislative process, group theory influences the study of which interest groups have the most power over the making of public policy. In the party reform era, the question for the Democratic Party was which demographic and socioeconomic groups should gain representation in the important decisionmaking bodies of the national party, including especially presidential nominating conventions.

A second and more complex form of representation is what Pitkin terms the "acting-for" dimension. This dimension is also called substantive representation, to indicate its emphasis on the public policy and the ideological issues involved. Here, the representative goes to Washington or the state capital to cast a vote that reflects the political values that would guide constituents if they were personally present in the political arena. Representative government, or the republican form, requires this kind of behavior from those we choose to represent us (or at least a majority or plurality of us). The assumption is that if these representatives fail to do this, they will also fail to be reelected. Operationalizing this dimension of representation is much more difficult for the researcher than is measuring descriptive representation. It requires ascertaining what the views and values of the representatives are and then comparing them with those of the population they are supposed to represent. Some classic political science research by Warren Miller and Donald Stokes (1963) was the first to explore this principle in the context of Congress. The Miller and Stokes study remains a standard by which representation is measured and the circumstances under which a member of Congress will follow his or her conscience versus voting the constituency, or both, and their research still illuminates the essential problems of representative democracy.

The Empirical Study

The empirical study for this book focuses on the delegates to the national conventions of the two major parties (see appendix A, this volume). The role of delegate is, of course, also intimately tied to the concept of representation. We intuitively understand that a delegate is sent from a group to represent that group in a larger setting. In this case, the delegates are chosen by and sent from state and local political parties to represent those geographic and organizational units in the national councils of party government. Being a delegate to a Republican or a Democratic national convention is an opportunity to participate in the highest plenary councils of the national party while at the same time choosing the party's nominee for the highest office in the land. It is a rare opportunity, and most party activists take their responsibilities as delegates quite seriously and value the opportunity to go to the national conventions. These are prized positions, eagerly sought by many people.

Most of the initial focus in the selection process is on the geographical unit from which the delegates are chosen, which is usually the congressional district. Typically, only three to seven people will be chosen from the average congressional district, as delegates to the national conventions. A handful of other party leaders and activists will also be chosen at the state level to round out the slate. The latter are supposed to represent state interests, while the other delegates often represent the interests of the candidates. Since the 1970s, under current reform rules presidential candidates usually try to recruit an attractive slate of delegates to run in a particular congressional district or from the targeted state. While the media focus is frequently on the "beauty contest"—that is, the presidential popularity poll in each state—the real battle is about identifying delegates who will advance the interests of (and vote for) a particular candidate.

In the older, "unreformed," and pragmatic era—before the McGovern-Fraser rules were instituted—the party organizational leadership at the state and local levels largely determined who among the party faithful had earned the right to go to the national convention. The result was that most delegates were white, male, and middle-class or upper-middle-class party stalwarts loyal to the party leader or the party organization sponsoring their trip to the national convention. Big city mayors like Richard J. Daley of Chicago had extraordinary control over these party "regulars," and thus they were able to deliver blocs of delegate votes for the favored candidates or for specific platform proposals. This is why the national conventions of those days were marked by intense bargaining among major party leaders and jockeying for position among the most competitive presidential candidates. This was popularly called a brokered convention, and party leaders were usually the brokers.

In those conventions there was the potential for multiple ballots and for a deadlock among the frontrunners, and an entirely different candidate could emerge unexpectedly. The most extreme example of this dynamic was in 1924, when the Democrats deadlocked for two weeks and finally settled, on the 104th ballot, on John W. Davis as their nominee. The last national convention requiring multiple ballots to choose a nominee was the 1952 Democratic convention, but the potential for such a result continued up through 1968. The party bosses continued to wheel and deal over the nominee, the platforms, and the seating of contested delegations up through the 1968 conventions in both parties.

All of this changed in the aftermath of the 1968–72-era reforms. The McGovern-Fraser rules put a premium on selecting national convention delegates through procedures that complied with the new national party rules. The new rules made it much more rational for a state to adopt a state primary to ensure that state's delegation arriving at the national convention with an uncontested slate, one that would be seated without challenges by the Credentials Committee or on the floor of the convention. That the times and the rules had changed dramatically was not entirely clear until the 1972 Democratic National Convention refused to seat Daley's Illinois delegation. While that delegation had been selected in the Illinois primary—it was held in March 1972 in a manner that comported with Illinois law—the selection violated a number of the key provisions of the new McGovern-Fraser Commission rules, so a rival delegation (led by Chicago alderman William Singer and the Reverend Jesse Jackson) was seated instead. The courts later upheld this decision, thus establishing the fundamental rule that national party law took precedence over state law in the selection of national convention delegates (*Cousins* v. *Wigoda;* see also *Democratic Party of the U.S.* v. *Wisconsin ex rel. LaFollette*).

From the 1972 Democratic National Convention forward, the die was cast, and state and local parties were on notice that they had to select their national convention delegates in ways that met the standards of the national party's rules and regulations. In addition, as a result of the changes in the rules requiring more pledged, as opposed to uncommitted, delegates, and the advent of more and more state primaries, the days of the brokered convention were done. There was some talk among Democrats about a brokered convention in 2008, since the contest between Hillary Clinton and Barack Obama was so close. As it was, the race was not settled until the last day of the primary

Table 4-1. *Delegates Selected through Primaries, by Party, 1912–2012*[a]

	Democratic Party		Republican Party	
Year	Number of primaries	Delegates (percent)	Number of primaries	Delegates (percent)
1912	12	32.9	13	41.7
1916	20	53.5	20	58.9
1920	16	44.6	20	57.8
1924	14	35.5	17	45.3
1928	16	42.2	15	44.9
1932	16	40.0	14	37.7
1936	14	36.5	12	37.5
1940	13	35.8	13	38.8
1944	14	36.7	13	38.7
1948	14	36.3	12	36.0
1952	16	38.7	13	39.0
1956	19	42.7	19	44.8
1960	16	38.3	15	38.6
1964	16	45.7	16	45.6
1968	15	40.2	15	38.1
1972	21	65.3	20	56.8
1976	27	76.0	26	71.0
1980	34	71.8	34	76.0
1984	29	52.4	25	71.0
1988	36	66.6	36	76.9
1992	39	66.9	38	83.9
1996	35	65.3	42	84.6
2000	40	64.6	43	83.8
2004	37	67.5	27	55.5
2008	38	68.9	39	79.8
2012	26	47.2	36	71.3

Source: Stanley and Niemi, 2013–14, 56.
a. The number of primaries held includes those in which delegates are elected and pledged to specific candidates. A few states also held "beauty contest" primaries, which are nonbinding; in those states, pledged delegates were selected in caucuses.

season, and was one of the closest in history. However, it was not brokered but was settled by the results of primaries, mainly, and to a lesser extent caucuses and superdelegates. Talk of a brokered convention returned again briefly in 2012, when Mitt Romney was having trouble wrapping up the Republican nomination; however, the suggestion was made moot by several Romney primary victories. This has been the pattern in the post-reform era.

While Democrats led the way in reforming the delegate selection process, Republicans followed soon thereafter. Republicans tend to leave it to the states to select national convention delegates, but they understand that their national party law will take precedence in any dispute. By 1972 most Democratic Party leaders had drawn the most obvious conclusion from the McGovern-Fraser rules: namely, that delegations that were the product of state primaries were more easily defended in national convention conflicts than delegations that were the product of caucuses and state conventions. The Illinois case from 1972 illustrates that some national party standards must be met by presidential primaries, so on balance it seemed prudent for the states to turn to primaries as their best defense against challenge. The result was a significant shift in the direction of states adopting the direct party primary for the selection of national convention delegations. Table 4-1 tells that story in more detail.

The nation went from having less than half of the delegates to both parties' national conventions in 1968 selected in state primaries to 65 percent of Democratic delegates and 57 percent of Republican delegates being chosen through primaries four years later. The number and percentage in both parties continued to grow steadily larger, with both parties eventually reaching over three-quarters of their delegates produced by the primaries. There has been some downturn in those percentages for the Democratic Party, with the percentage dropping to 47 percent in 2012, as a number of states canceled their primaries since there was no contest (which happens when the incumbent president is unchallenged; see Stanley and Niemi, 2013–14, 56).

Republicans topped out with about 80 percent of their delegates produced by primaries in 1992, 1996, and 2000. There was a decline on the Republican side in 2004 because President George W. Bush was not seriously challenged in the primaries. The number of state primaries and the percentage of delegates selected in them increased again in 2008. In 2008, as befits the hotly contested nominations season in both parties, there were thirty-nine Republican presidential primaries, with almost 80 percent of the GOP delegates selected in them, and thirty-eight Democratic primaries, in which nearly 70 percent of the delegates were selected. Perhaps one harbinger of the fall election was the fact that in 2008 almost 37 million votes were cast in the Democratic primaries, an increase of more than 20 million over Democratic turnout in 2004, and that total was also almost 17 million more than voted in the Republican primaries, which augured badly for the GOP in the fall. Only thirteen states used the caucus method to select their delegates in 2008. Most of them were small states, though they still accounted for almost one-third of Democratic delegates and were a key to the Obama victory (Stanley and Niemi, 2009–10, 55; CQ, 2001, 13). Texas selected its delegates using a combination of state primary and caucuses, all held the same evening. The increase in the use of primaries in 2008 was predictable, since both parties were vying for an open seat in the presidential race with no incumbent competing.

The basic fact is that national convention delegates are now selected mostly through presidential primaries, whereas in the pre-reform era the primaries were secondary. To survive the rigors of primary races (or caucuses), one must bring to the battle some special personal and political resources, among them an understanding of the rules of the game.

Demographic Representation

One of the major goals of the McGovern-Fraser Commission reforms was demographic representation in order to include certain social groups. Before the reforms the average delegate was likely to be a white, middle-aged male from the middle or upper-middle class. Women, minorities, and the young were sparsely represented in the national conventions of both parties between 1912 and 1968 (David, Goldman, and Bain, 1964, chap. 12). The McGovern-Fraser Commission rules in 1972 required representation for these three groups "in reasonable relationship to their presence in the population."

For the Democrats, this led to a quota system for those three demographic groups, as the states attempted, with varying degrees of fervor, to meet that mathematical formula for seating at the 1972 national convention. The rule carried over into subsequent conventions. This effort was based on the philosophical position that these three groups had been discriminated against previously and that either quotas or at least strong affirmative action measures would be required for the parties to overcome the effects of this past discrimination. Implicit in this argument was the assumption that opening the party would help ensure that these major demographic groups would gravitate toward the Democrats. In essence, this drive for demographic representation would increase the number of Democratic votes. Hannah Pitkin (1987) calls this approach descriptive representation or the standing-for dimension of representation. That is, she contends that, in the larger councils of the party or in any other political decisionmaking arena, women can best represent women, African Americans can best represent African Americans, and young people can best represent young people. The premise is that there is something unique about the experience of race or gender or generation that renders those outside of that experience incapable of representing the group.

This premise about standing-for representation is very controversial and has certainly not been adopted by all the major political groups. Republicans in particular are very skeptical. They denounced the Democrats' emphasis on such representation in 1972, labeling it "quotas" and promising never to adopt it themselves. Democrats retorted that Republicans had already adopted quotas, as had the Democrats, for their national committee by appointing one man and one woman from each state. In spite of abjuring quotas, Republicans did join Democrats in 1972 (through their Delegates and Organization Committee) in their effort to open up the national conventions to more women, minorities, and young delegates (Delegates and Organizations Committee, 1971). The Republican approach was more one of moral suasion than rule making, though. In taking the softer approach, Republicans were acting consistently with their long-standing stance in favor of states' rights and their skepticism about national power. It may also have been that Republican leaders thought that a low-key and decentralized approach would appeal to the white males who dominated their party's base in state and local parties and that, indirectly, this stance could encourage white males to stay with the party.

The fact is that both parties realized electoral benefits from the rules-oriented strategies they adopted. It is also now clear that the two parties have been going through a major realignment of their demographic bases over the three closing decades of the twentieth century and that this realignment is largely complete. The white South now overwhelmingly supports Republicans. The black South, and African Americans throughout the nation, now very heavily favor Democrats. While the gender gap is not nearly so dramatic, about 10 percent more women vote for Democrats and the same portion of men favor Republicans. This has been true across all elections since Ronald Reagan defeated Jimmy Carter. Only young people temporarily fell off the radar screen in this competition for delegate seats and, indirectly, for votes, but this voting bloc reappeared in 2008 and 2012, heavily and disproportionately supporting Obama.

Eighteen-year-olds were ensured the vote by the Twenty-Sixth Amendment, passed in 1971 but not operational until 1972. In spite of this new voting bloc, young voters did not attract much attention from the two major parties in their delegation selections. The parties did continue to have youth divisions and to support the Young Democrats and the Young Republicans; however, neither attempted to recruit youthful delegates in anything like their percentage of the nation's total population. Perhaps it is not surprising, then, that the youth vote has waxed and waned for both parties, depending mostly on who was running for president in a particular year. More important, turnout among young people declined drastically after the heady days when eighteen-year-olds first got the vote in 1972. From 1976 until 2000 the percentage of young people voting declined then made something of a comeback in 2000 and 2004, perhaps because of the increased emphasis on the youth vote among youth-oriented media outlets, such as the Rock the Vote campaign. However, the turnout of young people still remained considerably below that of their elders. This fact, too, made it less likely that the two parties would give young voters any special consideration in the development of their rules and in assignment of seats at the conventions. All that changed, however, in 2008, when Obama made a concerted effort to attract the vote and energy of young people and succeeded in mobilizing them at a level of turnout that was high compared to recent elections.

The Effect of Rules Changes: Women and Superdelegates

The story of women on the Democratic side is marked by an almost linear increase in the percentage of women delegates at Democratic national conventions (table 4-2). In 1952 women held only 13 percent of delegate seats. Sixteen years later, in 1968, women still held only 13 percent of them. Given the fact that women constitute, then and now, somewhat more than 50 percent of the national population, it is evident that they were not even close to enjoying representation proportional to their numbers.

Under the impetus of the McGovern-Fraser rules, the proportion of women increased dramatically, to 40 percent in 1972. While this is only four-fifths of what women could expect from a strict interpretation of the rules, it is nevertheless an enormous increase over the level of 1968, and it marked a turning point in the Democratic Party's attention to attracting women to the elite ranks as well as to trying to get their electoral support. The percentage declined to 33 percent in 1976 under the influence of two rules changes. First, the national party that year specifically eschewed any attempt at quotas and instead relied on affirmative action for women (and minorities). This decision was taken by the party's internal reform commission of that year, called the Mikulski Commission, named for its chair, Barbara Mikulski, who later became U.S. senator from Maryland. The affirmative action decision was made partially in response to vigorous criticism of the party from Republicans and partially in response to pressure from women's groups.

The 1976 national convention also gave specific recognition to party and public officials like governors, senators, and House members who were guaranteed seats or special access at the national convention by virtue of their office. Among other reasons for this change was the view that these officials were the backbone of the party organization and that they were needed at the general election. The theory was that if they participated, they would take ownership of the party platform and the nominee, work hard for the ticket

Table 4-2. *National Convention Delegates, by Demography and Party,*
1952–2008

Percent

Characteristic	1952 D	1952 R	1968 D	1968 R	1972 D	1972 R	1976 D	1976 R	1980 D	1980 R	1984 D	1984 R
Female	13	11	13	16	40	29	33	31	49	29	49	44
African American	2	3	5	2	15	4	11	3	15	3	18	4
Under thirty years old	N.A.	N.A.	3	4	22	6	15	7	11	5	8	4

Characteristic	1988 D	1988 R	1992 D	1992 R	1996 D	1996 R	2000 D	2000 R	2004 D	2004 R	2008 D	2008 R
Female	48	33	48	43	50	36	48	35	50	43	49	32
African American	23	4	16	5	19	3	19	4	18	6	23	2
Under thirty years old	4	3	6	N.A.	6	2	4	3	7	4	7	3

Source: Data for 1968–2008 based on *CBS News/New York Times,* 2008a, 2008b; data for 1952 based on David, Goldman, and Bain, 1964, 231, 232.

N.A. = Not available

in the election, and then be loyal to the president after the election. (This rationale is also put forward for women's representation.) These superdelegates have had an impact on the nomination in some years. In 1984 they favored Walter Mondale, the candidate of the party establishment, over challenger Gary Hart, and they helped provide Mondale's winning margin.

It was notable in 2008 how many people were unaware of the rules and seemingly had lost sight of the potential of superdelegates. A seemingly innocuous rule helped settle the closest race in recent presidential nominations history. These rules sometimes lie in wait for use by the candidates and campaigns that can make the most rational or strategic use of them long after they have been forgotten. The well-planned campaign will recognize the opportunities inherent in the rules structures and will take advantage of them in assembling a majority of the votes on the first ballot of the convention. The importance of making such strategic plans was never as clear as the nominations battle between Hillary Clinton and Barack Obama in 2008.

By 1980 the Democrats were under the leadership of yet another internal reform commission, this time the Winograd Commission, named for its chair, Michigan Democratic Party chair, Morley Winograd. The Winograd Commission mandated equal representation for women in Democratic national convention delegations. In short, the commission returned to quotas for women, and those quotas had to be met at the congressional, district, and state levels of delegate selection. This resulted in an immediate increase in female Democratic delegates (table 4-2). From 33 percent in 1976, women delegates increased to 49 percent in 1980. The 50 percent goal was achieved in 1996 and 2004, but it fell again to 49 percent in 2008. This record indicates that demographic representation can be achieved only through a sustained effort by the party's leadership and by the enactment and enforcement of specific rules designed to achieve that objective. Whether the objective is desirable or rational is a more debatable proposition, as the Republican Party's experience indicates. Nevertheless, it is clear that the Democratic Party has bet on representation for women and minorities and has spent some political capital to achieve that representation.

As is evident from table 4-2, the Republican Party has also given significant attention to increasing representation for women and has made some progress in that direction. However, the party has not reached the 50 percent marker and apparently has not aspired to do so. The pre-reform conventions of 1952 and 1968 show that Republican female delegates constituted 11 percent and 16 percent of the total (David, Goldman, and Bain, 1964; Stanley and Niemi, 2009–10, 68). In fact, it is notable that, in 1968, female Republican delegates had a 3 percent advantage over female Democratic delegates. It is perhaps a related fact that in the 1950s and 1960s, to the extent that any gender gap existed, it was in the direction of women voters being slightly more pro-Republican than male voters (Campbell and others, 1960). There may well have been more Republican women active in the state and local parties of that era than their counterparts in the Democratic Party. Regardless, from 16 percent in 1968, Republican women increased to 29 percent in the 1972 Republican National Convention, under the urging both of the party's DO Committee and of the Republican National Committee. The increase was not so dramatic as the Democrats experienced, but it was significant at that time.

Republican women delegates increased again in 1976, to 31 percent, and then dropped back to 29 percent in 1980. This was probably about the maximum level Republican women could expect under their national party's looser system, which used informal persuasion and low-key affirmative action. The Reagan campaign emphasized the recruitment of Republican women in 1984 partially in response to the marked gender gap among women in the 1980 vote. There was a substantial increase in Republican women delegates in 1984, with 44 percent of the delegate slots. Again, an organizational initiative, this time from the Democrats at the national party level, prompted a defensive reaction among Republicans. Nevertheless, this initiative was not sustained, and from 1988 through 2004 women delegates at the Republican National Convention did not exceed 43 percent. In 2008 this level dropped to 32 percent. John McCain's convention may have nominated a woman to be vice president, but less than one-third of its delegates were women.

Without a quota or pressure for affirmative action from the national party and the presidential campaign, the proportion of Republican women delegates seems to range between 33 and 40 percent. Given the Republicans' developing advantage with male voters, the flip side of the gender gap, Republican Party elites have little incentive to emulate the Democrats with a hard and fast rule regarding women's representation—this despite the fact that Republicans had a quota in place for women serving on the Republican National Committee since 1924. But, in fact, they have developed a rhetorical position against quotas, which they and their supporters in the mass media associate with the Democratic Party. This, like many other facets of the 1970s, became fodder for the ideological wars that date from that era.

Does the level of women delegates really matter, except symbolically? The data indicate that the answer is yes. Several studies find that, within the political elite, women hold different political values than men in some issue areas. In many issue areas, however, gender does not seem to make any difference. Research by Jody McMullen and Barbara Norrander (2000, 197) reports that female national convention delegates in 1992, both Republican and Democratic, were more liberal than male delegates. These ideological differences, moreover, were consistent across a range of issues. Thus if both parties are increasingly recruiting women delegates, the ideological composition of the two conventions may become more liberal. Of course, these findings predate the advent of Sarah Palin and Michele Bachman and the Tea Party influence in the Republican Party. Republican women who are identified with Palin and Bachman promise to be a very conservative influence in the Republican Party for years to come. However, ordinarily, even Republican women are more liberal than their male counterparts. If men still significantly outnumber women at Republican conventions, this may tip the scales in a somewhat more conservative direction than would be the case with equal gender representation.

Other authorities point to the increased role of women in politics and the influence of women's groups and feminists on the Democratic Party over the past two decades. There is no question that rules changes were important in bringing about this transformation (Baer and Bositis, 1988). The fight between Clinton and Obama in 2008 was initially predicated on a somewhat higher level of support for Clinton among activist women, and it provided an initial challenge for Obama to overcome and win back the trust of disappointed Clinton supporters. The fact that he was ultimately able to do so and to benefit from another gender gap, with women in his favor in the general election, underscores the importance of party rules. These rules are rarely neutral. Systematically including representatives of one demographic group has the effect of excluding representatives of other demographic groups as well as altering the values and issues mixture at the conventions.

The Effect of Rules Changes: Ethnic Minorities

The story of minority representation, especially African American, at the national conventions is somewhat more complicated than that of women. As table 4-2 indicates, the increases have been fairly dramatic and sustained over the years, mostly for the Democrats; there has not been much change in Republican national convention representation by African Americans. Black representation in the pre-reform baseline year of 1968 was 5 percent among Democrats and 2 percent among Republicans. A study from 1952 finds black representation at 3 percent among Republicans and only 2 percent among the Democrats. This gap may be explained by the fact that, before 1960 and 1964, the Republican Party was still thought of as the party of Lincoln and attracted sizable proportions of black voters in presidential elections during the period from the Civil War through the Eisenhower years.

The African American vote began to change, however, during the presidency of Franklin Roosevelt and then more dramatically in Lyndon Johnson's 1964 campaign after the passage of the Civil Rights Act of that year. This era had opened during the 1960 presidential campaign with the dramatic gesture John F. Kennedy made by contacting Martin Luther King while he was in jail for civil rights activities. This appeal, plus the Democratic Party's traditional strength in urban areas, resulted in Kennedy attracting 68 percent of the nonwhite vote in 1960. Lyndon Johnson took up the Kennedy mantle and his unfinished legislative program in 1963. Republican losses among African American voters continued after the Republican nominee, Barry Goldwater, opposed the 1964 Civil Rights Act. As a result of that high-profile policy disagreement between Goldwater and Johnson, the Democrats won 94 percent of the black vote in 1964 (Stanley and Niemi, 2000, 118). It was also at the 1964 Democratic National Convention that the Mississippi Freedom Party called on Democrats to stop the seating of all-white, or segregated, delegations in future national conventions. The Democrats, under pressure from the Johnson-Humphrey campaign, agreed—promising that no more all-white delegations would be seated in subsequent national conventions.

At the 1968 Democratic National Convention, 5 percent of the delegates were African Americans. This was the result of the state party autonomy approach to increasing minority representation, which the Democrats had always used. The McGovern-Fraser Commission recommendations for 1972 dramatically changed this laissez-faire approach. The new national party rules required minority representation at the national conventions "in reasonable relationship to that group's percentage of the state's population." The Democrats' percentage of black delegates almost tripled under these rules, going from 5 to 15 percent in one four-year election cycle. While debate developed over the proper measure—whether the percentage of the black national population (approximately 12 percent then) or the percentage of the party's base that was black (more than 12 percent for Democrats)—the increase to 15 percent in 1972 was remarkable.

Since the reforms of 1972, every Democratic national convention except one has met or exceeded the national population standard in terms of African American delegates. The exception was 1976, when black representation dropped to 11 percent overall. The range otherwise has been between 15 and 23 percent; the 23 percent level was reached in 1988, the year in which Jesse Jackson made his most concerted attempt to obtain the Democratic Party's presidential nomination. He won the Super Tuesday primaries, which were mostly in the South that year, and was the closest competitor Michael Dukakis faced for the Democratic Party's nomination. These results indicate that the candidate can have some short-term impact on the composition of the delegations, even though official rules and political factors are the more important long-term influences on the delegations' composition. Black convention representation stood steady at 16–19 percent between 1992 and 2004. In fact, the percentages have been consistent enough to suggest that the Democratic Party had reached a fairly stable plateau in the numbers of black delegates under the existing rules, a pattern that seemed likely to persist in the absence of either further rules changes or a viable African American candidate.

In 2008 that viable African American candidate appeared in the person of Barack Obama. For the first time since Jesse Jackson's 1988 challenge a black candidate appeared to have a real chance of being nominated. Of course, Obama went on not only to achieve the nomination but also to win the general election, something that would have been unthinkable in the pre–civil rights era. Not surprisingly, given the highly organized nature of the Obama campaign, there was also a high level of black delegates (23 percent) in 2008, equaling the level of black delegates at the 1988 Democratic National Convention (Stanley and Niemi, 2013–14, 67). Not all of these were Obama supporters, since Senator Clinton had her own cadre of black backers. But after Obama's victory in the Iowa caucuses demonstrated that he could win among white voters, the black community increasingly supported him in the primary elections. This trend continued in the fall, when he racked up a near record of 95 percent of the black vote in the general election. Obama almost replicated this record in 2012, when he took 93 percent of the black vote (Stanley and Niemi, 2013–14, 116).

This historic level of black representation in the national conventions was reached through what is essentially an "affirmative action" rule for black delegates. While there is a procedural quota of 50 percent required for women, there is no such quota for African Americans or other minorities. State parties are required to demonstrate that the selection process is open and transparent and that all races are encouraged to participate; however, they are not required to meet any particular target for black or other minority delegates. Such a target must come from state and local party leaders, and it must be supported by the national campaigns of the candidates. Most recently, the major concern regarding minority group representation has been about Hispanic voters. This is the fastest growing minority group in the United States, outnumbering African Americans. Not surprisingly, the leaders of both major parties spend enormous resources on recruiting Hispanic leaders. For Democrats, 11 percent of the national convention delegates in 2008 listed themselves as being from Hispanic or Latino backgrounds (Stanley and Niemi, 2013–14, 67). It was a record for this group.

President George W. Bush made the recruitment of Hispanics a special mission for the Republicans in both 2000 and 2004. His efforts paid some dividends when 44 percent of Hispanic voters supported him in 2004. By 2006, however, the percentage of Hispanic voters supporting Republican candidates in the midterm congressional elections declined dramatically. Many observers thought that this decline was linked to the harsh rhetoric regarding illegal immigrants by Republican candidates. These candidates also overwhelmingly opposed President Bush's immigration bill, which some termed amnesty, for the estimated 12 million immigrants in the United States without proper documentation. One of the hottest topics in the Republican presidential debates of 2007 and early 2008 was what to do about illegal immigration, and the only agreement seemed to be on building a longer and more effective wall on the nation's border with Mexico. That debate continues still. Many in the Republican Party worry quite publicly that such political posturing might play poorly with the party's base voters, while alienating one of the key new constituencies they had hoped to attract. Their fears appeared to be confirmed when Hispanic voting for the 2008 Republican candidate, John McCain, was only 31 percent—despite McCain's having been one of the two initial sponsors of an immigration reform bill in Congress. The bill, championed by President Bush, provided a realistic route for undocumented immigrants, especially children, to gain U.S. citizenship.

The harsh Republican reaction to this proposed legislation (some termed it amnesty for illegal aliens) was led by such Republican Party members as Representative Tom Tancredo of Colorado, an early candidate for the presidential nomination in 2008. All the Republican candidates for president in the early debates in 2008 seemed to adopt Tancredo's position. None of the Republican primary candidates talked about a pathway to citizenship during the presidential nominations. The pressure became so intense that McCain himself ultimately disavowed the bill he had initially cosponsored. Many Hispanic leaders reacted negatively to McCain's campaign at that point, and ultimately many Hispanic voters followed suit in the general election by voting for the Democrats at much higher rates than they did in 2004.

This Republican swing to the hard right was exacerbated by Mitt Romney's campaign in 2012. In Republican Party debates in the primary season of that year, Romney took the harshest tone of all the candidates in his rhetoric concerning what to do about illegal immigrants. His suggestion that self-deportation might solve the problem for the estimated 12 million undocumented immigrants did not go down well in the Hispanic community. Romney was never able to overcome this deficit by taking a more moderate stance in the fall campaign. He received only 27 percent of the Hispanic vote in the general election of 2012 (Stanley and Niemi, 2013–14, 116). The debate within the Republican Party over immigration only intensified in the prelude to the 2016 elections.

There is clearly an electoral price at the ballot box for what party leaders do and say about minorities. Party leaders certainly think that offering party positions to high-profile Hispanic candidates and supporting Hispanic causes will garner support among Latino voters. However, if the Hispanic cause is seen as hostile to white interests, as was true of the McCain immigration bill, there is also a price to be paid among white voters. This is especially true in the South and the Southwest, where illegal immigrants tend to cluster and where the white backlash against them has taken the form of restrictive and punitive state legislation. Politics is about conflict and making these hard choices, with trade-offs on both sides. It is up to party leaders and public officials to weigh the costs and benefits carefully as they apply to the party's interests while presumably also keeping in mind what may be in the long-term best interest of the nation as a whole. It is also clear that party officials, interested in taking the most rational action to build the party's base and enhance its diversity, have little or no control over what that party's elected officials and candidates for office will do, in their own pursuit of office, in a particular constituency.

For Republicans, in the area of race, a natural equilibrium of sorts has apparently been reached regarding African American delegates. Republicans started with 2 percent black delegates in 1968 and doubled this to 4 percent in 1972, under the impetus of the DO Committee. That is approximately where black representation stands; the range was 3–6 percent between 1976 and 2004. In 2008 it was 2 percent. Only 5 percent were Hispanics in that year, leaving the rest of the delegation, or 93 percent, white. Not much has changed since then, and the Republican leadership probably sees little reason for any changes. There have been reports in the national media of Republican leaders over the years, usually in response to inquiry and implied criticism from the media or from Democrats, stating that their level of black representation may be about right, given the low level of support that black voters typically give to Republican presidential candidates, ordinarily in the 10–15 percent range. This argument is not entirely persuasive if one applies the mathematical method that Democrats have adopted; however, Republicans eschew such mathematical standards, denouncing them as quotas.

Whatever the philosophical and ideological considerations, pragmatic politics have probably worked to the Republicans' net advantage over the past four decades. Up until 2006 and 2008 the electoral results since 1968 have not been particularly negative for Republican presidential or congressional candidates. Their more laissez-faire and states' rights approach certainly fits the Republican Party's ideology and value commitments, and it has not done them great electoral harm, as winning the white South has been their biggest coup in the past generation. Thus from its perspective, the Republican Party leadership at the national level (the Republican National Committee, first and foremost, the White House, when Republicans have the presidency, and Republican congressional campaign committees) generally has acted strategically and rationally in the recruitment of new demographic groups, although this may not hold true of the party's treatment of Hispanic voters. The question of how to appeal to minorities, especially Hispanics—and to a lesser extent African Americans—continues to divide the modern Republican Party.

In 2005, after the George W. Bush reelection victory, the Republican National Committee chair, Ken Mehlman, announced that he was initiating a new outreach to African American voters and began to visit with various black groups and leaders in an effort to broaden the party's base. He and White House adviser Karl Rove clearly wanted to create a much larger Republican majority and adopted this new outreach plan as one way to accomplish that goal. Republicans are now faced with the issue of how to recruit both Hispanic elites and mass voters, which both parties want to incorporate into their coalition. Like Democrats, Republicans did a number of highly symbolic things, under the leadership of President George W. Bush, to recruit Hispanic voters. After the 2004 elections the Republican National Committee and other party officials took Spanish lessons in order to communicate with Hispanic voters. In addition, Bush engineered the appointment of Senator Mel Martinez, a Cuban American from Florida, to be the chair of the Republican National Committee during his second term; however, Senator Martinez was ousted after only one year at the helm. In 2009 the Republican National Committee chose an African American, Michael Steele, to be its chair. His tenure was a rocky one, and he only lasted through one two-year term before being ousted; Republican gains among African Americans were not evident.

For all the effectiveness of symbolic politics in this country, when the conversation turns to public policy issues, the two parties must take into account the policy agendas of the minority voters in question, and the parties must make some hard choices about which side of those issues they are on. The fierce debate over President Bush's immigration legislation in 2007–08 illustrates this point. This debate continued throughout President Obama's first term and well into his second term, as Congress refused to pass any immigration reform legislation. Both major parties must hone their message, and their legislative agendas, at both the national and state levels, to appeal to a large and varied group like the Hispanic voters. Some policy positions, like stances on immigration laws and on English-only language restrictions, have special relevance to Hispanic communities. On other issues, this bloc of voters may not differ from the national population. Hispanic voters tend to be culturally conservative on a number of social and religious issues. On the other hand, they are operational liberals on many socioeconomic and educational policy issues.

The point is that difficult strategic choices must be made by officials of both parties, and those strategic choices must be made with an eye toward building the party's coalition and adding diversity, while at the same time not alienating the party's current base. It is a delicate balancing act that requires constant calibration.

The Effect of Rules Changes: Youth

Young voters were originally of interest to party leaders because of the Vietnam War and the electoral fallout from it. It was mostly the young who demonstrated against the war in Grant Park at the Democratic National Convention of 1968 (Nelson, 2011). The Democrats and Hubert Humphrey lost that year because the party was deeply divided, because the nation was deeply divided, and because Hubert Humphrey's campaign attracted more of the blame for that division than Richard Nixon's campaign did. The Democrats also lost that year because of the bloody and anarchical confrontations between the Chicago police and the young demonstrators at the Democratic National Convention, confrontations played out before a national audience on television. As a result, by 1972 party elders desperately wanted the young people to be inside the hall, participating in the process, rather than outside, protesting, and they used the McGovern-Fraser rules to ensure that at least a significant bloc of the 1972 delegates would be young people. They called for a "reasonable relationship to that group's percentage of the state population," just like the rule for women and African Americans that year.

The data in table 4-2 indicate that their objective was largely reached. The Democrats went from 3 percent of delegates being under thirty years old in 1968 to 22 percent under thirty in 1972. This is one of the most dramatic changes for a demographic group on record. In addition, Republicans went from 4 percent under thirty in 1968 to 6 percent just four years later. After 1972, the drive stalled, and the percentages of young people in both conventions began to decline. Since 1976 the percentage of representation for young delegates has been in the single digits at most conventions and well below the youth cohort in the population at large. For example, in the 2000 census, 22 percent of the population was under thirty. By that standard, in 1972 only Democrats reached the national norms. The reasons for those failures of demographic representation are complex.

By 1976 the war in Vietnam had ended; young people aged eighteen and older had the vote; the draft was no longer in force; and the interests of young people had changed as had the interests of party leaders. Young people are not a coherent group in American politics. With the possible exception of a war and the draft, there is little to unite them or to hold their attention for long; and of course, they are not young for very long. There is always another cohort coming along at the bottom of the age ladder, and those once at the bottom are soon in the middle. Thus the youth movement of the 1970s, to the extent there ever was one, failed to be sustained into the 1980s and 1990s as any kind of coherent force in American politics. Indeed, the major political hallmark of the young in these latter decades of American electoral politics is their apathy. Generation X became synonymous with very low levels of voter turnout, low levels of political interest and involvement, and high levels of political distrust and alienation. There was some renewed interest during the 1990s and the early twenty-first century, which brought some young people back into the political process. Bill Clinton's campaign made some targeted efforts at the youth vote in 1992, as did George W. Bush's 2000 and 2004 campaigns. John Kerry also made a concerted effort to court the youth vote in 2004. In addition, MTV's 1992 Rock the Vote campaign was an effort to increase the abysmally low voter interest and turnout among the younger generation; however, its impact is not clear, and turnout among this group remained low in 1996 and 2000.

By 2004, and again in 2008, the percentage of young delegates in the Democratic National Convention did increase—to 7 percent. It may be that the divisiveness of the Iraq War, as well as conflict over social and domestic issues, again piqued the interest of the young. They had favored Gore over Bush in 2000 by a narrow margin of 48 to 46 percent (Stanley and Niemi, 2006, 124). Exit poll data indicate that people under thirty years old voted for Kerry over Bush in 2004 by a margin of 54 to 45 percent (Stanley and Niemi, 2006, 124). In 2008 the groundwork laid by the Kerry campaign paid dividends for Obama, who had tremendous appeal to young voters. The Obama campaign also used modern technology to mobilize young voters and get them involved, using social networks like Facebook and YouTube. As a result, young people voted for Obama by a 2-1, or 66–32 percent, margin (Stanley and Niemi, 2009–10, 114). Young people voted almost as heavily for Obama in 2012, when they gave him a margin of 60–37 percent over Romney (Stanley and Niemi, 2013–14, 116). This constitutes an age gap of unprecedented proportions, echoing the gender gap.

It is unclear whether the young are a coherent cohort, one that a party can build on. A whole age group seldom becomes a permanent and loyal part of a party coalition in the way the Depression-era generation was for decades a dependable component of Franklin Roosevelt's New Deal coalition. It can be done, but it usually takes cataclysmic events in a nation's history. The war in Iraq, followed by the Great Recession of 2007–09, could prove to be such a transforming national experience for the millennium generation; however, it is unclear at this point if that group will be a lasting influence on American party politics.

Occupation, Education, and Religion

Table 4-3 reports the occupation of the delegates to both national conventions during the period under study. It is clear that the number and percentage of lawyers at both conventions declined somewhat. This decline is particularly notable in comparison with the base year of 1948, when 35 percent of Democratic delegates and 36 percent of Republican delegates were attorneys (David, Goldman, and Bain, 1964, 239), but this decline is also

Table 4-3. *National Convention Delegates, Occupation, by Party, 1968–2008*
Percent

Occupation	1968		1972		1976		1980		1984		1988	
	D	R	D	R	D	R	D	R	D	R	D	R
Lawyer	28	22	12	N.A.	16	15	13	15	17	14	16	17
Teacher	8	2	11	N.A.	12	4	15	4	16	6	14	5
Union member	N.A.	N.A.	16	N.A.	21	3	27	4	25	4	25	3

	1992		1996		2000		2004		2008	
	D	R	D	R	D	R	D	R	D	R
Lawyer	14	13	10	11	9	9	13	N.A.	17	16
Teacher	9	4	9	2	7	2	13	N.A.	8	5
Union member	26	N.A.	35	4	31	4	25	3	24	N.A.

Source: Based on *CBS News/New York Times,* 2008a, 2008b. Data for 1992 Republicans and 2008 Republican union members based on author surveys.
N.A. = Not available

clear if the base year is 1968, when about a quarter of the delegates to both conventions were lawyers. Dropping from more than a third of convention delegates originally, the percentage of lawyers has been mostly in the 10–17 percent range in recent conventions. It is noteworthy that the lowest participation by lawyers was in 2000, at just 9 percent. This low figure is congruent with the decrease in attorneys in Congress and state legislatures, although in that arena lawyers are still the modal category. While lawyers' brokering abilities are important, many other occupations also have that skill. Nevertheless, lawyers made a comeback of sorts in 2008, when 17 percent of Democratic delegates and 16 percent of Republican delegates served (Stanley and Niemi, 2009–10, 68).

One occupational group that has increased representation is teachers, who composed 8 percent of Democratic delegates and 2 percent of Republican delegates in 1968. That percentage increased to the 11–16 percent range for Democrats from 1972 through 1988. The percentage of schoolteachers also more than doubled in the Republican national conventions from 1968 forward; however, their percentage in the Republican conventions is consistently well below that in Democratic delegations. This increase is in line with the much noted efforts by the National Education Association and the American Federation of Teachers to increase their political power by urging teachers to seek access to the political process. Republicans frequently charge that Democrats have been "captured" by the teachers' unions and that the unions dictate Democrats' positions on such controversial issues as school vouchers. If that is true, the Democrats have been captured by a relatively small group, representing just under 10 percent of the delegates in most recent years.

Union members constitute another notable occupational group with representation at the Democratic Party's national convention. Democrats are widely regarded to be the party of organized labor. The data for union members in the pre-reform era are sketchy; however, the seminal study of the 1948 convention indicates that only 2.1 percent of the Democratic delegates and just 0.2 percent of the Republican delegates were labor union representatives (David, Goldman, and Bain, 1964, 239). The post-reform data indicate that union delegates have grown to a fairly stable contingent among Democrats. In 1972, 16 percent of Democrats were union members. This was George McGovern's convention, and it was not thought to be particularly hospitable to mainline labor union members, given McGovern's opposition to the Vietnam War, which most labor leaders supported. Union member representation increased to 21 percent at Jimmy Carter's 1976 convention, and it has remained around one-fourth of the Democratic delegation since that time. From one-fourth to one-third of the delegates is probably about the current equilibrium level for labor delegates, given the very important role they play in the Democratic Party's overall national coalition. The portion of delegates who are Republican union members ranges from 3 to 4 percent in the years for which data are available.

It has long been recognized that those who get heavily involved in political parties, especially to the extent of having the personal and political resources necessary to become national convention delegates, are not likely representative of the American population. Political activists are much more likely to show an upper-middle-class socioeconomic bias. Virtually all the studies of political elites demonstrate that they are likely to come from the better-educated strata of society. National convention delegates are likely to reflect that bias, and it is clear from table 4-4 that those with at least some college are the most likely to be selected as delegates. Those with a high school or lesser level of educational attainment are represented in both conventions, but at levels in the 4–22 percent range. It is clear, moreover, that the educational attainment of the delegates in both parties has been increasing over the past several presidential election cycles. To be a delegate entails a demanding and rigorous regimen, and it is not for everyone. The cognitive and social skills required are often formidable, as the prospective delegate wends his or her way through a labyrinth of rules and regulations and politics. This is especially true in caucus states, which require a lot of long meetings at multiple levels, where the activist's ambitions to become a national convention delegate

Table 4-4. *National Convention Delegates, Education, by Party, 1948–2008*
Percent

Education	1948		1972		1976		1980		1984		1988	
	D	R	D	R	D	R	D	R	D	R	D	R
High school or less	22	18	17	13	10	N.A.	12	10	20	17	18	15
Some college	22	23	27	28	19	N.A.	22	27	15	21	4	3
Bachelor's degree	22	25	27	27	16	N.A.	31	34	25	37	28	42
Graduate or professional degree	34	34	29	33	55	N.A.	35	30	41	26	50	42

	1992		1996		2000		2004		2008	
	D	R	D	R	D	R	D	R	D	R
High school or less	9	8	10	5	7	6	7	5	7	4
Some college	20	20	17	17	16	18	15	19	12	16
Bachelor's degree	28	37	42	36	26	36	68	71	29	37
Graduate or professional degree	43	35	42	36	51	40	10	5	53	42

Source: Data for 1948 based on David, Goldman, and Bain, 1964, 234–35; data for 1972 based on Kirkpatrick, 1976; data for 1980–2008 based on author surveys.
N.A. = Not available

can be stymied. Just getting endorsed by the candidate to be on the primary ballot and then choosing the right candidate at the right time can also be a formidable task. These demands are increasingly tilting the playing field in the direction of those who have the advantages of more advanced education.

Obviously, this phenomenon also indicates something about the kind of political parties we now have. The older and more pragmatic parties were often populated by blue-collar and working-class people, who were in it for the material and social rewards provided by the old-style political machine (Wilson, 1962). Those days are mostly over, and the newer and more programmatic parties are driven by activists who are ideologically committed, are sophisticated about the issues, know where they stand on those issues, and know which candidates represent their views and values. These qualities, too, are more likely to be held by those with more advanced levels of education. While this trend is understandable, it also ensures that, at least on some dimensions, the political elites will be dramatically out of step and unrepresentative of the mass public.

Table 4-5 reports on religion and indicates where there is both continuity and change. The religious categories used in this table are fairly broad and do not allow for more precise analysis, since the early studies simply asked for Protestant, Catholic, and Jewish identifications. For Democrats, the Protestant vote fell from 64 percent in 1948 to 43 percent in both 2004 and 2008. Catholic representation, on the other hand, has held steady, being 28 percent

Table 4-5. *National Convention Delegates, Religious Denomination, by Party, 1948–2008*

Percent

Religious denomination	1948		1972		1976		1980		1984		1988	
	D	R	D	R	D	R	D	R	D	R	D	R
Protestant	64	87	42	N.A.	47	73	47	72	49	71	50	69
Catholic	28	6	26	N.A.	34	18	37	22	29	22	30	22
Jewish	2	1	9	N.A.	9	3	8	3	8	2	7	2

	1992		1996		2000		2004		2008	
	D	R	D	R	D	R	D	R	D	R
Protestant	47	N.A.	47	62	47	63	43	65	43	57
Catholic	30	N.A.	30	25	30	27	32	26	26	30
Jewish	10	N.A.	6	3	8	2	8	2	9	3

Source: Data for 1948 based on David, Goldman, and Bain, 1964, 233–34; data for 1972–2008 based on *CBS News/New York Times*, 2008a, 2008b.

N.A. = Not available

in 1948 and 26 percent in 2008. Jewish representation has also held steady, at about 9 percent.

For Republicans, as expected, the Protestant category is by far the dominant religious identity. In the benchmark year of 1948, 87 percent of the delegates were Protestant. Republicans had always been the WASP (white, Anglo-Saxon, Protestant) party. However, the Protestant percentage has been declining among the Republicans because other categories, particularly the Catholic category, have been increasing. Catholics were at 30 percent in 2008, the highest it has ever been among the Republicans. That year Catholic representation at the Republican convention exceeded Catholic representation at the Democratic convention. Certainly, Republicans have been courting the Catholic vote and church hierarchy, especially on social issues, most notably women's right to abortions. These data indicate that Republicans may have made some progress at the party elite levels and to a lesser extent at the mass voter level.

In 2004 John Kerry was the first Catholic to receive the Democratic Party's nomination since John Kennedy in 1960, but the results among mass voters was quite different for the two candidates. While Kennedy carried the Catholic vote handily, 78–22 percent, John Kerry lost the Catholic vote to George W. Bush by a margin of 55–45 percent (Stanley and Niemi, 2000, 118). Democrats' standing among Catholic voters improved somewhat in 2008, as 54 percent supported Obama (Stanley and Niemi, 2009–10, 114). Still, Democratic losses and Republican gains among Catholics seem evident in these data. In 2012 the Catholic vote was split, with a slight cant toward Obama (at 50 percent) compared to Romney (at 48 percent; Stanley and Niemi, 2013–14, 116). This was better than how John Kerry did in 2004; however, compared to the New Deal era, when Catholics formed a significant component of the Democratic Party's coalition, the losses for Democrats and the gains for Republicans are significant.

Among Jewish activists, the story is more stable. In 1948, 2 percent of the Democratic delegates were Jewish, and a miniscule 0.7 percent of Republican delegates were Jewish. The Jewish delegation among Republicans was at 2 or 3 percent most years, compared to 9 or 10 percent among Democrats. Clearly the Jewish presence among Democratic Party activists is fairly stable and consistent and is about three times that among Republican activists. Democratic presidential candidates are favored heavily among Jewish voters. Typically, about three-fourths of those who identify themselves as Jewish vote for the Democratic candidate. In 1996 this percentage was 78 percent; in 2000 it was 79 percent; in 2004 it was 74 percent; in 2008 it was 78 percent; and in 2012 it was 69 percent (Stanley and Niemi, 2013–14, 116). In spite of a slight slippage away from Obama in 2012, the Jewish vote is one of the most loyal and consistent components of the Democratic coalition. This is one group that has not changed its voting pattern significantly since Roosevelt stitched together the New Deal coalition. It is perhaps not surprising that Jewish voters favor the Democratic Party heavily. Jewish people have a strong cultural and religious commitment to social justice issues and to the moral obligation to help the poor and less fortunate. They have long identified with liberal and progressive community groups and causes, and they support such groups financially and with their votes. Thus religious values reinforce cultural and political values for the Jewish community.

The important changes on both sides of the partisan divide can be shown with a more refined classification scheme, especially the generic category of Protestant. Table 4-6 provides that more refined look at religious and political identification.

The Republican Party since its inception has been the party of Protestants of various stripes. Protestants were attracted to the Republican Party, just as Catholics and Jews were attracted to the Democratic Party, because of their cultural and religious values, their shared history, and peer group reinforcement. Religion was a defining characteristic of both parties, but the dominant groups making up the generic category Protestant have shifted in ways that are politically important. The Protestants who originally formed the core of Republican Party strength were Episcopalians, Presbyterians, and Lutherans. These

Table 4-6. *National Convention Delegates, Religious and Political Background, by Party, Selected Years 1988–2008*

Percent

Religious or political affiliation	1988		1996		2000		2004		2008	
	D	R	D	R	D	R	D	R	D	R
Fundamentalist	1	9	3	12	2	7	5	12	1	6
Evangelical	9	13	2	18	2	17	5	21	4	22
Charismatic or Pentecostal	2	3	1	5	2	3	2	5	8	5
Mainline	N.A.	N.A.	28	33	25	36	22	34	19	29
Liberal or progressive	N.A.	N.A.	23	2	26	2	31	2	27	2
None	N.A.	N.A.	35	19	37	25	34	24	33	16
Other	N.A.	N.A.	9	13	7	10	2	2	10	20

Source: Author surveys.
N.A. = Not available

churches, along with Methodists, are usually called mainline churches today, an appellation that separates them from evangelical and fundamentalist churches. These latter churches, especially Baptist and Pentecostal, and especially in the South, have become active in politics over the past two or three decades. Most of that political activity has accrued to the benefit of the Republican Party (Kohut and others, 2000). It is worth noting that George H. W. Bush is identified as an Episcopalian, while George W. Bush followed his wife into the Methodist Church, and he assiduously courted evangelical leaders, especially those from the Southern Baptist Convention. Likewise, John McCain was raised in the Episcopalian tradition, but for years he attended a mega-church in Phoenix associated with the Baptist denomination. Both men reflect the dominant religious identification of members of the Republican Party.

The situation is significantly different for Democrats. In some ways this difference is encapsulated by President Obama's religious journey. Since 1996 about a fourth of Democratic delegates have considered themselves to be liberal or progressive Protestants. Another 19–36 percent are mainline Protestants. Both of these groups are exceeded, however, in most years by delegates who do not identify with any organized religion. Barack Obama came from such a secular background; his mother was essentially a nonbeliever and his father, who did not raise him, was a Muslim. Obama converted to Christianity as a young man working on the South Side of Chicago, where his membership in a liberal United Church of Christ under the tutelage of Dr. Jeremiah Wright became a well-known and then controversial part of his religious odyssey.

Obama's history is the exception among recent presidents, and while other American presidents have come from essentially secular backgrounds, and many very rarely attended church, nominees in the modern era have increasingly come to identify publicly with a mainline or evangelical denomination by the time the campaign opens. Obama's church membership and his controversial minister became fodder for much of the denomination-related conflict that threatened to engulf the Obama campaign in the 2008 primary. While he got past the immediate crisis during the primary season, his religious identification, and especially the charge that he was a Muslim, continued to be raised against Obama by his opponents during his entire first term. Religious identification questions and conflict probably were used against Obama more than any other modern American president. For example, a Gallup poll conducted on June 22, 2012, almost at the end of his first term, found that only 34 percent of Americans could correctly name Christian as Obama's religion, compared to 44 percent who said they didn't know, 11 percent who said he was a Muslim, and 8 percent who said he had no religion. Religious identification and frequency of church attendance are powerful influences on a vast segment of American voters.

This increased role for religion is also evident among mass voters. In 2000, exit polls showed that Protestant voters favored George W. Bush over Al Gore by 55 to 42 percent. This religion gap grew in 2004 when Protestants favored George W. Bush over John Kerry by a whopping 62 to 38 percent (Stanley and Niemi, 2006, 123). In 2008 white Protestants favored John McCain over Obama by a 65-34 percent margin (Stanley and Niemi, 2009–10, 114). This religion gap was even more marked in 2012, when white Protestants voted for Mitt Romney over Barack Obama by a 69–30 margin (Stanley and Niemi, 2013–14, 116).

In addition, frequency of church attendance and other markers of evangelical Protestantism, such as literal belief in the Bible, are now reliable predictors of voting for the Republican Party (White, 2003; Balz and Johnson, 2009; Putnam and Campbell, 2010). Thus evangelical and fundamentalist Protestants play an increasingly important role in the Republican Party and in presidential election outcomes (Kohut and others, 2000; Wilcox, 2000). Secular or nonreligious delegates and those from liberal or progressive church backgrounds have come to play a more important role in the Democratic Party's conventions and in the Democratic Party as a whole. The major exception to this rule is the African American community, which heavily identifies with evangelical churches and yet is deeply loyal to the Democratic Party.

Conclusion

Since the party reform era began, both political parties have increased diversity among their convention delegates. This eclectic permeability is evident at both the elite and the mass levels of the parties. This increased diversity was influenced by the changes wrought by the McGovern-Fraser rules for the 1972 Democratic convention. It was reinforced by demographic trends that have emphasized diversity and decisionmaking at the national level. Democrats have changed more obviously than Republicans in terms of demographic representation, with the face of the national convention increasingly being that of an African American or woman delegate. This change was never more dramatically displayed than when the television cameras scanned the delegates to the Democratic National Convention in Denver in 2008 and in Charlotte in 2012. Teachers' unions are also an important part of the Democratic coalition, although perhaps not as dominant as their critics often charge.

On the Republican side the faces were mostly white when the cameras scanned the convention hall in 2008. The number and percentage of women have increased, although not to the extent evident among Democrats. The number and percentage of lawyers have declined among Republicans, perhaps a reflection of the party's war with trial lawyers over tort reform. Most notably, the number and percentage of fundamentalist and evangelical church members have increased decidedly for the GOP. The original research, surveying national convention delegates, was by Paul T. David and his associates (David, Goldman, and Bain, 1964). It shows that the typical national convention delegate for both parties then was likely an upper-middle-class white male who had long years of service to the party. That description was also true for most holders of political power in any arena during that era of American politics. At the beginning of the twenty-first century there was still some truth to this finding, and the upper and middle classes still have significant advantages in gaining political power. But the reality now is much more complicated as a result of the changes instituted in the 1960s and 1970s.

As Samuel Eldersveld (1964) maintains, the two major political parties have proved to be remarkably "porous." They have been willing, even eager, to take in new constituents and to give them a role in the selection of the nation's highest official as well as in the writing of the party's platform and rules. This porous nature—this ability to expand the coalitional base—is a key to the ability of the two major parties to adapt to the external pressures they face for greater access for new social groups and new claimants on political power. The old stereotype of the highest levels of party power being dominated by upper-middle-class white males needs major modification to conform with the empirical results presented in this chapter. There is some continuity, but there is definitely significant change. These twin themes of continuity and change are revisited in subsequent chapters of this book.

5

On Political Values

This chapter examines the political values of Democratic and Republican elites who have led their party organizations through the past four decades. As noted in the previous chapter, it is relatively easy to ascertain the level of demographic representation in a legislative body or in the national conventions. Race, gender, socioeconomic class, religion, and occupation are familiar categories of what Hannah Pitkin (1987) terms "descriptive" or "standing-for" dimensions of representation. These are important components of representation in both a symbolic and a substantive sense of the word. Those social groups that have felt excluded, and that have in fact been excluded in the past from the inner councils of public power, frequently demand a form of descriptive representation as recognition of their status and newly gained political currency. This is the most prominent and obvious form of representation.

Nevertheless, as important as this dimension is, the more important test of the representative nature of the legislative or party body is whether those chosen accurately and fairly reflect and share the political values and views of their constituents. There is no more damaging charge in the American political lexicon than the charge that a political leader has "lost touch" with the people who elected him or her. It is a constant charge heard in this country: that once people are elected to office they immediately start acting in their own best interests, or for the interest groups who fund their campaigns, or for the "elites," without regard to the needs of the people. This is a form of political distrust and alienation that has been widespread in the American political culture almost since its inception (Hofstadter, 1996). It is a strain that seems to be growing in our contemporary era, when political discourse is dominated by talk radio and cable television pundits whose words are widely distributed through a viral network of angry bloggers. Attacking the government and those who are in charge of it is the dominant motif in most of the mass media in today's political world.

The very essence of mass democracy lies in the question of how well the political elites represent the values of the base and whether that link between the decisionmakers and the people is seen as viable and legitimate. It is essential that the representative broadly reflect the political beliefs, policy preferences, and values of the constituents, because this allows the decisionmaker to truly represent what is important to the constituents in the myriad of votes, exchanges, and decisions that the public or party official engages in. This linkage is necessary to maintain legitimacy in a mass democracy that takes a republican form. In Pitkin's terminology, the sharing of basic values is a mark of substantive representation. It is this quality that enables the representative to "act for" rather than simply "stand for" those whom he or she endeavors to represent. This chapter explores what it means to be a representative in the highest party councils, the beliefs and values the representative takes into the decisionmaking arena.

Political Ideology

Table 5-1 provides an overview of the self-identified ideology of those who attended the national conventions between 1972 and 2008. There are limitations to the measurement of political ideology through this self-identification scale. Certainly, the concepts of *liberal* and *conservative* mean different things to different people, and there are several well-recognized dimensions to these concepts. People can be liberal on one dimension and conservative on another and feel absolutely no incongruity in their lack of what Philip Converse (1964) terms *constraint* in their belief systems. Studies have also amply demonstrated that there can be a disconnect between some people's self-identified position on the ideological scale and their various public policy issue stances. So one should not expect this one measure to tell us all we need to know about the basic values of these political decisionmakers.

That limitation of the indicator of ideology having been acknowledged, it is still a worthwhile measure to use here. The subjects of this study are, after all, political party activists and leaders. They are experienced and sophisticated people who have been around politics long enough to rise to one of the

Table 5-1. *Ideology of National Convention Delegates, 1972–2008*[a]

Percent

Ideology	1972		1976		1980		1984		1988	
	D	R	D	R	D	R	D	R	D	R
Liberal	79	10	40	3	38	1	43	2	51	3
Moderate	13	35	47	45	53	34	50	31	42	27
Conservative	8	57	8	48	9	65	7	68	7	70

	1992		1996		2000		2004		2008	
	D	R	D	R	D	R	D	R	D	R
Liberal	57	1	51	0	54	1	51	0	60	1
Moderate	41	27	45	18	43	24	47	21	37	18
Conservative	3	71	4	82	4	76	3	78	3	81

Source: Data from 1980 through 2008 are based on author surveys. Data for 1976 are based on *CBS News/New York Times*, 2008a, 2008b; data for 1972 are based on Kirkpatrick, 1976, 168.

a. Responses were on a 5-point self-identification scale, with 1–2 = liberal, 3 = moderate, and 4–5 = conservative.

more widely sought-after positions in the two major parties. As we saw in the previous chapter, they are also better educated and more politically articulate than the American public in general. Many of them are what Jeane Kirkpatrick (1976), in her seminal work on these "presidential elites," terms "symbol specialists." Thus these political elites can be expected to judge candidates, the issues, and their own political positions through an ideological prism. In addition, these political activists help shape the image and the message of their political party to the external world. Mass voters see the parties and form their impressions of them partially through their perceptions and evaluations of the people who represent the parties by serving in positions of prominence and distinction in the party organization.

The data on the ideological views of the political elites before 1972 are sketchy, so it is impossible to be definitive about any pre-reform versus post-reform comparisons. Nevertheless, it is probably correct to pinpoint the development of a more ideologically polarized group of partisans representing their constituent state parties as beginning with the 1972 conventions. Certainly, the import of the various rules changes, as well as the demographic changes in the delegations of that year, would lead one to that conclusion. The fact that the Democrats overwhelmingly selected George McGovern, arguably one of the most liberal politicians in the modern era, to be their standard-bearer would also lead in that direction. From 1972 through 2008 the pattern is consistent and unmistakable. That is, the two major parties, at the leadership level, separated themselves on the ideological continuum and have become very polarized on self-identified ideology. Put simply, the Democrats are predominantly the liberal-to-moderate alternative and the Republicans are predominantly conservative with a much smaller group of moderates, if one judges by what these party leaders choose to call themselves ideologically. Again, these are people accustomed to dealing with these two concepts, and over the course of the research none of them had a problem adopting one of the three labels. Ideology is a currency in which political elites are accustomed to dealing, and they are not shy about attaching the label to themselves and others.

Liberal delegates reached their zenith of 79 percent in the 1972 Democratic convention, which nominated George McGovern (Kirkpatrick, 1976). From there, the liberal delegates declined to 40 percent in 1976 and were certainly outnumbered by moderates, at 47 percent. Since this was the convention that nominated an avowed moderate southern governor, Jimmy Carter, that marked ideological change is not surprising. It simply illustrates the point that the presidential candidate and the issues and short-term conflicts of the moment will have some effect on the ideology of the delegates to any particular convention. In spite of that short-term perturbation, however, longitudinal trends in party leadership are notable across these ten data points and across these thirty-six years of American presidential politics (table 5-1). Data from 1980 through 2008 indicate that a sort of ideological equilibrium was reached at the end of the century, with the proportion of liberal delegates ranging from 38 percent in Carter's renomination year to 51 percent in the 1996 convention that renominated Clinton.

The moderate category in 2000 and 2004 began to rival the level of liberal representation among Democrats. Its dropping to 37 percent at the Obama convention of 2008 reflects the dramatic increase in liberals that year. The sizable moderate contingent at the Democratic conventions may show the influence during much of that era of the Democratic Leadership Council. The DLC was organized as the voice of moderation in the party and was prominent in Clinton's original nomination drive and played a role in his administration. From its inception, the DLC and the liberals fought a spirited intraparty battle over who would define the future of the Democratic Party. At times, from the rhetoric of the two sides of this fraternal fight, it seems as though each regarded the other faction as a greater threat to the future of the Democratic Party than their Republican opponents. Although the DLC has declined recently as the moderates have lost elections and power, there is still ideological factionalism within the party. That is not uncommon in the internecine warfare that often breaks out in political parties, especially when they are out of power, as the Democrats were from 1980 through 1992 and from 2000 through 2008. The reduction of conservatives to almost nonexistent status in the party, ranging from 8 percent of the delegates in 1972 down to only 3 or 4 percent in the most recent Democratic national conventions, provides proof that the two major parties have largely purged themselves of those who "misidentify" with them. Conservatives have almost disappeared among Democrats, and liberals have almost disappeared among Republicans.

This realignment also, of course, reflects the almost total realignment of the South. No other mass partisan movement is as important in recent American politics as the transformation of white southerners from being the foundation of the Democratic Party's national majorities to their role as the foundation of the Republican Party's national electoral majorities. This realignment is reflected in the parties' ideological polarization. While there is debate in the literature on how extensive the "values divide" and the "culture war" are among mass voters, there can be little doubt of their contours among the party elites (Fiorina, Abrams, and Pope, 2005; White, 2003; Greenberg, 2004). In 2008, when Democrats nominated Barack Obama—generally regarded as one of the most liberal senators in Congress—60 percent of the delegates defined themselves as liberal.

Ideological sorting and polarization are even more notable among Republicans across this time period. From 57 percent conservative and 10 percent liberal in 1972, the Republicans went as high as 82 percent conservative and as low as 0 percent liberal in 1996. One could hardly ask for more ideological consistency. This is a particular trend among the moderates of the Republican Party. In 1972 Republican delegates were 35 percent moderate. That portion decreased to 18 percent in 1996 and to 18 percent again in 2008, a year when 81 percent of these delegates called themselves conservatives. Since 1980 only 1 to 3 percent of the delegates called themselves liberal, and in some years there were none. Again, the dominance of the avowed conservative group among Republicans is marked and growing. In 1964 their presidential nominee, Barry Goldwater, in his acceptance speech, told the national convention, "Moderation in the pursuit of freedom is no virtue and extremism in the pursuit of liberty is no vice." From one-fifth to one-third of his party's delegates at succeeding national conventions would probably not agree with this aphorism, yet it is also notable how many Republican delegates consistently describe themselves as conservatives. My data indicate that the 1996 and 2008 Republican conventions were the two most conservative in the party's history. Likewise, the 2008 Democratic convention was the most liberal since 1972. The polarization of the two-party system seems not only clear but almost complete.

It may be, as some observers claim, that the moderates in both parties have become uncomfortable with the ideological tenor of convention delegations. Ironically, it was thought during the era when party literature predicted the demise of the two-party system that one major source of fraction was the committed ideologues within both parties who were said to be alienated by the moderation of the two major parties. Indeed, the thrust of the American Political Science Association's famous report calling for a more responsible two-party system was that the two major parties should offer more coherent and more programmatic alternatives (Committee on Political Parties of the American Political Science Association, 1950).The APSA report challenged the pragmatic party model, dominant at that time and throughout much of American history. It argued instead for a more ideological and programmatic model. For years scholars advocated and predicted an ideological realignment of the two major parties. It is evident from the data presented here and from many other scholarly studies—for example, studies on party unity and on the increasing party support in Congress—that the ideological polarization of the two major parties is fairly advanced. How to evaluate that transformation, and whether it is functional for the continuation of the party system and for American politics, are much more difficult and controversial questions. At least on this particular dimension, we have seen a partisan realignment in American politics probably unprecedented in American history. How well that realignment allows for effective government, and whether it is a good thing or a bad thing for the nation, will continue to divide scholars and activists alike. One leading scholar, John W. Kingdon (1999), after reviewing the ideological polarization of the two major parties, evaluated the change negatively. He maintains that the majority of the American people are in the vast middle of the ideological spectrum and that they are repelled by the intense ideologically based partisanship that has developed in Washington. Kingdon's recommendation is for moderation on the part of leaders of both parties.

Thus, we have gone from the blandness of the two parties being one of the problems with the American system to its opposite. Critics now routinely decry ideological polarization, which has become one of the hallmarks of the current American party system. This critique of partisanship is one thing that Barack Obama and his challenger, John McCain, agreed on in the 2008 campaign. Each promised to defang the poisonous partisanship in Washington and to seek bipartisan solutions to the nation's problems. When elected, Barack Obama found this ambition impossible to realize. Partisan polarization continued and increased in the Obama era. Obama hardly talked about how to overcome polarization at all during his 2012 campaign. Mitt Romney occasionally claimed that he could overcome the divisions; however, short of electing a Republican majority in both houses of Congress, he offered few specifics as to how he could accomplish this feat.

Party and ideological polarization is now so deep that some in Congress are willing to risk the full faith and credit of the American government and its credit rating to make their point, no matter what the cost is to the economy. Others are literally willing to close down the government in order to repeal or delay the Affordable Care Act in an attempt to win with this leverage what they could not achieve using the normal channels of the legislative process. This is essentially what happened in the first half of October 2013, when party polarization, and lack of compromise, closed down the federal government and sent 800,000 "nonessential" employees home. The threat of default on the nation's financial obligations became very real, before a last-minute deal was finally struck with the help of the Senate leadership in both parties. In spite of the evident costs, the same scenario was at least possible for January 15, 2014, when the temporary truce ran out, although it was ultimately avoided by another cliff-hanger compromise. This high-profile political gridlock was a central factor in the public's historically low regard for Congress and its evident distrust of legislative leaders.

There has been a long-standing discussion in the political science literature as to whether the ideology of the party elites matches that of the party rank and file. Most studies find that the mass membership of the party is considerably more moderate than the party leadership. This finding is suggested by Kingdon but was originally documented by Herbert McClosky and his associates over fifty years ago (McClosky, Hoffman, and O'Hara, 1960). The basic pattern shows a majority of the leadership of the two major parties (as represented by their convention delegates) on the ideological extremes, with a majority of the identifiers and the mass public being in the middle. This pattern is referred to in the literature as the McClosky distribution (Baer and Bositis, 1988). I examine that theme in chapter 6.

Public Policy Issues

Tables 5-2 through 5-8 take up some of the specific public policy issues that have divided the American people over the past three decades. These divisions are especially evident at the leadership levels of the two major parties. Some critics of political parties contend that the two major parties unnecessarily magnify and exacerbate the divisions in American society and that this is one of the things wrong with the American political system (Dennis, 1976).

Defenders of parties point out that although there are indeed divisions of political opinion and interest in American society, it is the legitimate role of political parties to articulate those differences. In fact, this position goes back to James Madison and his famous disquisition on "factions" in the *Federalist Papers,* No. 51. It has been a consistent theme in modern political science literature.

The tables show a certain continuity in longitudinal data, so it seems that the American voter long ago made the distinction between long term and short term (Campbell and others, 1960). The data in the tables indicate that such a distinction applies as well to party elites. Although in the main their views are fairly stable from election to election, there is also room for social learning. Both phenomena are in evidence in these tables (Hershey, 1984).

Scope and Size of Government

Table 5-2 concerns the size and scope of the federal government, an issue that has been important on the national agenda during the last two decades. The proper role of the federal government has been a defining issue in American politics at least since Franklin Roosevelt's New Deal and fundamentally since the writing of the Constitution. Critics of Roosevelt decried his large expansion of the federal role and his intervention into the workings of the marketplace as a form of creeping socialism. Roosevelt's supporters retorted that the Great Depression as well as mobilization for World War II were existential challenges to the nation, which required a massive response on the part of the federal government, and that the market could not heal itself without governmental help. Whatever the labels, there is no question that the size and scope of the federal government grew significantly under Roosevelt and Truman.

The political debate grew more intense with the advent of Lyndon Johnson's Great Society, a package of domestic legislation that extended the reach and scope of the federal government. Ronald Reagan was committed to reducing that role. He famously announced that government was not the solution to the problem but was itself the problem. However, Reagan was either not able or not willing to follow through on some of the promises he made, such as reducing the size of the federal bureaucracy, reducing the number of cabinet-level departments that deal with domestic policy, and—most important—reducing the national deficit and debt, which ballooned under his administration. If the report of his former budget director, David Stockman, is correct, Reagan gave up on those objectives in favor of his tax cuts after the first two years in office (Stockman, 1984).

The size and scope of the national government continue to be one of the major ideological and partisan divisions in the United States. As late as 1994,

Table 5-2. *National Convention Delegates, Position on Government Services, 1980–2008*[a]

Percent

Delegate position	1980		1984		1988		1992		1996		2000		2004		2008	
	D	R	D	R	D	R	D	R	D	R	D	R	D	R	D	R
Continue	60	7	71	13	78	13	75	6	80	5	91	17	85	16	86	11
Neutral	16	10	16	21	12	17	11	14	11	8	6	23	9	22	8	15
Fewer	25	83	14	66	10	71	14	81	8	88	4	61	6	62	5	74

Source: Author surveys.

a. The question read, "Some people think/feel the government should provide fewer services, even in areas such as health and education, in order to reduce spending. Other people feel it is important for the government to continue the services it now provides even if it means no reduction in spending. Where would you place yourself on this scale?" Responses were on a 7-point scale, with 1 = provide fewer services, 7 = continue services.

in his Contract with America, Representative Newt Gingrich and his allies in the Republican-controlled House of Representatives promised a significant reduction in the scope of the domestic side of the American government (Gingrich, 1994). The Democrats in Congress and President Bill Clinton aggressively resisted many of these attempted reductions. The two partial shutdowns of the federal government over a budgetary fight in late 1995 and early 1996 helped Clinton and the Democrats in Congress to regain some of their power and saddled the Republicans with the political bill attendant on lost governmental services, as the public blamed the Republicans far more than the Democrats (Pika and Maltese, 2002, 98). The debate continued throughout the 1990s and into the 2000–12 presidential elections.

The size and role of the federal government were certainly two of the things fueling the mass protest movement led by the Tea Party in its post-2008 expansion. The data in table 5-2 indicate that this question taps a profound partisan division, and it is one that is likely to continue for the foreseeable future given the deep divisions between the two parties.

These data begin with the 1980 presidential elections, the contest between Jimmy Carter and Ronald Reagan. The results in table 5-2 indicate that the political party leaders and activists attending the two national conventions that year were widely separated on this important issue. Six in ten of the Democratic delegates favored keeping the services of the federal government intact, while only 7 percent of the Reagan Republicans responded in the same way. The opposite side is that 83 percent of the Reagan Republicans opted for fewer government services, while only 25 percent of the Carter delegates chose the same option. Clearly, the two parties were highly polarized that year, despite the complaints of the Kennedy wing of the Democratic Party that Carter was too moderate and that he had abandoned the party's core liberal constituency. Indeed, that complaint was the major basis for the challenge Senator Edward Kennedy mounted against President Carter in the Democratic primary season in 1980. That division also illustrates the fundamental dilemma of any candidate: the challenge of keeping the party's core constituency happy while at the same time reaching out to the more moderate middle of the political spectrum. On this issue the two parties have chosen to emphasize their signature approach rather than bunching up in the middle of the spectrum, as the Downsian perspective would hypothesize (Downs, 1957). That ideological division was marked in the 1980 results, and it has grown steadily since then.

By 1992 and 1996 the two parties seemed deeply entrenched in their ideological division on the scope of the federal government. Almost nine of ten of all Republican delegates in 1996 were in favor of a reduction in government services, while eight in ten of all Democratic delegates opposed any reduction in government services. One could hardly find a more polarized distribution of opinion than that represented in these results. This division continued to be evident in the 2000 election cycle for the Democrats, with fully 91 percent opposed to a reduction in government services. The Republican results in 2000 provide an exception to the general rule, when only 61 percent of the Republican delegates that year chose the more conservative option; 23 percent chose the moderate option, and 17 percent chose the "continue services" option. This is one indication that the 2000 convention that nominated George W. Bush may have been composed of somewhat more moderate delegates than its predecessors. Perhaps these Republicans of 2000 took seriously their need to put a more moderate and less aggressively conservative face on the national convention that year in order to appeal to a broader base in the general election. Certainly, George W. Bush's claim in 2000 to be a "compassionate conservative" was recognition of the need to appeal to an audience that was wider than the core conservative base of the Republican Party.

In 2004 these distributions in the Republican Party remained almost the same. This slight moderation of the Republican elites' ardor for public service reductions may also reflect their experience of being in power. In 2008 this distribution returned to a more conservative tenor.

Universal Health Insurance

At least since the administration of President Harry S. Truman, the provision of health insurance has been a divisive domestic policy issue. Various Democratic Party leaders have proposed doing something to provide more widespread health insurance coverage. They point out that the United States

Table 5-3. *National Convention Delegates, Position on National Health Insurance, 1980–2008*[a]

Percent

Delegate position	1980 D	1980 R	1984 D	1984 R	1988 D	1988 R	1992 D	1992 R	1996 D	1996 R	2000 D	2000 R	2004 D	2004 R	2008 D	2008 R
Government insurance	59	5	59	5	74	13	82	10	69	4	71	7	81	9	82	5
Neutral	12	6	16	10	13	12	9	13	18	6	16	6	12	7	8	11
Private insurance	30	89	24	82	13	75	9	77	13	90	13	87	6	84	7	87

Source: Author surveys.

a. The question read, "There is much concern about the rapid rise in medical and hospital costs. Some people feel that there should be a government insurance plan that would cover all medical and hospital expenses for everyone. Others feel that all medical expenses should be paid by individuals, and through private insurance plans like Blue Cross or other company-paid plans. Where would you place yourself on this scale?" Responses were on a 7-point, scale, with 1 = favor government insurance, 7 = favor private insurance.

is the only industrial nation without some form of universal health insurance. A proposal for a national health insurance plan has long been popular with labor unions, various liberal groups, and advocates for old people and children. More recently, even some major corporations have joined in the chorus, as they worry about the ever-increasing costs they incur in trying to provide health care to their workers. General Motors estimates that $1,500 is added to the price of each car it builds in the United States in order to cover the employee health insurance plan, and that cars built in Canada have a competitive advantage because of Canada's national health care plan.

Opponents of universal health insurance are, however, determined to stop what they believe to be a step toward socialized medicine, and they claim that the United States has the best health care in the world under the system already in effect—before the Affordable Care Act of 2010. When the Clintons tried to devise a national solution to this problem in 1993–94, a powerful combination of insurance companies and health care providers spent enormous amounts of money to defeat their plan. Over the long term, Republicans have been strong supporters of the private sector providing for health insurance, generally through the workplace, and the Democrats have supported more government intervention, especially for those who do not get health insurance through their workplace. The results in table 5-3 show that these differences were generally reflected in the views of the national convention delegations. The table indicates substantial polarization between the two major parties. Well over a majority of the Democratic activists have been in favor of a government-sponsored insurance plan since at least 1980, and that majority has grown steadily. There was little middle ground.

During his first term, President George W. Bush became a leading advocate for providing prescription drug coverage for senior citizens through the existing Medicare program. His emphasis, however, was on private companies competing for the business of each individual senior citizen to provide a package of drug benefits that fit his or her needs and ability to pay. In addition, the bill made it illegal for the federal government to use its purchasing power to negotiate lower drug rates from the companies. This proposal passed Congress, was signed into law by President Bush in 2003, and became effective in 2005. It provided Bush with an effective appeal to senior citizens in the 2004 election. This was the most significant expansion of the Medicare program since it was created by Lyndon Johnson in the mid-1960s. It also angered some of Bush's more conservative constituents, who charged that the new program was a sellout to the Democrats and another step toward the socialization of medicine in the United States. It is interesting to note that, between 1980 and 2008, between 75 percent and 90 percent of Republican elites have favored the private insurance approach, while only 13 percent or less have been willing to endorse any kind of government insurance program.

Democrats, on the other hand, have long been in favor of the government taking on this vital role for all Americans. They consistently emphasized that over 47 million Americans had no health care plan and that these uninsured people placed an enormous burden on emergency rooms, which wind up treating many of the uninsured. The divisions between the two parties remain deep on this important issue across all the conventions studied. In 1992, 82 percent of Democrats favored government insurance, while only 9 percent were in favor of going the private insurance route. Democratic support for a government insurance plan dropped to 69 percent in 1996 and 71 percent in 2000 but shot right back up to 81 percent in 2004. This minor aberration in 1996 and 2000 perhaps reflects the party's experience with the Clinton health care plan of 1993–94—and losing control of Congress partly because of it.

Nevertheless, the continuity among Democrats across these six election cycles, across the presidential candidates, from Jimmy Carter and Ronald Reagan to Al Gore and John Kerry and George W. Bush, and across a changing cast of national convention delegations (see chapter 7) underscores the intensity of the party's commitment to this position.

In 2008 the division between the parties continued. Barack Obama and Hillary Clinton made the provision of some kind of national health insurance plan a central feature of their primary campaigns, although they differed over the precise role of the government. During the 2008 fall campaign Democrats promised a new national health care plan, a promise that President Obama followed through on as his new administration began in 2009. His commit-ment continued a long Democratic tradition that extends back to Lyndon Johnson and Harry Truman.

Opposition to a national health care plan among Republicans also extends back to the 1950s, and they have been consistent in this position, with the exception of the stance taken by George W. Bush in the expansion of the Medicare subsidy for drugs. Republicans in Congress were almost completely united as they fought the Obama administration and the Democrats in Con-gress over the health care plan. Even after Obama's Affordable Care Act passed Congress in March 2010 and was signed into law, the proposal continued to roil the political waters. Republicans made it a centerpiece of their success-ful campaign to take over the U.S. House in November 2010, and one of the first actions the new House took in 2011 was passage of a bill repealing the new health care law. Only the Democratic majority in the Senate saved President Obama the trouble of having to veto the repeal if it had passed both houses. Republican candidates for president and Congress in 2012 continued to campaign avidly against "Obamacare." In 2012 and 2013 the Republican majority in the House of Representatives voted over forty times to repeal the act. Failing this, they then promised to make opposition to Obamacare the centerpiece of their campaign for Congress in the 2014 mid-term elections.

The two major parties are clearly offering significant policy differences in this important area of the national policy debate, with the leadership levels of the two parties deeply polarized over the best answer to this major policy chal-lenge. While these differences on one policy matter alone do not constitute a revolution in the ideology of the two-party system, the change from the old pragmatic party model is nevertheless striking. It is also a significant indicator of the development of the responsible party model among party elites.

Aid to Minorities

Table 5-4 provides longitudinal data for another highly contentious issue on the American political agenda over this span of eight presidential elections. Issues of race and the relations between the races have always been a significant source of conflict in American politics. As far back as the 1940s the Swedish sociologist Gunnar Myrdal (1944) called U.S. race relations "an American Dilemma." The American federal system literally came unglued in the 1860s, ending with a civil war that cost the country over 600,000 dead—the bloodi-est war by body count in American history. Slavery, along with economic issues and states' rights issues, drove the conflict.

Table 5-4. *National Convention Delegates, Position on Government Aid to Minorities, 1980–2008*[a]

Percent

Delegate position	1980		1984		1988		1992		1996		2000		2004		2008	
	D	R	D	R	D	R	D	R	D	R	D	R	D	R	D	R
Government help	52	17	57	12	66	24	76	28	71	12	73	23	76	18	66	11
Neutral	21	25	22	22	16	20	16	23	14	13	14	17	13	20	19	13
Help selves	27	58	22	67	18	56	8	50	16	75	13	60	12	62	15	76

Source: Author surveys.

a. The question read, "Some people feel that the government in Washington should make every possible effort to improve the social and economic position of blacks and other minority groups, even if it means giving them preferential treatment. Others feel that the government should not make any special effort to help minorities because they should help themselves. Where would you place yourself on this scale?" Responses were on a 7-point scale, with 1 = government should help, 7 = minority groups should help themselves. (In 1992 the wording was "no special help"; in 2000 and 2004 the wording was "no special treatment.")

The issues of that war divided the two major political parties for many generations, even though the two parties have effectively switched places on some aspects of the race issue. The echo of racial division is still clearly heard in American politics today, in spite of the unprecedented election of Barack Obama in 2008. Race and some of its related issues couched as states' rights, the power of the central government, affirmative action, and "reverse discrimination" still provide much of the content of the platforms of the two major parties and of the content of the campaigns of the major party presidential and congressional candidates. It is not surprising, then, to find that issues of race are another major divide among delegates to the two national conventions. Whether the national government should help racial minorities or leave them to help themselves was the question posed to these delegates across eight national conventions. The answer came back in a consistently polarized fashion. In 1980, 52 percent of the Democratic delegates opted for the liberal answer while only 17 percent of the Republican delegates chose that position. They were opposed by 58 percent of the Republican delegates, who believed that minorities should "help themselves." Only 27 percent of the Democrats shared that view. The differences between the two parties inched upward steadily from 1980 through the turn of the century.

Between 1996 and 2008, the percentages grew markedly more polarized. Well over a majority of each party's national convention delegations identified with their party's expected position. We have already noted the realignment of the white South with the Republican Party during this almost three-decade span of American history and the attendant realignment of the black voters with the Democratic Party. Certainly it is clear on this rather blatant, racially tinged, issue that a concurrent working majority has now taken the party's signature position as its own.

While there is some academic debate about the potential for the realignment or de-alignment of the two parties, there can be little doubt about these elite-level differences. On race and racially charged matters related to the power and scope of the national government, the two major parties are now pretty clearly realigned, and that realignment has persisted across a number and variety of political seasons featuring a remarkable array of presidential candidates and elections. Here, too, if the American people are looking for important policy-driven choices, the two major parties are providing those choices in the views of the delegates—as well as the parties' platforms (Pomper, 2001). While these results may not indicate a shift to a responsible party model, they provide evidence of a notable departure from the first 120 years of history of the pragmatic party model. There are definite policy agendas being offered by the two major parties, and those agendas are notably different.

Defense Spending

This same party and policy polarization is evident when the focus shifts from the domestic to the foreign policy field, as indicated in table 5-5. Although it shows more deviation from the party position than other issues, significant party polarization is also evident. The Democratic Party in 1980 was deeply divided on defense-related matters, with 29 percent wanting to decrease spending and 41 percent wanting to increase spending. One could hardly find a more internally divided party. This was the era of the Iranian hostage crisis, when questions about the military response versus diplomatic and economic pressure deeply divided the nation and the Democratic Party. These differences perhaps also reflect the deep divisions between the Carter and Kennedy wings of the party that year. This division into two camps probably contributed to President Carter's defeat in 1980.

Republicans that year suffered little from internal division over foreign policy. Almost nine out of every ten Republican delegates wanted to increase defense spending, which, of course, was Ronald Reagan's position. As president, Reagan made good on that promise, with a massive buildup in national defense, and that general position is usually the stance taken by subsequent Republican presidential aspirants of all stripes. Only in 1988 and 1992 was there much ambivalence or internal division within the Republican ranks. Those were the years after the Reagan defense buildup and after the winding down of the cold war and the breakup of the former Soviet Union. Those two periods found the Republicans divided, with somewhat less than a majority

Table 5-5. *National Convention Delegates, Position on Defense Spending, 1980–2008*[a]

Percent

Delegate position	1980 D	1980 R	1984 D	1984 R	1988 D	1988 R	1992 D	1992 R	1996 D	1996 R	2000 D	2000 R	2004 D	2004 R	2008 D	2008 R
Decrease	29	5	65	9	69	12	83	30	72	11	32	2	47	3	82	5
Neutral	30	7	25	31	26	42	11	46	22	23	44	8	35	18	9	8
Increase	41	88	11	60	5	46	7	24	6	66	24	91	18	79	9	87

Source: Author surveys.

a. The question read, "Some people believe/feel that we should spend much less money for defense. Suppose these people are at one end of the scale at point 1. Others feel that defense spending should be greatly increased. Suppose these people are at the end, at point 7. And, of course, some people have opinions in between at points 2, 3, 4, 5, or 6. Where would you place yourself on this scale?" Points 1–3 = decrease, 4 = neutral, 5–7 = increase.

wanting to increase defense spending in 1988 and only 24 percent voting for this option in 1992.

This was the era in which the George H. W. Bush administration was in charge of the Defense Department and its budget. Undoubtedly the Republican delegates of 1992 thought the first Bush administration had defense expenditure levels about right at that time. It is remarkable that only 24 percent of the Republican delegates that year supported an increase in defense spending. This is certainly uncharacteristic of the consistent Republican support for more defense spending, but this was after eight years of Reagan in office and after four years of the George H. W. Bush administration making the key defense spending decisions. It was also an era when the national deficit and debt had soared, partially under the weight of significantly increased defense expenditures during the Reagan administration.

This perturbation in the general pattern suggests that party elites sometimes change their specific issue-oriented stances to reflect the changes in the external policy and political environment. They are particularly attuned to their party's presidential candidates and their record. The party elites are not so committed to their ideological mind-set as to ignore the demands of the external environment. With the end of the cold war there was general support in the Bush administration for lower levels of armaments—and even discussion of a "peace dividend," that is, defense funds that could now be applied to domestic needs. This was clearly the hope of the vast majority of Democrats and one that was shared by roughly 30–40 percent of Republicans. The cutbacks in the Defense Department budget of the 1990s actually began under George H. W. Bush.

Nevertheless, by 1996 circumstances, within the United States and in the external environment, had changed. By then the Clinton administration had been in power for four years, and Republicans had become convinced that the Defense Department budget had been reduced to a dangerous degree. This charge became a major tenet of Robert Dole's campaign that year. Fully two-thirds of the Republican delegates at the 1996 convention supported a defense buildup. They faced opposition by the Democratic convention, though, as almost three-fourths of those delegates wanted to decrease defense expenditures.

In 2000 and 2004, the Democrats were much more ambivalent about decreasing defense spending, with 32 percent and 47 percent, respectively, taking this position. Among Republicans, by 2000 and 2004, over 90 percent and 79 percent, respectively, were in favor of increasing the budget of the Defense Department; this was also the position of President Bush.

The September 11, 2001, attacks on the United States by terrorists made support of the Defense Department the accepted position in the nation as a whole. Republicans made the war on terrorism the centerpiece of President Bush's reelection campaign in 2004 as well as the message of most Republicans running for Congress. There was little of the ambivalence about increasing defense expenditures among Republicans that they exhibited during the later Reagan years and George H. W. Bush's single term. Not surprisingly, then, President George W. Bush and the Republicans in Congress pushed through a massive Defense Department budget. The budget became associated with the war on terrorism and, by extension, the wars in both Iraq and Afghanistan.

It was only during his second term that President George W. Bush began to face some opposition to this military buildup within his own party, as some "deficit hawks" began to complain about the debt the nation had accumulated. By 2008 the position of the parties was very much their signature position over the long term. On the Democratic side, 82 percent were in favor of reducing defense expenditures, while 9 percent were in favor of increases. On the Republican side, 87 percent favored significant increases in defense expenditures, with only 5 percent favoring decreases. This result may initially be somewhat surprising, since George W. Bush had been in the White House eight years at that point and the defense budget had been dramatically increased under the impact of two wars and the generalized war on terror. But it attests to how powerful the defense spending ideology had become for the Republican Party. This has become one of the signature issues associated with the Republican brand.

Women's Right to Abortion

Of all the issues currently part of the national political agenda, perhaps none has been as difficult to process as the conflict over abortion. The pro-life versus pro-choice debate has been long and acrimonious. The conflict reached a climax of sorts in the landmark U.S. Supreme Court ruling of *Roe* v. *Wade* in 1973. In that ruling a majority of the court held that a woman's privacy rights included the right to have an abortion in the first trimester of a pregnancy. With any Supreme Court ruling there is the possibility that the conflict represented in the immediate case will be settled, that the general constitutional rule announced by the court in the case will prevail, and that political controversy will move on to other issues.

Alternatively, there is always the chance that the supposedly final and definitive constitutional ruling by the Supreme Court will only spark renewed conflict in the two other branches of the government and that the political elites will lead the populace to a new round of conflict. This happened in the racial desegregation decisions, and it has become the record in the abortion controversy. Included in that potential for continuing the conflict is the possibility of insistent calls by the losing side for a change in the composition of the court. That latter scenario is, of course, what happened in the wake of *Roe* v. *Wade*. Both sides felt that they had deep moral and personal principles on their side. The pro-life people believe that life begins at conception. Any attempt to halt that life is murder to them. For many, their pro-life conviction reflects their religious views as well. The Catholic Church and many fundamentalist Protestant churches take an adamant and aggressive stand against abortion. Those of the pro-choice persuasion feel just as strongly that a woman's right to control her own body includes not bearing an unwanted child and that this is based on the important principle of personal rights. The potential of bearing a child who is the product of rape or incest, for example, and the potential for returning to "back-alley abortions," which was the situation before *Roe* v. *Wade*, were often used in the political rhetoric of the pro-choice forces.

When the two sides to a political question are so diametrically opposite and are framed in the language of basic personal or religious rights, it is difficult for the political system to deal with the conflict in the ways it ordinarily handles conflict. When each side believes that it has morality and religion and personal principle on its side, normal give-and-take, half-a-loaf, incrementally oriented American politics no longer work. This is the case with the abortion debate. Table 5-6 provides the positions of party delegates between 1984, when we first asked the question, and 2008.

Table 5-6 contains some expected data, based on the record of political conflict over the past two decades. But it contains some surprises as well. Under the party brand name concept, the two parties have clearly become the advocates for the two different positions on abortion. Democrats embraced

Table 5-6. *National Convention Delegates, Position on Abortion, 1984–2008*[a]

Percent

Delegate position	1984		1988		1992		1996		2000		2004		2008	
	D	R	D	R	D	R	D	R	D	R	D	R	D	R
Never permitted	2	7	3	5	0	9	1	18	1	18	1	17	1	26
Only in special circumstances (rape/ incest or health of mother)	44	69	39	75	12	65	16	63	9	57	23	68	20	62
Always permitted	53	23	59	20	88	25	82	19	90	26	76	15	79	12

Source: Author surveys.

a. The question wording and response categories varied depending on the year. For 1980 and 1984 the response categories of "health of the mother" and "difficulties raising the child" were collapsed into "only in special circumstances." Between 1992 and 2008 the response categories for special circumstances were separate for rape and incest and health of the mother.

the pro-choice position, and many of the most ardent supporters of that policy position have been very active in the Democratic Party over the past several election cycles. Feminists and the women's movement have gravitated toward the Democratic Party and have poured their energy and resources into the election of Democratic candidates, especially presidential candidates. Likewise, the Republican Party has clearly become the home of the pro-life movement. Traditional women—those who work in the home and those who are members of the more conservative churches—and men who are strongly committed to the pro-life position have increasingly become active in state, local, and national Republican Party circles. This is especially true in the South and has been a part of the driving force behind the realignment of the white South. It is also true in the Mountain West and other more rural states.

The platforms of the two major parties could not be more clear-cut on this difference, which has been evident in the two party platforms since 1980. In addition, the varying promises of the candidates for president of the two major parties reflect this polarized reality. In 2000 Al Gore suggested that the future of *Roe* v. *Wade* was up for grabs in that election and that he would look for Supreme Court candidates who would uphold a woman's right to choose. Even more strongly, George W. Bush said that his ideal for the kind of candidate he would appoint to the Supreme Court were current justices Antonin Scalia and Clarence Thomas, the two most conservative members of the court and the two most prominently identified with attempts to overturn *Roe* v. *Wade*. While Bush also maintained that there would be no "litmus test" with respect to his selection of judges, his assurances to conservative church people left little doubt about the kinds of judge he was promising to name. He reiterated that position in his 2004 campaign, while Kerry reflected his party's strong support for the pro-choice position. Indeed, Kerry got into some trouble with leaders of the Catholic Church for his pro-choice stand, and at least one bishop stated that Kerry should not be given communion by the church. Kerry lost the Catholic vote, narrowly, to George W. Bush in 2004. For the Democrats to lose the Catholic vote in a presidential election was a marker of how much the earlier New Deal coalition had come unraveled.

This debate continued in 2008, when John McCain and Barack Obama differed clearly on pro-choice versus pro-life issues, a difference also reflected in the platforms adopted by both parties. Once again there was talk about Supreme Court nominees and the kinds of justices each candidate was likely to select and what this meant for the future of *Roe* v. *Wade*. This difference was hardly lost on the American public. The public policy pronouncements and positions of the two national parties could hardly be more starkly different on this most divisive issue, and generally the mass public understands those differences.

Despite these pronounced and very public differences between the two major parties, their platforms, and their recent standard-bearers, there is more ambivalence on the part of these party elites than might be expected. When one collapses all the intermediate-level answers to the survey, answers that have to do with abortions in the case of rape and incest and abortions if the mother's life is in danger, a surprising division emerges within Republican Party elites' responses. Only 18 percent of the 2000 delegates who nominated George W. Bush chose the "Never permitted," or most extreme, pro-life option, while 26 percent were on the pro-choice end of the continuum (with the remaining 57 percent choosing "Only in special circumstances"). In 2004, 15 percent of the Republican delegates took the "Always permitted," or pure pro-choice, position, while only 17 percent took the clear "Never permitted" choice. In 2008 these internal divisions continued, although that year the percent of Republicans taking the "Never permitted" position rose over the four years since the last convention: from 17 to 26 percent. Still, even with this probably the most conservative Republican delegation ever, almost two-thirds of the delegates were in the more moderate category.

There is more ambivalence on the Republican side in these data than their national platforms and the content of their presidential rhetoric would lead one to expect. Perhaps in their desire to find some grounds for compromise in what many see as a fight beyond compromise, these activist Republicans more accurately reflect the ambivalent views of the American people. The fact that the Republicans have been ambivalent over much of this period is another surprising finding. When President George W. Bush actually got the opportunity to nominate two Supreme Court candidates in 2005, his choices reflected some of this ambivalence. In the case of both John Roberts to be chief justice and Harriett Miers as his first choice for associate justice, President Bush insisted again that there was no litmus test and that he did not know how either of them would rule on *Roe* v. *Wade.*

However, Karl Rove and other White House operatives assured right-to-life groups and fundamentalist church groups that these nominees shared their policy positions. This two-pronged strategy succeeded in the case of Roberts and failed in that of Miers, perhaps because questions of credentials and basic philosophy were also raised in the Miers case. Many Republicans on the conservative end of the continuum insisted that Miers was insufficiently dedicated to conservative causes and not a "movement conservative." Ultimately the White House caved in to this opposition, and the Miers nomination was withdrawn in favor of the more consistently conservative Samuel Alito, who was then easily confirmed. (He has, incidentally, lived up to his conservative billing.) The fault lines within the Republican Party were clearly on display during the fight over the Miers nomination. Some of that internal division is presaged in the data presented in this table.

Until 2004 the Democratic Party's elites exhibited no such propensity toward moving to the middle of the road on the matter of abortion. In 2000 they were 90 percent pro-choice. (Only 1 percent took the pro-life position.) This has been more or less the case since at least 1984 and 1988, when well over a majority favored the pro-choice position and almost none took the pro-life position. Only in 2004 did the Democrats indicate a bit more diversity on this issue, with only 76 percent of the delegates in the pro-choice category. In 2008 this distribution remained essentially the same.

One could hardly find a more consistent and coherent issue position than that taken by the Democratic Party elites and standard-bearers on this signature issue: the right of women to choose. Moreover, one also could not find a more clear-cut difference in the platforms adopted by both major parties in all their recent conventions. It is notable, however, that the two parties were in essential agreement on this issue in their platforms until 1980, when the Republicans adopted a pro-life plank and the Democrats adopted a pro-choice plank (Craig and O'Brien, 1993). Before that, both parties could effectively be termed pro-choice after the *Roe* v. *Wade* decision was rendered.

Even in this era, however, the opinions of some of the Republican Party leaders included in this study diverge from the Republican majority. In fact, an intense and mobilized minority is clearly taking an alternative stance and defining the party in ways not supported by a majority of the most active

Table 5-7. *National Convention Delegates, Position on School Choice, 1992–2008*[a]

Percent

Delegate position	1992		1996		2000		2004		2008	
	D	R	D	R	D	R	D	R	D	R
Oppose	52	11	85	13	89	15	86	17	83	18
Neutral	15	10	6	11	4	5	8	9	7	6
Support	33	80	10	77	8	79	7	74	10	76

Source: Author surveys.

a. The question read, "Would you support a voucher system where parents would get money from the government to send their children to the public, private, or parochial school of their choice?" Responses were on a 7-point scale, with 1 = favor vouchers and 7 = oppose vouchers.

echelon of the national party's leadership. To the extent that the gender gap works against the interests of the Republican Party, candidates have suffered an electoral disadvantage. Overall, however, this is a price Republican leaders have been willing to pay in order to keep their core constituents in the fold.

School Choice

Table 5-7 provides the party activists' views on the contentious issue of school choice. Respondents were asked their position on providing choices for parents with children in the public schools. This has long been a divisive issue in American politics, and it includes some of our most sensitive personal values involving our children. It frequently carries the additional freight of both race and religion, since many of the alternatives to public schools are religiously affiliated private schools or are private but publicly funded schools that have replaced failing inner-city schools. The Democrats have become staunch defenders of the public schools, and that party is now home to the politically mobilized teachers' unions. Republicans are equally adamant critics of the public schools, and various Republican presidents and governors have promised alternatives to the current public school systems, or major reforms of the schools, as a way to address the shortcomings they perceive in public education. It is clear that the partisan divisions on this issue are deep and abiding. In most of the years this question was asked on our survey, between 80 and 85 percent of Democratic delegates were against school choice, and only 7 to 10 percent favored it. Republicans are almost as united on the other side of the question, with over three-fourths consistently favoring school choice and 11 to 18 percent opposing it.

In light of this near consensus among Republicans, it is perhaps not surprising that one major component of President George W. Bush's No Child

Table 5-8. *National Convention Delegates, Position on Term Limits, 1992–2004*[a]

Percent

Delegate position	1992		1996		2000		2004	
	D	R	D	R	D	R	D	R
Oppose	63	20	76	37	75	52	63	47
Neutral	11	8	7	10	9	12	20	14
Support	25	72	17	53	16	36	17	39

Source: Author surveys.

a. The term limits question was not asked in the 2008 study or before 1992. The question read, "Some people feel terms of service in legislatures should be limited. Others oppose any limitations on terms of service." Responses were a 7-point scale, with 1 = favor limits and 7 = oppose term limits.

Left Behind (NCLB) legislation, offered very early in his first administration and handily approved by Congress, is a provision that children in schools that consistently fail to meet federally mandated performance standards are given the opportunity to transfer to a school where the standards are being met. This is a form of school choice, although it provides for an alternative school assignment only for students from failing schools. For this reason, actually changing schools became a very difficult challenge in the implementation stage of NCLB. Democrats are consistent critics of this program and of the concept in general. The overall question of how to improve public education seems likely to stay on the national agenda for the foreseeable future, and the parties and their constituencies are likely to remain deeply divided on the answers.

Term Limits

Table 5-8 deals with term limits. The movement to provide automatic limits on the terms of office for state officials and members of Congress became huge in the early to mid-1990s. It was even a part of the 1994 Contract with America, the platform for Republican candidates for Congress that Speaker of the House Newt Gingrich (1994) used to swing the House of Representatives from a Democratic majority that had lasted for forty years to a Republican majority, which lasted over a decade.

In 1995 a decision by the U.S. Supreme Court stopped the drive toward state-imposed term limits for members of Congress (*U.S. Term Limits* v. *Thornton*, 1995). The majority of the court held that age, residency, and citizenship were the only criteria provided for members of Congress in the Constitution and that the states had no power to add to those criteria. The court said such a fundamental change could only be done by constitutional amendment. The drive for limitations on state legislative officers was constitutional, and ultimately twenty-one states adopted term limits in some form (Dye and MacManus, 2012, 63). Then much of the steam went out of the movement. Republicans took control of both the House and the Senate, and they lost much of their ardor for the concept at the federal level. Several members of Congress, originally elected in 1994 on the promise of self-imposed term limits, subsequently decided it was not such a good idea and reneged on their promises. Almost none suffered an electoral defeat as a result of not keeping their promise. A few voluntarily limited themselves to four or five terms and then moved on to other offices or left public service. At the state level, many legislators found that the constant turnover and the loss of expertise and institutional memory had negative consequences for the way the legislature operated. Some of the original supporters at the state level became advocates for returning to unlimited terms after they experienced some of the consequences. Currently only fifteen states have term limits (Dye and MacManus, 2012, 63–65, 219).

The data in table 5-8 reflect some of these changes among these party activists. It is clear that Democrats were heavily opposed to term limits from the beginning, and their opposition has not changed much over the years covered by this study. The interesting variation is among Republicans, who supported term limits in 1992 by a three-to-one margin but whose support dropped to only 36 and 39 percent, respectively, in 2000 and 2004. Given this shift, the question was not asked again in the 2008 survey. By then it seemed clear that the steam had gone out of the term limits movement and that it was not worth asking about. Republicans had largely abandoned the cause, and Democrats were mostly opposed to it from the outset. Changing times and circumstances provided the opportunity for party leaders to change their views or to be replaced with activists who held different views.

Conclusion

Party elites are predominantly fairly sophisticated on political matters. Many have worked in the party for years and have found reinforcement for their views among their party colleagues. They read specialized newspapers and journals, or increasingly blogs, watch television and cable news, and listen to those talk-radio personalities who reinforce their own personal views. They are usually well educated and able to handle complex concepts related to political issues and ideology. Most of them also exhibit a good deal of what Philip Converse (1964) once termed "constraint" in their views. In short, their issue-oriented positions and their ideological commitments are interrelated and cohere across broad dimensions. They are not likely to be buffeted by the winds of political change or enticed by passing fashion.

On the other hand, they are also not immune to the pressures and influences of the external world. Things change. Term limits looked great in 1992 and not so great in 2004. Presidents come and go, and the issues they advocate change or, in a different era, are seen in a different light. There is room for both continuity and change in this matrix. The public changes its mind; the elites circulate. On the one hand, it is remarkable that despite social and political changes there is so much stability in elite polarization and in their fidelity to the signature positions of the two parties. On the other hand, nothing is entirely set in concrete, and there are interesting variations on the theme of continuity, which is the major message of the data presented in this chapter.

The two parties are definitely different from what they were in the pre-reform era, and they are also very different from each other now. To paraphrase Barry Goldwater's 1964 campaign, they now offer "a choice, not an echo" to the voters of the twenty-first century. This is a different party system from the one that dominated American politics through the last half of the nineteenth century and through almost three-fourths of the twentieth. Liberal Republicans and conservative Democrats are almost all gone at the elite level. Those who constitute the party in government—that is, those who hold office, particularly at the national level and increasingly at the state levels—are now identifiable by their signature ideological positions. Their votes along party and ideological lines then follow quite predictably on most legislation.

As we will see in the following chapters, the masses have followed suit and have largely sorted themselves into two warring camps, although this process is not nearly as far advanced as it is at the elite level. The polarization of the two political parties, and of the entire governmental system, is so advanced and so widely recognized that the term itself is used as shorthand for this entire constellation of forces that have bedeviled American politics over the past two or three decades. We turn in the next chapter to where the mass voters locate themselves on many of these same questions.

6

Party Elites and Party Identifiers

Chapter 4 reviews Hannah Pitkin's (1987) concept of substantive representation, which points to the importance of attitudes and political values as they influence the behavior of the political decisionmakers. These long-term attitudinal and value commitments on the part of political elites influence their behavior in the political arena as they "act for" the people they represent. The theory of representation holds that the more closely aligned elites' values are with the values of their constituents, the greater the likelihood that there will be congruence between the political and public policy decisions of the elites and the wishes of the voters. Basic representational theory has always held that there should be relatively close alignment between the views and actions of the people in power and the views and values of the people in the constituency they represent. Under democratic theory, the elites are supposed to act for those they represent and to be held accountable for those actions, ultimately at the ballot box. Our data provide an empirical test of that theory for these leaders, who include both party and public officials.

Convention delegates are not necessarily also public officials, although some of them are, but as party officials and strong partisans they want their party to prosper. Ultimately in the American system this means winning elections and controlling public office. These delegates must represent the grass roots of their parties as well as other voters if they are going to succeed in the electoral wars. A party whose activists and leaders have lost contact with and the confidence of the base will be judged unresponsive to the public—out of touch, even elitist. That is a charge no party or candidate can afford for long, given the premium the American political culture places on at least symbolic egalitarianism. Voters do not really get to know the person running for office; they only know the image, which is mostly purveyed by television.

This image may be different from the reality; however, appearances count for a lot in an era of electronic mass politics. Bill Clinton's "I feel your pain" persona was effective because it was believable, even though Clinton had left his humble Arkansas roots behind long ago and had been a member of the national political elite for years. George H. W. Bush's 1992 presidential race against Clinton was harmed by a photo showing him apparently confused by the purpose of bar codes on groceries, as he attempted a staged checkout at a suburban Virginia supermarket. Republicans learned from this experience, and in 2008 they consistently charged that Obama was "an elitist" who could never see the views and realities of the common people. When Obama in an unguarded moment talked about the price of arugula (a salad green) in the grocery store, he seemed to play right into that stereotype. Indeed, it is often argued that the mass appeal of Sarah Palin is partially rooted in her ability to identify with the common people and to voice their resentments against the political and economic elites.

The elitist label was stuck on Mitt Romney in 2012. He was raised in a wealthy and privileged home in suburban Detroit, where his father, George Romney, was a car company executive who went into politics and then, as a former governor, ran for president in 1968. Mitt Romney amassed a formidable personal fortune of his own, and his family had several palatial homes in different states. None of this would have disqualified him from being competitive except that he also had a patrician and wooden manner when he campaigned, and this style cast him as being much closer to Al Gore than to George W. Bush in campaign appearances (Balz and Silberman, 2013; Simon, 2013). Being a member of the political elite class will not stop a candidate from succeeding, but the appearance of being an elitist will.

Elites in the American political system cannot afford to become complacent or removed from the opinions and values of the people who elect them. Even less can the major political parties afford to appear that they have gotten out of step with their supporters and the opinions of the American people. The "limousine liberal" image acquired by the national Democratic Party in the 1970s was based on the conservative charge that Democrats wanted everyone to attend the public schools except their own children, many of whom went to elite private schools in and around Washington, D.C. The allegation entailed enough substance that it stuck to Democrats for decades. The Obamas' enrollment of their daughters in an exclusive private school in

Table 6-1. *Ideology of Democratic Convention Delegates and Party Identifiers, 1972–2008*[a]

Percent

Ideology	1972 E	1972 I	1976 E	1976 I	1980 E	1980 I	1984 E	1984 I	1988 E	1988 I
Liberal	79	36	40	36	38	38	43	40	51	38
Moderate	13	39	47	39	53	34	50	38	42	35
Conservative	8	25	8	24	9	28	7	22	7	27

Ideology	1992 E	1992 I	1996 E	1996 I	2000 E	2000 I	2004 E	2004 I	2008 E	2008 I
Liberal	57	44	51	44	54	44	51	53	60	51
Moderate	41	32	45	35	43	36	47	36	37	37
Conservative	3	24	4	21	4	20	3	11	3	12

Source: Author surveys; American National Election Studies, various years.
a. Elite data are the same as Democratic data in table 5-1.

Washington in December 2008 seemed to confirm this charge. One difference between party elites and party identifiers is, then, about class differences, or perceived class differences. These differences are echoed in differences in opinion on a variety of issues, such as government services, national health insurance, government aid to minorities, defense spending, and abortion.

When compared to the party leadership, the parties' base is often considerably more moderate (tables 6-1 and 6-2). Other studies bear this out (see McClosky, Hoffman, and O'Hara, 1960). As John W. Kingdon (1999) suggested more recently, this tension between the views of political elites and those of mass voters poses a problem for a two-party system. The basic pattern—of a majority of the leadership of the two major parties (as represented by their convention delegates) being on the ideological extremes of the continuum and a majority of party identifiers being in the middle—has been widely recognized since McClosky's early research (see Baer and Bositis, 1988). Various other subsequent studies generally replicate this finding; however, which party leadership group is closer to its party's base and which is on the far extremes of the ideological continuum has varied with the year of the study, with the presidential candidates that year, and with the researcher. For example, McClosky and his associates found the Democratic leaders of the 1950s to be closer to the base of their own party than the Republicans were to theirs. Indeed, Democratic leaders were closer to the middle, and thus to Republican identifiers, than Republicans leaders were. It

Table 6-2. *Ideology of Republican Convention Delegates and Party Identifiers,*
1972–2008[a]

Percent

Ideology	1972		1976		1980		1984		1988	
	E	I	E	I	E	I	E	I	E	I
Liberal	10	13	3	9	1	10	2	11	3	10
Moderate	35	33	45	29	34	23	31	25	27	25
Conservative	57	53	48	62	65	67	68	63	70	65

	1992		1996		2000		2004		2008	
	E	I	E	I	E	I	E	I	E	I
Liberal	1	10	0	5	1	8	0	6	1	4
Moderate	27	26	18	21	24	24	21	24	18	12
Conservative	71	64	82	74	76	68	78	70	81	83

Source: Author surveys; American National Election Studies, various years.
a. Elite data are the same as Republican data in table 5-1.

was the Republican leadership that was far out of step with the mainstream
of popular opinion.

In the 1972 national conventions, Kirkpatrick (1976) found the opposite to be true, with the Democratic delegates being much more liberal, and
thus much more extreme, than their own followers—and more extreme than
the Republicans were that year. Later in the 1980s John S. Jackson and his
associates found that the Kirkpatrick results were an aberration induced by
the McGovern candidacy and the war in Vietnam; by then the more familiar McClosky distribution had reasserted itself (Jackson, Brown, and Bositis,
1982). Various other scholars have contributed to this academic discourse over
subsequent election cycles (Miller and Jennings, 1986; Miller, 1988; Hadley and Bowman, 1998; Maggiotto and Wekkin, 2000). A study by William
Crotty and associates covering the years 1984, 1988, and 1992 provides a
richer and more nuanced level of analysis of the differences between leaders
and followers (Crotty, Jackson, and Miller, 1999). Generally it shows that
Republican leaders were somewhat closer to their base than Democrats were
to theirs during this eight-year period. It also reaffirms the party polarization
thesis. By 1996 and 2000 the familiar McClosky distribution had reasserted
itself, and Democratic delegates were again somewhat closer to the mass identifiers of their party than Republican delegates were to theirs. The picture that
emerges shows that Republican elites had veered pretty far to the right even of
their own base, much less of the rest of public opinion.

The data set used in the Crotty, Jackson, and Miller research is part of the larger data set undergirding this book. The present study is the first to provide longitudinal data for a long stretch of party leadership at the national conventions. As such, it provides more than a snapshot. It is closer to a motion picture account of what have been continuity and changes in ideology among partisans, the mass public, and party leaders for four decades of American electoral history. In an era of party polarization it is expected that the middle of the political spectrum is unrepresented, since the political elites are expected to be on either extreme, even though the middle is thought to be the best strategic position for presidential candidates (Downs, 1957). This research is uniquely applicable to assessing those expectations.

Party Elites and Party Identifiers

The era of party polarization was well advanced in both parties at both mass and elite levels by the opening of the twenty-first century, as is evident in tables 6-1 and 6-2. The elites usually lead the masses in opinion formation, but the two groups can also reinforce each other (Zaller, 1992, 6–13). Party polarization at both mass and elite levels is one of the necessary ingredients for an ideologically based realignment of the parties. There are many empirical indicators that just such an ideological realignment did occur at the elite level during the last three decades of the twentieth century. In its careful analysis of mass attitudes and the voting of partisans in Congress, one research team demonstrates that polarization gained traction in the decade of the 1970s and has become more marked each decade since (McCarty, Poole, and Rosenthal, 2006). The study also demonstrates that polarization is partially driven and maintained by the income gap. Our data, as well as the work of other scholars, indicate that the realignment is well advanced among elites and that it has penetrated into the base of the two parties. Put simply, most liberals are now deeply embedded in the Democratic Party and most conservatives are safely in the Republican Party (Levendusky, 2009). The meaning of this for long-term party survival, for the permanent realignment of the two parties, and for the ability of either party to govern is more problematic.

At least since Kevin Phillips published his influential book in 1969 scholars have been predicting an ideological realignment. The identity of the new majority and the timing of the realignment vary, and the projections of identity and timing for the new majority party have been controversial (Burnham, 1970; Shafer, 1991; Judis and Teixeira, 2002). Certainly, the change of the conservative white South from predominantly Democratic to predominantly

Republican over the last three decades of the twentieth century was a major step in the direction of ideological realignment. The allegiance of the vast majority of African American voters to the Democratic Party also moves the system toward an ideological realignment. The results in tables 6-1 and 6-2, particularly for 2000 through 2008, indicate what such realignment should look like in any comparison between party elites and followers; they also indicate that ideological realignment was well advanced by the beginning of the twenty-first century.

The tables also show the results from the beginning of the reform era, in 1972 and 1976. Democratic delegates in 1972 were the forerunners of the truly polarized party system of the end of the century. The 1972 convention (George McGovern's convention), with 79 percent of Democratic delegates calling themselves liberals, was the first convention operating under the McGovern-Fraser reform rules. Given the intensity and bias of the antiwar sentiment of the time, it is not surprising that this convention was dramatically out of step with the party's base. The fact that Democratic identifiers in the electorate were deeply divided is underscored by their self-designation as 36 percent liberal, 39 percent moderate, and 25 percent conservative.

This convention was dominated by a party elite easy to caricature, which President Nixon's campaign did quite effectively—and, of course, Nixon went on to win a landslide victory over McGovern. Republican delegates that year were much more moderate than Democratic delegates and much more representative of their party's base. Jeane Kirkpatrick made this point in her seminal 1976 work on the 1972 convention—and she was right. However, the characteristics of the delegates in subsequent years indicate just how atypical Democratic delegates were in 1972. Indeed, there were more liberals at Miami in the 1972 convention than there have been at any convention since. Nevertheless, that year was the beginning point of this monumental change in American politics.

By 1976 moderates had become the plurality among Democratic delegates. This is not markedly different from the Democratic base, although again conservative delegates were underrepresented in 1976. Compared to party identifiers in the general electorate, Democratic delegates mirrored the party's base for liberals and moderates reasonably well, although there were still far more Democratic identifiers who considered themselves conservatives (24 percent) than there were elites representing them among the delegates (8 percent). Since 1976 was the convention that nominated Jimmy Carter, former governor of Georgia and widely seen as the moderate among other Democrats who sought the nomination, it is not surprising that his convention attracted a plurality of moderate Democratic delegates.

As table 6-2 demonstrates, moderates were stronger among Republican delegates in 1976 than among the Republican base (45 percent to 29 percent). This is a case of the grass roots being ahead of party elites in terms of the ideological realignment. Indeed, by that year 62 percent of Republican identifiers called themselves conservatives, compared to only 48 percent of Republican delegates. A Republican delegation in 1976, which was almost evenly split between moderates (45 percent) and conservatives (48 percent), nominated Gerald Ford, the incumbent, over the more conservative candidate, California governor Ronald Reagan, who challenged Ford vigorously for the nomination that year. While Ford won the nomination, he lost the general election in the fall. Some of Ford's problems clearly began with his failure to unify the party's more moderate and conservative wings during the primary and convention seasons. Despite Reagan's failure to capture the nomination, the conservative ascendancy was well under way by 1976 and was undoubtedly spurred on by Ford's loss; 1976 was the last year when less than a majority of Republican elites considered themselves to be conservatives. By 1976 the age of Ronald Reagan was dominant in the Republican Party. It had been initiated by the party-building effect of Barry Goldwater's 1964 candidacy.

By 1980 the Reagan revolution was well established in the Republican Party. Fully 67 percent of the Republican identifiers that year called themselves conservatives. Old-line East Coast establishment liberals of the Rockefeller, Javits, Mathias, and Scranton era were fading away or were changing parties. A slightly smaller percentage of delegates (65 percent) than party identifiers (67 percent) in 1980 claimed the conservative mantle, although conservative delegates were comfortably more than a majority by then. It is not surprising perhaps that this convention nominated the conservative Ronald Reagan over his principal challenger, George H. W. Bush, who was perceived to be the more moderate candidate. The era of party polarization was well on its way by 1980, led in the Republican Party by Ronald Reagan.

The Democratic Party was deeply divided in 1980, as it had been since 1972. This division is evident at both mass and elite levels. In 1980 Senator Edward Kennedy challenged the incumbent president, Jimmy Carter, in the Democratic primaries. Kennedy was considered to be more liberal than Carter, and his critique of Carter's presidency included criticism of Carter for being not liberal enough. Democratic identifiers in the electorate were almost equally divided between liberals (38 percent) and moderates (34 percent), while convention delegates were more moderate (53 percent) than liberal (38 percent). It was evident well before the national convention that Carter would win the nomination. The convention itself was very divisive, as the Kennedy forces challenged the Carter camp over the platform, the resolutions, and the basic rules. At the end of the convention, Carter had won the nomination but had been unable to unify the party. Plagued by divisions within his party's base, it is hardly surprising that Carter went on to lose the general election to Reagan in November. It is also ironic that while Carter and Kennedy never ended their feud, they were finally united under the same banner when both were early supporters of Barack Obama for the party's nomination in 2008. The two warring ideological components of the Democratic Party—the moderate and the liberal—have rarely been united for long at the national level. When they are united, as in 1992 and 1996 with Clinton and in 2008 and 2012 with Obama, they are able to win the presidency.

In the meantime, conservatives took control of the Republican Party, a control they maintained easily up through the first decade of the twenty-first century and that increased in the 2010 midterm elections, fueled by Tea Party enthusiasts. This conservative dominance became evident in 1980 and continued through the 1984 and 1988 elections. Those elections saw Ronald Reagan winning a landslide victory for reelection over Walter Mondale in 1984 and Reagan's vice president, George H. W. Bush, winning a much more narrow victory over Massachusetts governor Michael Dukakis in 1988. The Reagan campaign successfully depicted Mondale, who had been Jimmy Carter's vice president, as a liberal, and Mondale's voting record in the U.S. Senate lent credence to that charge. The Bush campaign successfully depicted Dukakis as a "Massachusetts liberal," in spite of the fact that Dukakis had a reputation as a pragmatic technocrat who had been a moderate in the way he governed his state. Either way, the two national Democratic campaigns in 1984 and 1988 were unsuccessful in an era when the label *liberal* was a liability.

The data provided in tables 6-1 and 6-2 show the problems the Democratic candidates faced. In 1984, 43 percent of the Democratic delegates were liberals, 50 percent were moderates, and only 7 percent were conservatives. These elites were a fairly close reflection of the base of the party, with 40 percent liberal, 38 percent moderate, and 22 percent conservative. In 1988 the Democratic delegates were 51 percent liberals and 42 percent moderate, and 7 percent conservative, with fewer liberals among identifiers. In both years the sizable conservative contingent among party identifiers was vastly underrepresented by party elites. Losing three elections in the 1980s led party elites to shift to the left. It is clear that, among Democrats, identifiers were more conservative and less liberal than elites and that Democrats were more diverse than Republicans.

The Democrats were opposed in 1984 and 1988 by a much more cohesive Republican delegate cadre, who were 68 percent conservative in 1984 and 70 percent conservative in 1988. This ideological realignment was not confined to the party elites but had penetrated into the party's grass roots. The Republican base was almost as conservative as the delegates in both of those years. Moreover, the 1980s were a time of realigment, with conservatives among political elites and the public gravitating toward the Republican Party. Yet even at the end of that decade 27 percent of Democratic identifiers thought of themselves as conservative. The realignment was well advanced at the elite level in both parties at the end of the 1980s, but it was still incomplete and in transition at the mass level, especially among Democrats. This diversity among Democrats and near consensus among Republicans grew in the 1990s. The Democratic base continued to be close to evenly divided between liberals and moderates, with a healthy dose of conservatives thrown in for 1992 and 1996. Among both elites and identifiers, liberals held only a narrow advantage. This pattern reflects the McClosky distribution, in which party elites are more on the ideological edges than party identifiers.

Bill Clinton's two presidential conventions, 1992 and 1996, represent these distributions. Clinton's complex mixture of philosophies and policy positions defied easy categorization. He often presented himself as a moderate, or a man of the middle, who sought a "third way," which was not identifiably liberal or conservative. He believed in a pragmatic and flexible approach that emphasized "what works," meaning programs and ideas that tackle real problems and, just as important, have a realistic chance of being passed by Congress (Clinton, 2004; Harris, 2005). He attempted this balancing act while keeping most of the liberals and moderates of his party on board and even gaining some crucial help from Republicans. In taking this approach, Clinton was probably bowing to the inevitable, given his lack of a majority in Congress and the power and unity of the Republican opposition (Eilperin, 2006). But he was also in fairly close synchronization with the Democratic Party's loyal identifiers and party leaders. Part of the genius of Bill Clinton is that he could straddle these ideological divisions within his party, synthesize the various positions into a coherent whole, and articulate the process clearly. By this means he achieved many of his policy goals. That Clinton got reelected rather handily in 1996 and survived Republican efforts to remove him from office in 1997 and 1998, with much Democratic elite-level help and the party's base solidly behind him, speaks to his ability to accurately read and represent public opinion. This combination is one of the keys to his success. Indeed, it is a key to the success of any politician who survives for long in American politics.

In the 2000–08 era Democrats continued to be more heterogeneous in comparison with Republicans. In 2000 Democratic convention delegates exhibited a fairly close division of 54 percent liberal and 43 percent moderate. This result was remarkably close to the 51 percent liberal and 47 percent moderate of 2004. Thus although Democratic elites leaned toward the liberal side of the continuum, it was not by a large margin. Party identifiers were similarly divided in 2000, with 44 percent liberal and 36 percent moderate. While the liberal and moderate percentages are fairly close to those among the party elites, the 20 percent of the Democratic identifiers who called themselves conservative were clearly unrepresented at the national conventions that year. Liberals among party identifiers grew to 53 percent in 2004, while the moderate category remained the same, at 36 percent, and the conservative category shrank to 11 percent. In 2008 liberals were 60 percent of Democratic delegates, the highest level of liberal representation since the McGovern convention of 1972. As table 6-1 shows, the Democrats were, throughout these years, much more ideologically diverse than their Republican counterparts (table 6-2). It may be that it is this diversity that makes it more difficult for Democratic presidential candidates to unite their party than is usually the case for Republicans.

Republicans, by contrast, were the conservative party and proud to be so labeled. We have to go all the way back to 1976 to find less than 60 percent of Republican elites who claimed the conservative mantle. In 1972, Richard Nixon's reelection year, 35 percent of party elites and 33 percent of identifiers were moderates. The moderates grew among delegates in 1976, although they declined among identifiers, an instance of elite opinion lagging mass opinion. As noted earlier, this was the convention when Gerald Ford won a narrow victory over Ronald Reagan, and by that year the party base had begun its shift to the right. In the decade of the 1980s approximately two-thirds of Republican elites and identifiers were conservatives. This was the decade when conservatives solidified their hold on the Republican Party at both the mass and elite levels and when the liberals almost disappeared at the elite level and, even at the mass level, attracted at most only 11 percent.

By 1992 the Republican Party exhibited considerable stability and cohesion at both elite and identifier levels, with 64 percent of the party's base calling themselves conservatives (see table 6-2). There were almost no liberals among the delegates in the conventions of 1992 and 1996, the latter being Robert Dole's convention. There was no doubt then about Dole's conservative credentials, although recently he has come to be seen as more moderate than the current group of Republican leaders. This dominance by conservatives among both delegates and party identifiers grew in the three elections held since the turn of the century, reaching its apex in 2008, when 81 percent of delegates and

83 percent of identifiers called themselves conservative. By then the moderates were shrinking dramatically and the liberals had almost disappeared. Clearly, conservatism was by far the most acceptable philosophy among Republican elites and identifiers during the last decade of the twentieth century and the first decade of the twenty-first. The term *liberal* carried the negative meanings that Republicans and conservatives had attached to the term—connotations that Democrats struggled to overcome (Jamieson and Waldman, 2003).

The purification and symbolic unity under way in this era were much more pronounced among Republicans than among Democrats. Republicans, at both the elite and mass levels, formed a near consensus that they were the conservative party and would provide a clear alternative to the Democrats and that this designation would lead them to electoral success. It intimated an adherence to a public policy agenda of which they could be proud. Republicans, particularly those running for office and their most active core constituencies, eagerly and proudly embraced the label of conservative, although there were some practical differences over what the term meant in the world of policymaking. Those differences, however, were more about nuance and priority rather than basic policy. For Republicans, factional fights were about who was the most pure.

Democrats, by contrast, were much more ambivalent and divided over their embrace of the liberal mantle. During most of this era they seemed constantly at odds over their best policy stances and the image they wanted to project. Some were liberals and proud of it. Others wanted to be called *progressives* because of the negative connotations of the term *liberal*. Others, especially from the South, the Midwest, and the mountain states of the West, claimed the moderate mantle, and a few even called themselves conservatives. They were organized by the moderate Democratic Leadership Council. They were also represented in Congress by the Blue Dog Coalition, which was determined to pull the Democratic Party toward the middle. A phalanx of liberal interest groups vigorously resisted that pull. The Clinton administration and then the Gore and Kerry campaigns were often caught in between and buffeted by both forces. These campaigns were particularly ineffective in uniting the partisan coalition; they also failed to appeal to the party base or to broaden it by an appeal to the middle and to independents (although both came very close in the popular vote). Indeed, his mastery of this balancing act was one reason Barack Obama won in 2008 when his two very capable predecessors had lost in 2000 and 2004.

The themes of consistent conservatism among Republicans and of bifurcation and struggle between liberals and moderates among Democrats continued through the first three elections of the twenty-first century. Among Republicans there was widespread symbolic unity around Ronald Reagan and around the label of conservatism, even though considerable operational disagreement occurred over what conservatism actually means. Most prominently, there are social conservatives and fiscal conservatives. There are libertarians and Tea Party populists and establishment Republicans. There are values voters and economic interest voters. These policy priorities are often difficult to reconcile, as the October 2013 shutdown of the government demonstrated. In that fight the Tea Party faction was determined not to give in to compromise in order to prevent default on the debt, while the establishment faction was adamant that this was the path to financial disaster for the nation and political disaster for the party. This debate continues and will help structure the 2016 election. However, almost no Republican today would reject the label of conservative outright, and some version of what it means to be a conservative is the dominant narrative within the Republican Party today. This symbolic unity over the label *conservative* and the Reagan legacy has generally worked well for Republicans and their supporters.

On the Democratic side, divisions between liberals and moderates have been more difficult to bridge. The moderate Blue Dog Coalition in Congress and the grassroots-oriented Democratic Leadership Council (DLC), on one side, versus a host of decidedly liberal interest groups and the congressional caucuses, on the other side, reinforce these differences, although moderate Democratic groups have been much weakened by recent elections, and the DLC folded in 2011. All Democratic candidates get scrutinized in terms of where they stand on this continuum. If they make moderate sounding pronouncements, it is interpreted as an attempt to appeal to business friendly interests and the Blue Dog Coalition. If they take a liberal stance, it appears that they are pandering to the liberal base of the party. Part of this electoral dilemma may stem from the fact that there are approximately twice as many conservatives as liberals in the United States. Part of it may also stem from the success of Republicans and conservatives in giving the label *liberal* a bad image during the 1970s and 1980s. As George H. W. Bush used to frame it, "the L word" is far more negative than positive for many Americans. Republicans have successfully framed their message regarding liberalism and a host of policy positions, and Democrats have failed to match them for the past three decades (Jamieson and Waldman, 2003). So, while both philosophical positions have their supporters and detractors and both represent venerable philosophical traditions, one clearly became dominant and the other subservient in the early twenty-first-century American political culture.

The electoral advantages of the disparity between these two positions are also evident in public opinion polls that consider the nation as a whole, as opposed to the partisan bases of both parties. During the early 2000s 31–37 percent of the American people designated themselves as conservatives, while only 24–25 percent claimed the liberal label (Stanley and Niemi, 2006, 120; 2009–10, 111). By 2010 the conservative identification had grown to around 40 percent, while liberals remained at about 20 percent (Gallup poll, June 2010). By the end of 2013 this conservative advantage had declined a bit, at 38 percent conservative, 23 percent liberal, and 34 percent moderate, but it was still a fifteen-point spread (Jones, 2014a, 2014b). This gap affords an immediate advantage to conservative candidates who seek to identify themselves and their opponents symbolically. It also means that both sides must work hard to unite and mobilize their base, the critical first step toward any winning coalition. The remainder of the battle must be fought for the middle, which has generally ranged from 35 to 38 percent of the American electorate (Stanley and Niemi, 2013–14, 113). While the middle is where the battle will be won, conservatives almost equal moderates most of the time and occasionally exceed them. This gives Republicans an initial strategic advantage in presidential politics and many other races where just symbolic self-identification is involved in evaluating candidates and parties, although some liberal social issues such as gay rights have gained traction recently.

The American public perceives the differences between the two major parties in these ideological terms, with Republicans generally recognized as the conservative party and Democrats the liberal party (Flanigan and Zingale, 2006, 152). It is possible to mark the polarization of the two parties as they shifted along the continuum driven by Barry Goldwater's 1964 election, the backlash against Lyndon Johnson's Great Society of the mid- to late 1960s, George McGovern's 1972 liberal campaign, Ronald Reagan's conservative ascendancy in the 1980s, and Barack Obama's elections in 2008 and 2012. The presidential campaigns and the administrations of Johnson and Reagan were particularly important factors in establishing those identities, and it is now well established that the two parties are significantly polarized in ideological terms at the elite level. While polarization at the mass level is more controversial, it appears from our data that this division is also real. The body of research upon which this book builds helps to document that ideological divergence at both levels.

Figure 6-1 compares the liberals in each group and shows unambiguously that Democratic Party elites were always the most liberal group, except for

Figure 6-1. *Ideologies of Liberal Party Elites and Party Identifiers, 1972–2008*

Percent

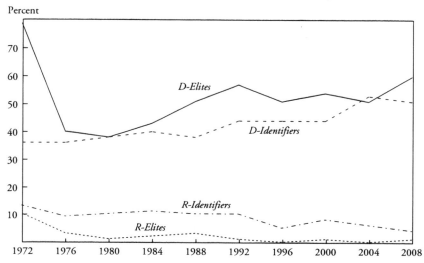

Source: American National Election Studies, various years; author surveys; *CBS News/New York Times,* 2008a, 2008b.

1980 and 2004. It is also notable how out of step with the party base the 1972 convention delegates were. This was the convention that nominated George McGovern over Edmund Muskie and that banished Chicago's mayor Richard J. Daley and his Illinois party regulars in favor of the delegation led by the Reverend Jesse Jackson and the alderman William Singer. This was the year of Jeane Kirkpatrick's monumental study (1976), which fixed the picture of a very liberal Democratic Party elite dramatically out of step with the party's base and mainstream voters. While that picture was accurate for 1972, the longitudinal data in figure 6-1 show just how time bound that picture was. It is also true, however, that the Democratic Party's elite leadership has been usually the most liberal group studied and that, in general, that liberal identification has grown, after taking a definite dip between 1972 and 1978. From 1976 on, the upward trend line of the Democratic Party elite is matched by a lower but steady upward trend for the party's base, which also now tends to identify as liberal; by 2004 liberals among the identifiers slightly exceeded liberals among the party elites. Although there are some slight dips (as among the Democratic elites in 1980 and 1996), the slope of both elite and mass lines is generally upward for Democrats from 1980 forward.

Figure 6-2. *Ideologies of Conservative Party Elites and Party Identifiers, 1972–2008*

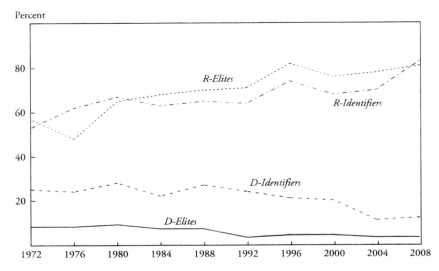

Source: American National Election Studies, various years; author surveys; *CBS News/New York Times*, 2008a, 2008b.

The Republican lines for elites and masses are the mirror image of the Democratic lines (figure 6-2). Republican elites are pretty consistently the most conservative and the least liberal group studied; however, in 1976 the party's base was substantially more conservative than the party's elites. That was the year in which the more moderate of the two candidates, Gerald Ford, was nominated over Ronald Reagan. This deviation fits the popular view of that historic era, but this is a rare case in which the base of the Republican Party was more conservative than party elites. These data show that the party's nominee had an impact on convention delegations: Gerald Ford in this case and George McGovern in the case of the Democrats in 1972. Both long-term and short-term effects are evident here. The 1980 Republican convention that nominated Ronald Reagan over George H. W. Bush is another example of this gap, albeit much smaller, between party elites and party identifiers, the latter being more conservative than the elites. Generally, however, Republican Party elites have been more conservative than the party's base—until 2008, when they were essentially tied. Needless to say, both groups have been far more conservative and less liberal than the Democratic identifiers and leadership. In addition, the level of conservative identification increased steadily for both

Figure 6-3. *Ideologies of Moderate Party Elites and Party Identifiers, 1972–2008*

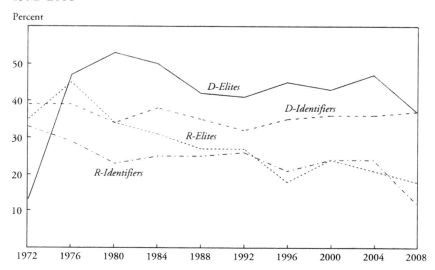

Percent

Source: American National Election Studies, various years; author surveys; *CBS News/New York Times*, 2008a, 2008b.

the party's leadership and its base over this period. With only slight perturbation, the line is consistently upward for Republican elites and followers alike during this era.

The moderate category is depicted in figure 6-3, where the line is the most erratic for Democratic Party elites. For them, 1972 was clearly a major aberration. In 1976 the percentage of Democratic Party elites who called themselves moderates shot up dramatically, to 47 percent in 1976 and to above 50 percent in 1980, which was Jimmy Carter's re-nomination convention. The line has been up and down somewhat since 1980, but as the liberal category expanded, the moderate and conservative categories contracted. The moderate range for Democratic Party identifiers has been a narrow one, consistently staying between 30 and 40 percent in every presidential election since 1972.

The pattern for moderates among the Republican Party's elites and identifiers is somewhat more erratic than for the other Republican ideological categories; however, the trend line for both groups is generally downward. It is clear that Gerald Ford's 1976 convention was the apogee of moderate strength among Republican elites. Moderates have been up and down since then among Republican elites. Indeed, by 1992 there was very little difference between the two groups. Put simply, during this era the Republican Party became the conservative alternative, and party leaders and identifiers agreed on that designation. This congruence makes it easier for Republican candidates to campaign wearing the conservative mantle, since there is near consensus among all ranks of the party on its positive appeal.

It is evident from these figures that the Republicans are more united in their embrace of the conservative label than the Democrats are of their liberal label. Moderates are a larger percentage of Democrats than of Republicans. That the three leading contenders for the Republican presidential nomination in 2008—John McCain, Rudolph Giuliani, and Mitt Romney—were once considered to have moderate views, at least on social issues, and that all of them then tried to shed these views and move to the right in preparation for the caucus and primary season, is proof of the dominance of the conservative label. Mitt Romney exhibited the same pattern in 2012. Both parties largely shed their misidentifiers during this period. They became much more homogeneous internally and much farther separated from each other ideologically than they were when this era began in the early 1970s. This homogeneity is more marked among Republicans than among Democrats.

Issues

The major parties are no longer the pragmatic electoral organizations of the previous era, when ideology and issues took a backseat to getting elected and when southern Democratic moderates and conservatives and northeastern Republican liberals had a place at the table and positions of power in their respective party councils. This modern post-reform era was marked by watershed realignments, at least on ideology, for both parties at both the mass and elite levels, although the ideological divide is greater at the elite level. Whether these divisions also cut across issue areas that have been important components of the political agenda in the United States for the last quarter of the twentieth century and the first decade of the twenty-first century is the question to which we now turn.

Government Services

Tables 6-3 and 6-4 present the positions of national convention delegates and party identifiers on the question of providing more or fewer government services. Clearly, the size and scope of government are defining differences between conservatives and liberals and has been since Franklin Roosevelt's

Table 6-3. *Democratic Convention Delegates and Party Identifiers, Position on Government Services, 1984–2008*[a]

Percent

Position	1984		1988		1992		1996		2000		2004		2008	
	E	I	E	I	E	I	E	I	E	I	E	I	E	I
Continue	71	49	78	52	75	49	80	44	91	64	85	65	86	67
Neutral	16	33	12	27	11	34	11	35	6	26	9	25	8	23
Fewer	14	19	10	21	14	18	8	21	4	10	6	10	5	10

Source: Author surveys; American National Election Studies, various years.
a. Elite data are the same as Democratic data in table 5-2.

New Deal expanded the scope of the national government in the 1930s. The results shown in these tables indicate that party elites are more extreme in their views than are party identifiers.

Among Democrats, 91 percent of convention delegates in 2000 and 85 percent in 2004 wanted the government to "continue or provide more services," which is to say they favored big government. Only 6 percent and 9 percent in those two years chose the neutral category. In 2008 the liberal response still dominated, with 86 percent selecting the "continue services" category. Only 4 percent, 6 percent, and 5 percent, respectively, of the 2000, 2004, and 2008 Democratic delegates selected the "fewer services" category, compared to 10 percent of the Democrats in the mass public in these years. It is notable, though, that only one in ten of Democratic identifiers selected the conservative response in those three years. In the twenty-first century the conservative position was clearly not popular among Democrats at either the elite or mass level. A plurality (in 1996 and 1984) and a consistent two-thirds majority (in 2000, 2004, and 2008) of the Democratic Party's base took the liberal position on this issue; 80 percent or more of the elites have taken this position since 1996.

On the other side of the aisle, just over 60 percent of Republican delegates at both the 2000 and 2004 conventions opted for the most conservative response of providing "fewer services," compared to 46 and 39 percent of the Republican mass electorate in those years. In 2008 almost three-fourths (74 percent) of the Republican delegates selected the conservative "provide fewer services" response, while only 11 percent selected the liberal "continue services" response. Republican elites are clearly much more conservative than their party's base on this issue. Indeed, almost one-fourth of Republican identifiers in 2000 (22 percent) and just under one-third in 2004 (32 percent) and 29 percent in 2008 chose the most liberal "continue or provide more

Table 6-4. *Republican Convention Delegates and Party Identifiers,*
Position on Government Services, 1984–2008[a]

Percent

	1984		1988		1992		1996		2000		2004		2008	
Position	*E*	*I*	*E*	*I*	*E*	*I*	*E*	*I*	*E*	*I*	*E*	*I*	*E*	*I*
Continue	13	20	13	24	6	22	5	26	17	22	16	32	11	29
Neutral	21	29	17	30	14	27	8	44	23	33	22	29	15	25
Fewer	66	50	71	46	81	50	88	30	61	46	62	39	74	47

Source: Author surveys; American National Election Studies, various years.
a. Elite data are the same as Republican data in table 5-2.

government services" response. In essence, among the mass public, including Republican identifiers, cutting government services was not much more
popular than tax increases. Very few outside the elite cadre wanted to cut
services or to increase taxes to pay for them. This position helped to create
the massive federal deficits that reappeared after 2001. Covering expanded
government, especially in the areas of homeland security and national defense
in the aftermath of the 9/11 attacks, with increased borrowing proved to be
irresistible to the Bush administration and Congress, and so it easily became
official government policy in 2001.

In the earlier years depicted in tables 6-3 and 6-4 the deep division between
Democrats and Republicans at the mass and elite levels already existed, so
polarization over the proper role of government has been evident as far back as
1980. Indeed, as a result of the 2010 midterm election losses for Democrats,
dealing with the deficit became a challenge for the Obama administration and
provided the backdrop for the run-up to the 2012 election.

In sum, Republican elites are markedly more enthusiastic about cutting
services than their party identifiers are, while Democratic elites are uniformly
the most liberal group and Democratic identifiers are in between. Clearly, the
American public as a whole was much less committed to cutting services than
Republican leaders were.

National Health Insurance

Views on national health insurance have been a litmus test issue, dividing
Democrats from Republicans in Congress and in the White House for several
generations. It came to a boil in 2009 and 2010, when President Obama
and his allies in Congress passed the national health care reform bill, officially known as the Patient Protection and Affordable Care Act (Balz and others, 2010). Generally, Republicans in federal office have favored reliance on

Table 6-5. *Democratic Convention Delegates and Party Identifiers,
Position on National Health Insurance, 1984–2008*[a]

Percent

Position	1984		1988		1992		1996		2000		2004		2008	
	E	I	E	I	E	I	E	I	E	I	E	I	E	I
Government insurance	59	45	74	52	82	65	69	51	71	55	81	60	82	61
Neutral	16	21	13	20	9	18	18	23	16	22	12	20	8	19
Private insurance	24	35	13	27	9	17	13	26	13	24	6	20	7	20

Source: Author surveys; American National Election Studies, various years.
a. Elite data are the same as Democratic data in table 5-3.

private insurance and on the marketplace to address the need for broad-based health insurance, while Democrats have favored some form of health insurance provided by the government or subsidized by the government. Tables 6-5 and 6-6 illustrate these divisions among the party elites and followers.

Among Republican identifiers, 28 percent in both 2000 and 2004 and 29 percent in 2008 favored the liberal position of reliance on government insurance. More party identifiers, though, supported private insurance (55, 52, and 55 percent). The party elite heavily supported private insurance in those years (87, 84, and 87 percent). The comparable level of "misidentification" among Democratic partisans is 24 percent in 2000 and 20 percent in 2004 and 2008. Over half of Democratic identifiers in 2000 and three-fifths of Democratic identifiers in 2004 and 2008 supported their party's characteristic position.

By 2008 these partisan differences at the elite level had become almost monolithic, with 82 percent of Democratic delegates favoring the government insurance option and 87 percent of Republican elites favoring the private insurance option. The parties could hardly have been more polarized than they were on this item.

It was clear in the 2008 general election that the platforms of the two parties as well as the rhetoric of the candidates articulated dramatically different agendas on this issue. The data in the remainder of the table show that this division is long-standing. By 1984 the two parties were already significantly polarized at the elite level on this issue. The base of both parties was also polarized, though this division is not as pronounced as that between the two elite groups. The current conflict probably goes all the way back to Lyndon Johnson's advocacy for Medicare and Medicaid in the mid-1960s, and the roots extend back to Harry Truman. In 1965 Johnson got Medicaid and Medicare through a compliant Democratic majority in Congress, but that coalition ended in the 1966 mid-term elections, when the Democrats lost a

Table 6-6. *Republican Convention Delegates and Identifiers,*
Position on National Health Insurance, 1984–2008[a]

Percent

Position	1984 E	1984 I	1988 E	1988 I	1992 E	1992 I	1996 E	1996 I	2000 E	2000 I	2004 E	2004 I	2008 E	2008 I
Government insurance	5	28	13	30	10	34	4	21	7	28	9	28	5	29
Neutral	10	21	12	17	13	22	6	18	6	18	7	20	11	15
Private insurance	82	50	75	53	77	44	90	60	87	55	84	52	87	55

Source: Author surveys; American National Election Studies, various years.
a. Elite data are the same as Republican data in table 5-3.

substantial number of seats in Congress. Much of the remaining Kennedy-Johnson domestic agenda languished until Bill Clinton revitalized it in 1993.

Despite their joint efforts Bill and Hillary Clinton were unable to get expanded coverage of national health insurance through Congress, even though Democrats had the majority in 1993–94. Then the Republican take-over of Congress in 1994 stopped such progressive domestic agenda plans cold. Clinton spent much of his remaining six years in office trying to persuade a generally hostile Congress to adopt some of his domestic programs. The reform of the welfare system in 1996 was a large and important shift in the scope of the national government; however, with that exception, which many Republicans supported and Democrats opposed, Clinton spent most of his final six years focused on incremental changes to existing domestic programs and trying to ward off impeachment. The Bush administration during the 2001–06 era is an example of what can be done if the government is unified under the same party.

This era of unified government illustrates an instance in which public officials, relevant interest groups, and the governing party (in this case, Republican) had only to preserve and defend the status quo in order to prevail on the issue of health care coverage. To change the health care system, the Clintons and the Democrats, by contrast, had to win over the mass public and get a bill through a hostile Congress after 1994. Those who wanted basic change may have assembled significant support among their own partisans, and they may have even attained the support of a sizable minority of the other party's identifiers, but it is very difficult to amass the political pressure necessary to assemble a coalition that can make basic and large-scale change in a policy like health care. The exception was the Bush administration's expansion of the prescription drug benefit for senior citizens under Medicare. This was a massive expansion of the Medicare program. The debates among the 2008 presidential candidates highlight the importance that many of the candidates placed on solving the nation's health care crisis.

This history was the backdrop to the great debate over the Obama health care plan in 2009–10. Needless to say, this was a highly polarized issue, and the plan that the Obama administration pushed through Congress attracted almost no Republican support in Congress (Balz and others, 2010). The parties had rarely been as divided as they were over this issue. Party elites and the majority of those holding public office are probably much more entrenched in their positions than the mass public, as much of the public would support doing something if the elites decided to move. This observation is confirmed by the public opinion polls of 2009 and 2010, taken at the height of the health care debate, and then in the summer and fall of 2010, after the plan had passed. The polls consistently show that the public was deeply divided over the issue. Depending on how the question was worded, a majority of the public, usually in the 50–60 percent range, opposed the president's plan when asked about the plan as a whole. However, when component parts of the plan were broken out and asked about separately, a majority, often a large majority, supported various of these major provisions. This inconsistency, or lack of coherence, leaves room for maneuver for public officeholders and invites them to do what they deem best for the nation as a whole. That is exactly what happened when a bare majority of congressional Democrats passed President Obama's health care proposal.

The out-of-power party can try to make a major issue out of such a far-reaching social policy change, which is what happened when the Republicans took on Obamacare as one of their major and favorite targets in the 2010 midterm elections. This conflict continued in the 2012 presidential election and extended well into 2013, despite Obama's 2012 reelection. In 2013 Republicans in Congress continued to take symbolic votes to repeal the Affordable Care Act, and most Republican governors tried to prevent its implementation in their states. In the fall of 2013 Republicans in the House, led by Senator Ted Cruz of Texas, forced the shutdown of the federal government over their demand that the Affordable Care Act not be funded. The White House and Democrats in Congress were just as intent on protecting the signal legislative accomplishment of Obama's first term. The intensity of that debate shows how deeply divided the two parties were on this matter. The Republicans then decided to make their opposition to the ACA a central feature of their strategic plan for the 2014 midterm congressional elections.

The data presented here show that this fight had been brewing for a long time and is one in which the party elites on each side were deeply committed

Table 6-7. *Democratic Convention Delegates and Party Identifiers, Position on Government Aid to Minorities, 1980–2008*[a]

Percent

Position	1980 E	1980 I	1984 E	1984 I	1988 E	1988 I	1992 E	1992 I	1996 E	1996 I	2000 E	2000 I	2004 E	2004 I	2008 E	2008 I
Government help	52	31	57	41	66	36	76	30	71	28	73	26	76	36	66	36
Neutral	21	29	22	38	16	25	16	29	14	26	14	30	13	29	19	27
Help selves	27	41	22	27	18	39	8	40	16	46	13	44	12	35	15	37

Source: Author surveys; American National Election Studies, various years.
a. Elite data are the same as Democratic data in table 5-4.

to their party's signature position. The base of the two parties was much more divided and supported the party's traditional position at lower levels, although more than a majority of these party identifiers held the party position, perhaps reflecting the bruising battle over the Clinton proposals of 1993–94. Since then, polarization has grown on this matter. Health care insurance has significantly contributed to the deep polarization of the nation during the era under study here.

Government Aid to Minorities

Another polarizing issue is government assistance to minorities. The American National Election Studies question refers to "blacks and other minority groups." We adopted the same wording for our survey. No other area of domestic policy has been as contentious and divisive in American life as racial politics, and this question certainly plumbs the depths of that issue. Not surprisingly, political elites are deeply divided on this question (tables 6-7 and 6-8). Democratic Party identifiers are also deeply and rather evenly divided in most years. Since 1988 from two-thirds to three-quarters of Democratic Party elites took the liberal position on this matter, and a majority or more of Republican elites took the conservative position. Party identifiers are much more ambivalent and divided on the Democratic side, but they are more united against government aid on the Republican side.

In 2000 Democratic identifiers were divided into 26 percent who took the liberal position, 30 percent who were neutral, and 44 percent who took the conservative position (see table 6-7). In 2004, 36 percent of Democratic identifiers were in favor of government assistance, 35 percent were opposed (saying they should help themselves), leaving 29 percent in the neutral category. In 2008, 36 percent of Democratic identifiers favored government help for minorities, which was almost equal to the 37 percent who wanted them

Table 6-8. *Republican Convention Delegates and Party Identifiers,*
Position on Government Aid to Minorities, 1980–2008[a]
Percent

Position	1980		1984		1988		1992		1996		2000		2004		2008	
	E	I	E	I	E	I	E	I	E	I	E	I	E	I	E	I
Government help	17	11	12	20	24	17	28	13	12	7	23	9	18	9	11	11
Neutral	25	29	22	31	20	24	23	24	13	20	17	21	20	21	13	18
Help selves	58	61	67	49	56	59	50	63	75	74	60	70	62	70	76	71

Source: Author surveys; American National Election Studies, various years.
a. Elite data are the same as Republican data in table 5-4.

to help themselves. Only Democratic elites were clearly the liberals, with from two-thirds to over three-fourths giving the most liberal answer in the two decades between 1988 and 2008. Going back to 1980 and 1984, the percentage of Democratic elites who took the liberal position was still over a majority, although it was considerably lower than it became in subsequent election years. Overall, then, Democratic Party identifiers were divided and inconsistent on this contentious matter, while the predominant position among Democratic delegates was the liberal choice. Certainly, Democratic identifiers do not manifest a consistently liberal position on this item. This is perhaps inevitable, since Democrats are the more diverse party, with liberal minorities, particularly African Americans, being a very large part of the core constituency of the party and with moderate groups an important component of the party's base.

There was much less disagreement among the Republican identifiers: in most years from two-thirds to nearly three-fourths took the conservative position (see table 6-8). Indeed, between 1980 and 2004 (with the exception of 1984 and 1996), Republican identifiers were more conservative than their party elites were on this issue. In 2008 slightly more Republican elites fell into the most conservative category than identifiers, but the difference was small (76 percent to 71 percent). In this instance polarization at the elite level rests on mass support for the Republican elite's position, while for the Democratic elites, the base is a considerably less solid and more diverse group, meaning that Democrats are more internally divided on this issue. Matters of race and proposed government assistance for minorities are much more difficult for Democrats to finesse than is true for the more united Republicans. Democratic elites appear to be the outliers in their liberal positions. Here too the diversity among Democrats suggests that their candidates must walk a tightrope between the liberal and the moderate components of the party. Intrinsic knowledge of the perils of being seen as too liberal and

Table 6-9. *Democratic Convention Delegates and Party Identifiers,*
Position on Defense Spending, 1980–2008[a]

Percent

Position	1980 E	1980 I	1984 E	1984 I	1988 E	1988 I	1992 E	1992 I	1996 E	1996 I	2000 E	2000 I	2004 E	2004 I	2008 E	2008 I
Decrease	29	15	65	45	69	44	83	56	72	40	32	22	47	30	82	40
Neutral	30	20	25	29	26	32	11	28	22	33	44	33	35	35	9	25
Increase	41	65	11	26	5	24	7	16	6	27	24	45	18	35	9	35

Source: Author surveys; American National Election Studies, various years.
a. Elite data are the same as Democratic data in table 5-5.

too eager to cater to his African American supporters may help explain the very low-key role that race played in Barack Obama's presidential campaigns of 2008 and 2012 and during his first administration. There was no specific advocacy for programs deliberately and clearly addressed to the needs of the minority community, and all of Obama's major speeches emphasized the common good over any appeal to interest groups or to what is sometimes called identity politics. It was only in the second administration, with issues like differential treatment of various drug offenses and the need for special attention to young males, that Obama started a very tentative outreach toward the African American community.

The longitudinal data here indicate that the deep division between the two parties on government aid to minorities extends back for almost three decades—and probably even farther, as the nation has struggled with racial matters throughout its history.

Defense Spending

Providing for an adequate military defense of the nation is never very controversial, reaching almost consensus status, at least at the general and symbolic level. Almost everyone is in favor of spending enough to provide for the common defense, but defining how much is adequate as well as how the funds should be spent, which threats to respond to, which countries or groups represent a genuine threat, which weapon systems to fund at what level, what is an ideal troop strength, how to define the basic defense doctrine, and where the strategic national interests lie are controversial questions in American politics. Tables 6-9 and 6-10 display the partisan sources and dimensions of some of those conflicts.

It is evident from table 6-9 that Democratic Party identifiers are decidedly divided on defense expenditures. In 2008, 40 percent of them wanted to decrease defense expenditures, 35 percent wanted to increase them, with

Table 6-10. *Republican Convention Delegates and Party Identifiers, Position on Defense Spending, 1980–2008*[a]

Percent

Position	1980 E	1980 I	1984 E	1984 I	1988 E	1988 I	1992 E	1992 I	1996 E	1996 I	2000 E	2000 I	2004 E	2004 I	2008 E	2008 I
Decrease	5	6	9	18	12	21	30	36	11	21	2	9	3	7	5	13
Neutral	7	13	31	36	42	36	46	40	23	33	8	23	18	19	8	29
Increase	88	81	60	47	46	46	24	24	66	46	91	68	79	75	87	59

Source: Author surveys; American National Election Studies, various years.
a. Elite data are the same as Republican data in table 5-5.

25 percent in the middle. Their answers to the question in 2000 and 2004 are also evenly divided.

Like those in the party electorate, Democratic delegates were also deeply divided in 2000 and 2004 with respect to defense spending, with a 47 percent plurality in 2004 favoring a decrease in defense spending and only 18 percent wanting an increase. A decrease in spending was favored by almost one-third of the 2000 delegates, a proposition on which 44 percent were neutral, with 24 percent in favor of an increase in spending. In 2008 Democratic elites' position on defense spending was an overwhelming 82 percent in favor of decreasing it. This near consensus probably stemmed from the Democrats' deep aversion to the war in Iraq and perhaps secondarily from their recognition of the costs of the war, given the ballooning deficits during and after the Bush years. This consensus of 2008 was not shared by Democratic identifiers, however, as they show a plurality of only 40 percent in favor of decreasing defense spending and 35 percent in favor of increasing it. Before 2008, the divisions among Democratic elites on this issue closely matched the base, although delegates were consistently more favorable toward cutting defense expenditures than party identifiers were. Data from earlier years show that, from 1984 through 1996, a steady two-thirds to more than three-fourths of Democratic elites wanted a decrease in defense spending. Democratic identifiers were much more divided on this issue during the 1984 through 1996 era. In other words, Democratic elites and Democratic identifiers were out of step with each other. By 2008 this gap between Democratic Party elites and Democratic Party identifiers was even wider.

The same was true in reverse for Republicans in 2008, when 87 percent of party elites were in favor of increased defense expenditures but only 59 percent of party identifiers took this position. Two-thirds to three-fourths of the party's base, however, had favored defense increases in 2000 and 2004.

The congruence between leaders and followers is close in both of these years, although it is closer in 2004. Under these circumstances, and with Republicans in charge of the White House and Congress, it was probably inevitable that defense expenditures would increase, even without the push provided by the September 11, 2001, terrorist attacks.

This is indeed what happened, with the Bush administration increasing defense spending to fight the wars in Iraq and Afghanistan. This pattern began in the 1980s, when Reagan substantially increased defense spending with the overwhelming support of the party elites. In 1980 he also had overwhelming support for that position from party identifiers, but that support had declined by 1984. In 1988 both Republican Party elites and identifiers were deeply divided over whether to increase or decrease defense expenditures, with the increase side gaining the plurality. During his administration George H. W. Bush cut defense spending in the wake of the fall of the Soviet Union in 1989 and 1990, and in 1992 the party was again divided over the issue at both mass and elite levels. By 2000 over nine out of ten Republican elites favored an increase in defense expenditures, and they were supported by over two-thirds of party identifiers. Not surprisingly, George W. Bush substantially increased the defense budget during his first term. In 2004 and 2008 it had become a basic tenet of the Republican faith that defense expenditures be increased. That faith was shared by the party's base, but not at the level exhibited by Republican elites.

In fact, longitudinal data show that, in 1984–96, Republican identifiers were a good deal less hawkish on increasing defense spending than party elites. Only in 1980, 2000, 2004, and 2008 did the position of increasing defense spending attract a majority of Republican identifiers, a level that sometimes exceeded Republican elite support. It is notable that 1980 and 2000 were elections when the Republicans took the White House after a Democratic administration had been in power, and the 2004 election was influenced by the terrorist attacks of September 11, 2001. Obviously, the Reagan era defense buildup still resonated with the Republican base in 1988, when a plurality of 46 percent wanted to increase defense spending. By 1992, however, this support for an increase had dropped to only 24 percent among both Republican identifiers and elites, after George H. W. Bush's term. So position on defense spending depends on who is in the White House and what the partisans are being told from that bully pulpit.

Abortion

Since the U.S. Supreme Court decided *Roe* v. *Wade* in 1973, the matter of abortion rights has been on the public agenda (Craig and O'Brien, 1993). It

Table 6-11. *Democratic Convention Delegates and Party Identifiers, Position on Abortion, 1984–2008*[a]

Percent

Position	1984		1988		1992		1996		2000		2004		2008	
	E	I	E	I	E	I	E	I	E	I	E	I	E	I
Never permitted	2	12	3	14	0	10	1	11	1	12	1	12	1	11
Only in special circumstances (rape/incest or health of mother)	44	49	39	52	12	38	16	41	9	38	23	43	20	41
Always permitted	53	39	59	34	88	52	82	48	90	50	76	46	79	48

Source: Author surveys; American National Election Studies, various years.

a. Elite data are the same as Democratic data in table 5-6. The exact question wording and response categories varied depending on the year.

has also become one of the most salient issues dividing the Republican Party from the Democratic Party (tables 6-11 and 6-12). This issue was not clearly partisan immediately after *Roe* v. *Wade* and initially both parties had people on both sides; however, since 1980 the Republican Party platform has been adamantly pro-life and the Democratic Party platform just as adamantly pro-choice (Craig and O'Brien, 1993). Since the 1980s, the parties have been consistently polarized on this issue in their national platforms and in the rhetoric of their candidates.

The results for Democratic Party elites show the sources of some of that polarization. In 2000, 90 percent of the Democratic convention delegates took the pure pro-choice position and in 2004, 76 percent took that position. Then in 2008, 79 percent of Democratic delegates were in the pure pro-choice position. Since 1984 there has been a range of only 1–3 percent of Democratic delegates in the pure pro-life category. So Democratic elites have evidenced a fairly large consensus on the side of the pro-choice position since we started asking the question in 1984. However, Democratic identifiers were split almost evenly in 2004 between the 46 percent who were pro-choice and the 43 percent in the middle, leaving only 12 percent in the absolutely pro-life position. In 2008, again, the division between the pure pro-choice position and the more mixed moderates was close. Democratic elites most certainly did not react to the consensus position of their party's base when they officially adopted the pro-choice position. A plurality of Democratic identifiers is found in the more ambivalent middle category, which allows for some regulation although it is still a pro-choice position.

The same is true for the Republicans. The moderate category attracted 56 percent of Republican identifiers in 2000, while the pure pro-life position

Table 6-12. *Republican Convention Delegates and Party Identifiers,*
Position on Abortion, 1984–2008[a]

Percent

	1984		1988		1992		1996		2000		2004		2008	
Position	E	I	E	I	E	I	E	I	E	I	E	I	E	I
Never permitted	7	16	5	12	9	13	18	14	18	14	17	19	26	17
Only in special circum-stances (rape/incest or health of mother)	69	52	75	54	65	49	63	55	57	56	68	55	62	53
Always permitted	23	33	20	34	25	38	19	31	26	30	15	26	12	30

Source: Author surveys; American National Election Studies, various years.
a. Elite data are the same as Republican data in table 5-6. The exact question wording and response categories varied depending on the year.

attracted only 14 percent of them, leaving 30 percent in the pure pro-choice position. This is comparable to the 55 percent of Republican identifiers in 2004 in the mixed or moderate group, with only 19 percent of them in the pure pro-life category and 26 percent in the pure pro-choice position. These results continued to be consistent in 2008. More than a majority, and often two-thirds to three-fourths, of Republican delegates since 1984 have been in the middle category. Again, the Republican Party base is much more moderate and conflicted on this contentious issue than the party's official pronouncements and candidate rhetoric would indicate.

This is an instance where a narrow top echelon of elites and their presidential candidates (on both sides) are fairly out of step with their bases, which are much more diverse. Longitudinal data indicate that the mass public on both sides of the aisle has always been less polarized and more in the middle than party rhetoric would suggest. That ambiguity and complexity shows up in public opinion polls, in which the American public proves much more moderate and more ambiguous on this issue than the party elites are. That ambiguity is also reflected in most of the controlling law where abortion is legal. Whether abortion is available depends on where the woman lives. Getting an abortion is also bound by numerous restrictions, particularly for minors, in many jurisdictions. And funding abortions for poor women is forbidden to come from the federal government and from many state governments.

With these predominantly moderate and ambiguous results, one might well wonder how party platforms and party leaders can take such clearly opposite positions on abortion. The answer seems to be that those who control the parties, write the party platforms at the conventions, and drive the public policy agenda are much more pure and decisive in their policy preferences than the people they represent at the grass roots. This is an instance where an intense minority, within the larger leadership cadre of the party, is driving the agenda for the entire party. The clarity of the pro-choice position among Democratic delegates holds sway in the party's inner councils, despite the fact that the party base and the American public are much more divided. The moderation of Republican delegates is a close match for the party's mass identifiers; however, it is no match for the mobilized interest groups and party insiders, who dominate Republican platforms and rhetoric, despite being unrepresentative of the party's rank and file and the American public. Here is a case where the images the two parties have created for themselves, and purveyed through the mass media, are widely at variance with what the party base, and even a plurality or majority of party elites, personally support. The politics of polarization on this issue demands a level of purity for both parties that borders on caricature. Polarization does produce and reinforce great fervor among those who are deeply committed to the pro-life or pro-choice positions. It aids recruitment and fund-raising for both sides and helps to energize and mobilize the faithful; however, these pure positions only represent an intense and mobilized minority on both sides of the aisle.

Here is a case where party elites have staked out a much more clear and pure party position in convention platforms and in the public positions taken by presidential candidates than the essentially ambiguous and even moderate position taken by both parties' base supporters. In an earlier era, the pragmatic party era, these differences in policy positions might have been ignored or papered over in the desire to appeal to the largest range of voters possible. In the more recent ideological party era, these differences are magnified by both the party elites and the presidential candidates of the two parties.

Conclusion

There has been a long-running debate about the role of public opinion in a mass democracy and a related debate over the proper relationship between the parties' elites and their masses, the rulers and the ruled. Does public opinion control the policymaking process in any meaningful sense? How can the public make its views felt in controlling the decisionmakers and holding them accountable for their actions? Is there any other method, outside periodic free elections, for such accountability to be exercised? How can the public force changes in some policies (such as the wars in Iraq and Afghanistan) even after elections have been held and the party in power is displaced, as happened to the Republican majority in Congress in 2006 and partially happened to the

Democratic congressional majority in 2010. Do political and economic elites lead the masses in all cases and so effectively shape their opinions that there is little role left for the public outside routine acquiescence coupled with sporadic voting? The data presented in this chapter suggest some tentative answers.

The picture one gets from the longitudinal data is one of distinct ideological and issue-based polarization, especially at the elite level. The majority of each party's elites are arrayed against the majority of the other party's elites on a wide variety of the most important contemporary political issues. This elite-level polarization has been in place since the 1970s for the most part, and it increased in the 1980–2008 era. The classic McClosky distribution—with Democratic elites on the liberal end of the spectrum, Republican elites on the conservative end, and party identifiers lined up in between but leaning toward their own party's signature position—has held true, broadly, across almost four decades. There are occasional exceptions; however, this is a pattern so frequently observed that it is one of those generalizations that the discipline of political science strives to produce: that cross-party divisions have increased at the mass and elite levels over time.

In addition, it appears that party elites lead party identifiers and shape their party's agenda. In some special cases, such as pro-choice versus pro-life positions, an intense and mobilized minority cadre within the party elite dictates the party platform and helps to recruit a presidential candidate willing to pledge allegiance to that platform. The positions taken on the platform might even be in opposition to the position of the party's less-powerful elites and of the party's base.

Only in nominating candidates do party identifiers, acting mostly through party primaries, play much of a role in presidential politics. But the candidates they choose and those they reject in the primaries (and to a lesser extent, the caucuses) are opportunities for the party's base to shape the party and its agenda and image for the next four years. After the primaries and conventions end, voters are left only with the ability to judge the candidates and platforms offered and to vote for the presidential candidates of one or the other party. It is take it or leave it at that point. The role of party identifiers is not inconsequential; however, it is far removed from the direct shaping of public policy.

Put succinctly, the two parties' elites are now trending toward the ideological ends of the continuum, patterning some of the requirements of the classic responsible party model. These elites are likely to be either liberal Democrats or conservative Republicans, and they are likely to favor presidential candidates who hold their ideological values. At the same time, many party identifiers, particularly Democrats, are still in the classic pragmatic party model, although their ranks have declined recently. Identifiers are often found in the middle and are more comfortable with candidates who seem moderate or who craft their message to the issues and circumstances. There is a certain tension in the uneven evolution of these two components of the political parties. That tension can often be seen in the pull of presidential candidates toward the extreme ends of the ideological continuum during the primaries to please the party's core, all the while being aware of the need for flexibility so as to appeal to a more moderate and diverse electorate. Overall, however, the movement seems to be in the direction of the responsible party end of the continuum, especially from an elite perspective. Whether this tension between the two tendencies will be resolved any time soon remains to be seen. For now, the elites are in charge and dominate presidential politics and campaigns.

Mass voters are relegated to a support role, in which their main opportunity for influence is casting (or withholding) their votes for the party's candidates and programs, especially during primaries. The gap between what is realistic and what is expected in a representative form of government may lead to alienation and a mistrust of government and of those who govern. Much of the rhetoric of the modern-day Tea Party and Occupy Wall Street movements reflects that frustration, especially when such activists talk about "taking back" the government. Who they think they are taking back the government from seems to be political leaders and elites, most of whom were chosen in popular elections. It may be that representative democracy comes with a certain level of political alienation and mistrust. There is always and inevitably a gap between the party's base and its leadership. Just choosing candidates to hold public office singles out these officeholders as different from those they purport to lead. We do not have direct democracy on most matters. Nevertheless, the ideological commitment to the rhetoric and ideals of direct democracy is a source of continuing disappointment to those who advocate a government where "the people" rule.

The people do not rule in any direct sense of the word, and they have not done so since the foundation of the republic. They exercise indirect control through the candidates they support and elect and through the actions of those who represent them in the political parties.

7

Party and Political History of the Delegates

We already know something about the political attitudes and values of the delegates as well as their socioeconomic and demographic backgrounds. The next question addresses their party and political histories. How did they attain the status of political elites? What paths did they take to these positions of prominence? What party and political experiences shaped their views? What are their views on the future of their party and how can they ensure that their party prospers in a competitive environment? This chapter examines their responses to these questions.

It is clear from other research that political elites go through political socialization experiences that tend to set them apart from the average voter (Easton and Dennis, 1969; Almond and Verba 1963; Verba and Nie, 1972; Milbrath and Goel, 1977; Prewitt, 1970; Eulau and Prewitt, 1973; Flanigan and Zingale, 2006). They are more likely to come from families that value politics and public service and that encourage political discussion and participation. It is also clear from earlier studies of convention delegates that they are specifically recruited for this particular role and that they bring some special qualities to it (Kirkpatrick, 1976; Miller and Jennings, 1986; Miller, 1988). It is a difficult and challenging road to a delegate seat at the conventions, and relatively few local party activists are able to make their way successfully through the various decision points they must pass.

Data Analysis

Prior studies demonstrate that it takes perseverance and political acumen to negotiate the labyrinth of political obstacles that face those who want to attend

Figure 7-1. *Delegates Attending Their First Conventon, by Party, 1952–2008*

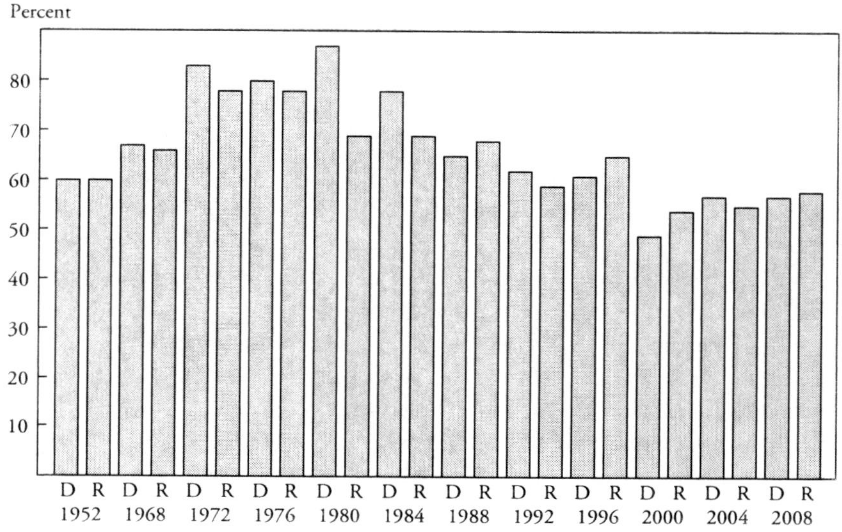

Percent

Source: *CBS News/New York Times Polls*, 2008a, 2008b; David, Goldman, and Bain, 1964, 243; author surveys.

the national conventions and be selected as a delegate (Kirkpatrick, 1976; Miller and Jennings, 1986; Miller, 1988; Maggiotto and Wekkin, 2000). The present study updates the existing literature with the advantage of a much longer time perspective.

Delegates at First Convention

The first question asked whether the delegates had attended an earlier convention (figure 7-1). Warren Miller and M. Kent Jennings built their important study of political party elites on the theoretical proposition that a circulation of elites is crucial for understanding party change and transition. The importance of this concept is captured in the following: "Much of our interest in mapping the circulation of presidential campaign elites is grounded in the fact that whatever the causes of replacement within elites, their circulation often produces changes in the motives, goals, ideals, ideas, and patterns of organizational behavior that characterize national presidential politics" (Miller and Jennings, 1986, 19).

The circulation of elites is a concept with an intellectual life that traces back to Vilfredo Pareto (1935). Part of the impetus for this current research was the desire to document and place into political context the changes among party elites and the circulation of elites taking place in the modern Democratic and Republican Parties. If there is going to be circulation of elites, spaces must be made available for the new people. If new people are going to be seeking access to power, one of the most productive points of access is through electoral politics, especially through involvement in presidential elections. Alternatively, if the parties are closed and not permeable at the top, if the current holders of power positions will not yield some places to the new aspirants, a quite different perspective arises on the potential for new groups and interests to share power. If important party councils, such as the national conventions, are essentially closed and self-perpetuating, the party system itself is likely to be much less responsive to the tides of public opinion and to the demands of new claimants on the one structure that is supposed to link citizens and interest groups to their government(Almond 1960; Leiserson, 1958). Indeed, the level of circulation of elites has for generations been an indicator of level of democracy in a nation and polity (Pareto, 1935). An analyst can document organizational change by documenting changes in the composition and characteristics of those who make up the organization's leadership. The definitive original study on national convention delegates was by Paul T. David and his associates. They found that 40 percent of the Republican and Democratic national convention delegates in 1952 had been delegates at least once before, thus leaving approximately 60 percent who were inexperienced delegates (David, Goldman, and Bain, 1964, 243). While this turnover provides considerable room for circulation of party elites, it also indicates a fairly high level of continuity from convention to convention.

An important study on delegate turnover in the 1944 through 1968 conventions, by Loch Johnson and Harlan Hahn (1973), establishes a benchmark for the pre-reform presidential selection era. Most delegates at those conventions were attending their first national convention. Indeed, over that period an average of 65 percent of Republicans and 64 percent of Democrats were first-time delegates (Johnson and Hahn, 1973, 148–49). Thus almost two-thirds of the delegates to each convention were inexperienced at that level of party service. In 1968, the last year before the reform era, 65 percent of Democratic delegates and 63 percent of Republicans were first-timers. Johnson and Hahn added 1972 to their analysis by interviewing official party sources. That year there was an increase in newcomers on both sides, with only 20 percent of Democrats and 33 percent of Republicans having attended prior conventions.

This comports with Kirkpatrick's seminal work on the 1972 conventions. Using survey data rather than official party sources, Kirkpatrick finds that even fewer Democratic delegates (17 percent) had been to earlier conventions.

This is a 20 percent increase in turnover for the Democrats in 1972, compared to the average for the twenty-four years preceding the reforms. This increase emphasizes how different the 1972 Democratic National Convention's delegates were from those at previous conventions, at least as far as fist-time attendance is concerned. This finding also contrasts with 30 percent of the Republicans who had previously been delegates. The 70 percent of newcomers at the GOP convention was only slightly greater than the typical turnover rate for the Republicans. Kirkpatrick attributed this disparity to the effects of George McGovern's largely antiwar insurgent candidacy and the impact it had on the Democratic Party in 1972.

Miller and Jennings's quasi-longitudinal research (1986, 29, 30, 37) on the 1972, 1976, and 1980 Republican and Democratic national conventions shows high rates of turnover across the three conventions. Only 13 percent of the delegates were repeaters—people who had been delegates previously. Miller and Jennings also found a high rate of continuity in campaign activism among the 1972 delegates. Among Republicans, only one in six of that year's delegates dropped out or failed to continue as a party activist in the subsequent years, compared to one in four of Democrats. This reinforces Kirkpatrick's finding from 1972, which shows substantially more veteran delegates among Republicans than among Democrats. When one broadens the scope of the question to ask, as Miller and Jennings did, whether the delegates had been active participants in the previous presidential campaigns (beyond being delegates), fully 70 percent of Republicans said they had been active in all three presidential elections between 1972 and 1980. The rate of consistent presidential campaign participation of delegates across the elections spanning George McGovern's 1972 race to Jimmy Carter's campaign for reelection in 1980 was lower. Only 57 percent of Democratic delegates participated continuously across all three of those elections. This finding demonstrates that the candidates, issues, and circumstances of a particular presidential year, and especially an unusual year like 1972, can attract newly energized participants, some of whom will turn out to be long-term recruits and some of whom will fall out of the organizational ranks quickly after their candidate passes from the scene. On balance, early studies show continuous elite participation at some level for both parties across several elections. Republican elites were more stable and somewhat more likely to show consistent commitment to their party's activities than Democrats, who were more likely to see their numbers augmented by newcomers.

As Miller and Jennings and other authorities emphasize, the circulation of political elites is an important source of both political change and renewal for the political parties. New party elites with access to the party's most basic and important functions bring new energy, new enthusiasm, and new ideas into the party's positions of power. If new recruits are to be satisfied, there must be openings made for them, a seat at the table provided, and their views valued. Those who seek the presidency provide the prism through which millions of ordinary voters view and evaluate the political parties. There are always new candidates and new coalitions of supporters eager to claim that prize in each national election, and there are always new candidates getting ready to make a run in the next election. These new candidates and their supporters want to put their brand name, their stamp, on the party if they succeed in winning the nomination. In that sense, then, change and the replenishment of the parties is almost guaranteed.

At the same time, if the national parties are to have continuity, institutional memory, and the advantages of political relationships built up over years of party work, a certain number of delegate slots must go to the veterans of earlier conventions. These veterans arrive at the conventions with friendships and networks already established. They know what to expect, know how to get things done, and provide continuity and stability. On the other hand, newcomers provide the potential for change. Thus there is an institutional value in a mix of veterans and newcomers.

Attaining the position of national convention delegate is not simple or easy. It usually requires some history of local party service, usually some political prominence in the local community and party, some statewide and national political connections, the support of crucial interest groups, and the personal resources to afford a very expensive week in a big city. It also requires the personal motivation to run for the position of delegate and the political and personal resources to be elected or selected. If it is a caucus state, delegations may be made up of people who have offered their candidacy several times at multiple stages of the process and have spent hours and days in the required meetings. If it is a primary state, a great deal of prior planning and resource commitment goes into winning a spot on the ballot and then winning the requisite votes on election day. Most important, being a delegate now requires an ability to make careful strategic political calculations, which are often quite sophisticated and demanding, and those calculations must be made early in the prenomination season. Most delegates must file a petition of candidacy far in advance of the announced date of the primaries, and they must pick a presidential candidate to back who will still be viable when their primary or caucus is held.

The window of opportunity to be a viable delegate is only open for a brief period, a few weeks at the most, usually in the fall of the year before the presidential election season begins. Ordinarily the prospective delegate must connect with the right presidential campaign at the right time and stay with that candidate through a local and then a congressional district or statewide race in order to reach a successful conclusion in achieving one of those coveted delegate slots. Alternatively, in many states a few delegate candidates get named to the ticket late, but they usually are those with special clout or who are needed to balance the ticket with the requisite demographic or political traits. It is little surprise then that only 30–40 percent of the delegates each year have ever attended more than one national convention as a delegate.

In the 1952 and 1968 conventions 60–67 percent of the delegates claimed to be attending their first convention. That percentage jumped considerably in 1972, the first post-reform conventions, when 83 percent of Democrats and 78 percent of Republicans indicated that they were at their first national conventions. This is not unexpected, since the object of the reforms in the Democratic Party was to open up the party so newcomers could more readily participate, and we know that those reforms had some spillover effect on the Republicans. These fairly high levels of newcomers continued for the Democrats in 1976, 1980, and 1984, although they declined somewhat for the Republicans in 1980 and 1984. The levels of newcomers declined again for both parties in 1988 and 1992. We know that Democrats had by 1984 instituted the superdelegate provision, which was designed to put more public and party officials back into the mix. That change appears to have made some difference in the number of newcomers after 1984; the effect was even more pronounced for Republicans. In addition, for Democrats, party regulars began a more concerted effort to get back in the game after the 1980 election, when Carter lost in a landslide to Reagan. So by the middle and last election of the decade of the 1980s, the rate of newcomers had declined and the veterans had increased for both parties. By 1992 around 60 percent of the delegates were newcomers in both parties, and this level of newcomers remained in the 50 to almost 60 percent range through 2000, 2004, and 2008.

In general, Democrats have had more first-time delegates than Republicans have had, although most years the differences are not major. For the entire period between 1972 and 1984 newcomers among Democratic delegates outnumbered those among Republican delegates. In 1988 Republicans had the highest level of newcomers, at 68 percent, compared to 65 percent for Democrats. In 1992, 62 percent of Democratic delegates said they were attending their first convention, compared to 59 percent of Republican delegates. This relatively high level of party veterans for Republicans could have reflected the fact that this convention featured George H. W. Bush, the incumbent, running for reelection against Bill Clinton, the challenger.

In 1996, 61 percent of Democratic delegates claimed it was their first convention, compared to 65 percent of Republican delegates. Then in the 2000–08 conventions the percent of newcomers compared to veterans was almost the same for both parties, with from 49 to 58 percent claiming to be newcomers and around 40–50 percent claiming to be veterans. Initially, Democrats were more open to the recruitment of new issue and interest group advocates during the era under study, a manifestation of the more porous nature of the national party. In fact, the rules adopted by Democrats during the McGovern-Fraser era were explicitly designed to foster this openness and to encourage greater participation from previously disadvantaged groups.

The data indicate that both Democrats and Republicans have had a fairly high rate of turnover in their national conventions, giving emphasis to the "change" side of the equation. The exceptions to this rule are instructive, since they were all Republican: in 1988, the first George H. W. Bush convention and an open seat; in 1996, when Robert Dole challenged the incumbent, Bill Clinton; in 2000, the George W. Bush inaugural convention and an open seat; and in 2008, the John McCain convention and an open seat. However, partisan differences in all three years were small. In all of these cases there was an open seat for the Republican nomination, and perhaps a new cohort of Republican activists was attracted to a new presidential contender. For Democrats, the rate of newcomers is usually above 50 percent. It is almost equally high in some years for Republicans, depending on which party is in the White House and whether there is an incumbent running. When there is an open seat, or when the party is out of power, the chances of newcomers making it into the coveted delegate slots are somewhat greater. These are the times when there are more opportunities for those who have not been in before to gain access.

The rules for both parties are complex as they intersect with state law and local norms, and they are particularly burdensome for Democrats, since they require gender equity, usually at both the congressional district level and the state level. The rules also require that prospective delegates declare their candidate preferences and that those preferences be public so primary voters and caucus attenders can know which presidential candidate they are supporting with their vote. Democrats also require proportional representation at the congressional district and state levels, where the final selection of delegates takes place.

All of these rules, plus candidate strategies, interact in complicated fashion, making it hard for an individual delegate candidate to ensure a place at the national convention. It is a challenge to negotiate such a regulatory minefield and become a delegate. It is also a challenge for a candidate for office to amass a majority of delegates across fifty states and several territories. It is little wonder then that Democratic conventions tend to be populated by delegates who are first-timers, people attracted to a candidate and determined to go to the conventions and represent that candidate's interests and views. (To be sure, Democratic conventions also have a core of experienced activists who are battle-hardened veterans.)

For Republican conventions, this mixture of veterans and newcomers is also common; however, there are slightly more years when they have a higher quotient of veterans. When they do not, it is because the presidency is an open seat for Republicans, thus inviting a wider selection of newcomers to enter national party politics. This mixture of newcomers and veterans for Republicans provides both elite circulation and elite stability, and it provides for both continuity and change for both parties, but the balance is tipped more toward the continuity side of the equation for Republicans and toward change for Democrats. In a system where the Republicans represent the conservative end of the political spectrum and the Democrats the liberal end, this probably depicts the expected level of circulation of party elites. It is to be expected that Democrats would be more open to nominating a newcomer, or party outsider, and Republicans to choose a candidate who has run before. With the advent of the more activist Tea Party enthusiasts, there was the potential that this could all change for the Republicans in 2012; however, candidates who were better known and had run for president previously (Mitt Romney and Ron Paul) had the decided advantage. Given Republicans' past patterns of behavior, it was not surprising that Mitt Romney—the original party favorite and the candidate who had run previously, in 2008—won the Republican nomination in 2012.

Delegates and Party Work

The specific question we used for party commitment and loyalty was whether the delegate worked for the party "year after year, win or lose, whether or not you like the candidates or issues" or whether the delegate worked for the party "only when there is a particularly worthwhile candidate or issue." This question attempted to get at the well-known dichotomy between amateurs and professionals among party elites (Clark and Wilson, 1961). A similar dichotomy is that between the purists and the politicians, to adopt Aaron

Figure 7-2. *Delegates' Characterization of Party Work, 1988–2008*

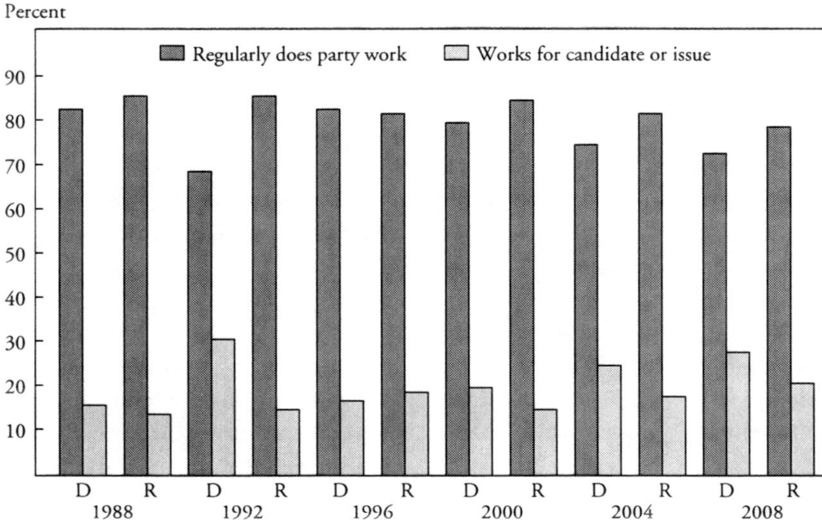

Percent

Source: Author surveys.

Wildavsky's (1965) terminology. As U.S. campaigns have become more candidate centered and more issue oriented, the general theme in much of the literature is that candidate-oriented and issue-oriented political activists may have only tenuous ties to the political party (Kirkpatrick, 1976). Some studies show that the proportion of political amateurs increased and that of political professionals decreased in many reaches of party service during the 1960s and 1970s (Kirkpatrick, 1976). The consequence, projected by critics of reform, was the weakening of political parties during those decades. Since the 1970s this has been a recurring theme in the literature regarding political change in the parties, especially at the elite level.

Figure 7-2 provides longitudinal data for the years between 1988 and 2008. They show that, according to this indicator, the overwhelming majority of delegates from all years for both parties fit the professional model. That is, delegates work for the party year after year, win or lose, whether or not they like the candidates or issues. These are largely people who have a fundamental attachment to the party and who have a long-term commitment to the party's partisan causes. In most cases over 80 percent of the delegates qualify as professionals. The differences between the two parties on this indicator are not sharp, but they are instructive. With one minor exception, Republican delegates claim to be party loyalists at a rate somewhat higher than Democratic delegates. The one exception is in 1996, when the difference is 83 percent professionals for Democrats versus 82 percent for Republicans. This is a minor difference at the most; in fact, that year was essentially a tie. However, 1996 was the year of President Clinton (his reelection campaign for a second term) versus Senator Robert Dole. With a sitting president on the Democratic side and a challenger on the Republican side, it may be understandable that the Democrats would have slightly more professional delegates that year. The opposite situation prevailed in 1992, when only 69 percent of Democratic delegates claimed to regularly do party work, which may be an indicator of new and more amateur delegates attracted by Clinton.

In an era when many new people are going to the conventions every year, and when circulation of elites at the national conventions is fairly high, these results indicate that circulation and elite replacement at the national conventions are still largely among party activists who are committed to their favorite party and to the ideologies and causes for which the two parties have come to stand. These findings have profound implications for the political party system in the modern era in the United States.

Such loyalty and commitment among party activists fueled the growth of the polarized party system of the late twentieth century and the first decade of the twenty-first century. These party loyalists form the core constituencies of the two parties. They are also the foundation for stability and continuity from year to year and election to election. There are delegates who say they only work for the party when there is a particularly worthwhile candidate or issue, and they certainly fit the amateur model. This group ranges from 14 to 31 percent of delegates. They are drawn into the parties for only a short-term stint of political activism. When the issues or candidates change, they may move on to other more satisfying party activities at the state and local base, or they may become more active in interest groups and have an impact on politics through that medium. Given the high costs and the extensive energy required to become a delegate in the first place, it is not surprising that those with weaker commitments do not persist at the national levels. These people provide at least a part of the changing face of party activists, which is evident every four years at the national conventions. The lack of a repeat performance provides an easy source of some of the permeability among activists within the two parties. Their compatriots who have made long-term commitments provide a foundation that sustains continuity.

Figure 7-3. *Where Delegates Do Party Work, 1980–2008*

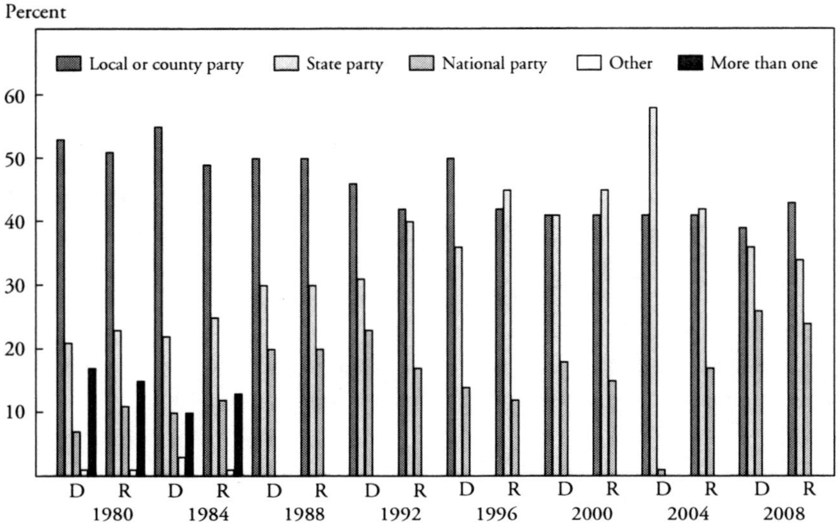

Percent

Source: Author surveys. The "more than one" option was offered only in 1980 and 1984.

Where Delegates Do Party Work

Figure 7-3 continues the inquiry into the delegates' party record and experience. This figure presents the data from responses to the question "If you had to choose one, would you say your current party service is mostly devoted to (a) local or county party activity, (b) state party activities, or (c) national party activities."

The responses are from delegates to the national party conventions who hold the plenary power of the national party in their hands for one week every four years. In that very important sense, they are both the national party elite and the presidential elite. Most of them are at the same time committed to and embedded in state and local party service. It is widely recognized in the academic literature that political parties in the United States historically have been highly decentralized both politically and institutionally. For generations standard textbooks have described the county party as the bedrock of party organization (Sorauf and Beck, 1988, chap. 3). Power is described as decentralized and flowing from the bottom of the organizational pyramid upward at least as forcefully as it flows downhill from the organizational apex of the two national party organizations (Cotter and Hennessy, 1964). This was the prevailing view of party power despite the parties being organized in a hierarchical pyramid.

Over the past two or three decades, parties' literature has changed, as descriptions of party organizations have shifted toward an emphasis on growth of power nearer to the top of the pyramid (Huckshorn and Bibby, 1983; Gibson, Cotter, Bibby, and Huckshorn, 1985; Eldersveld and Walton, 2000). These studies emphasize the increased organizational vigor of the state and national parties. There is no doubt, for example, that big money, political expertise, and staffing patterns have favored state and the national parties over the past two decades (Herrnson, 1988; Pomper, 1980; Maisel, 1994; Sabato and Larson, 2002). This change in the balance of power has worked against local party organizations, and local organizations tend to be the weaker for it.

Our data here reflect these shifts away from the bottom-up pattern. Many delegates are still oriented toward local or county levels of service. County-level loyalists can be thought of as being on temporary duty, on loan, to the national party for the presidential election year exercise. But the line of progression in the data is steadily upward, especially since 2000. That is, more and more of these party activists say that their time is predominantly devoted to state parties and even to national parties. This shift is clearly an important trend and reflects a need to adjust our thinking about the center of gravity in party organizations. Longitudinal indicators show that party activists are increasingly giving their attention and their organizational efforts to state and national party causes. They may not be neglecting their county and local duties, but they are at best divided in their organizational loyalty and focus.

How Delegates Became Active

There is an extensive literature on both political socialization and political recruitment (Easton and Dennis, 1969; Jennings and Niemi, 1968; Jennings and Markus, 1984; Prewitt, 1970). That seminal literature presents the question of how political elites first became interested in politics and how they were recruited to become activists. From 1988 through 2008 the question asked consistently of the delegates was how they first became active in party work. The longitudinal results are displayed in figure 7-4.

The modal category for most years, for elites from both parties, is the attraction of "a particular candidate or public official that I really supported." Note that this finding is not necessarily contradictory to the findings about working for the party year after year regardless of the candidate or issues. It has long been noted that the initial attraction or motivation for any voluntary activity may well be different from the sustaining motivation (Clark and Wilson,

Figure 7-4. *How Delegates Became Active in Party, 1988–2008*

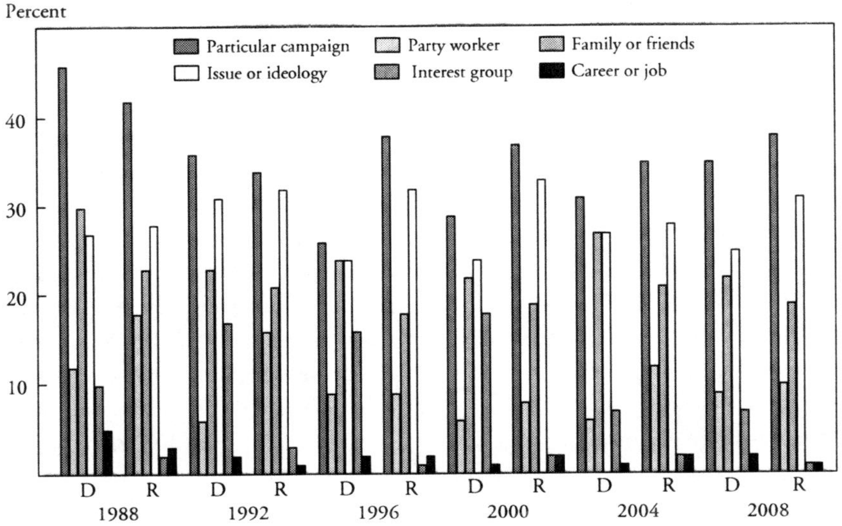

Percent

Source: Author surveys.

1961). Here, we are looking at the initial motivation; earlier we were examining sustaining motivation. The attraction of a particular candidate or public official is a familiar theme in an era of candidate-centered politics, the hallmark of the late twentieth-century electorate. Strong personalities and popular candidates have been successful in attracting activists into their party. Barry Goldwater, for example, recruited a great number of party activists into the Republican Party in the 1960s. Ronald Reagan's candidacies in 1976, 1980, and 1984 galvanized later activists; among these are delegates to the national conventions included in this study. For Democrats, John F. Kennedy was the attraction in the 1960s, at the beginning of the candidate-centered political era, and he helped to define that concept. Bill Clinton served that role in the 1990s. And in the 2008 presidential campaign, both Senator Barack Obama and Senator Hillary Clinton undoubtedly served the same candidate-centered recruitment role. Thus it is widely recognized that many people get involved in politics initially because a particularly charismatic candidate, one who is a strong advocate for their values, is running.

The candidate appeal response is followed closely by the related response "a commitment to an issue, ideology, or cause." Barry Goldwater and Ronald Reagan espoused conservative values. People who enlisted under their banners wore their ideological commitments on their sleeve and took pride in their ideological identification. In the modern era, marked by cultural wars and deep partisan polarization, ideological self-identification has come to be almost as important as party identification. This has been documented in the political science literature for years (see Campbell and others, 1960; Green, Palmquist, and Schickler, 2002; Gelman, 2008). In addition, during this era partisan and ideological cleavages have come to lie along the same fault lines in the American polity, with one reinforcing the other, whereas in an earlier generation partisanship and ideology often were cross-cutting cleavages for many voters. Put more directly, class, race, region, and religion used to cut across the political positions of various large groupings in American society, with the result that people were more likely to have cross pressures and parties were more ideologically diverse and pragmatic. Today, these demographic and socioeconomic cleavages tend to separate the same people the same ways, thus reinforcing and strengthening instead of diluting and moderating each other.

These data point to some of the roots of the red-state/blue-state divide and the cultural wars of the modern era (Fiorina, Abrams, and Pope, 2005; Greenberg, 2004; White, 2003; Gelman, 2008). While opinions in the literature differ over how deep those divisions are at the mass level, there is little doubt that they are quite deep at the elite level. Undoubtedly elite-level polarization drives much of the difference between the two parties (Hetherington, 2001; Carsey and Layman, 2006). Here again we find the roots of contemporary divisions, as elites on both sides were mobilized by their own party's signature ideologies. Put simply, if you are a conservative these days, you seek out the Republican Party; if you are a liberal you seek out the Democratic Party. There are fewer and fewer exceptions to that rule.

Not surprisingly, family and friends are also a great influence on a delegate's choice of party. A fifth to a third of respondents from both parties indicated this most years. The whole structure of political socialization studies at the mass level is built on the premise of the initial influence of the family, followed somewhat later by the influence of peers. It is thus not surprising that those agents are also influential in attracting political elites into party activism. Much less frequently respondents credited interest groups and considerations of career and job as their source of initial entry into party service. While these sources are theoretically viable as recruitment channels, they are also less laudable influences in the American political culture, which eschews both political parties and interest groups as worthy sources of political motivation. These are party elites, yet few of them claim to have been recruited into their activism by other party workers. Certainly, in other nations, particularly the strong party states of Western Europe, recruitment of party activists by other party activists would not be denied or be a source of embarrassment. This response may tell us a lot about the ambivalent status of political parties, which has always been a feature of the American political culture's distrust of political parties (Ranney, 1975). This response may also mean that parties do not explicitly and directly recruit the next generation of party activists.

Delegates and Public Officeholding

Figure 7-5 presents the data from responses to the question as to whether the delegate has ever held public office. Early research by Paul T. David and his associates found a high percentage of public officeholders and party officials among the delegates to the 1952 and 1956 conventions. Indeed, in 1952 almost 500 high-ranking officials and in 1956 over 600 party and public officials were convention delegates (David, Goldman, and Bain, 1964, 240–41). In this pre-reform era Democratic delegates numbered just over 1,100 and Republicans numbered just over 1,000 (Stanley and Niemi, 2006, 74). Party insiders and party bosses tended to dominate the conventions, in both numbers and influence. Conventions were the place for bargaining, a process that could even include the wording of resolutions and party platforms. They could begin not knowing who the presidential nominee would be. Perhaps multiple ballots would be cast, and party leaders would work out a compromise position. Bargaining among the factional and regional leaders of the party could make one candidate the presidential nominee and the remaining candidates also-rans—or, perhaps, the vice presidential nominee. In such a brokered convention, decisions were in the hands of the delegates.

Choosing the presidential candidate is now, after the reforms of the 1970s, the responsibility of primaries and caucuses (Ceaser, 1979; Crotty and Jackson, 1985; Shafer, 1988; Jackson and Crotty, 2001). Jeane Kirkpatrick's study (1976) of the 1972 convention caught the front edge of this wave of change. Her study shows how few public officials were delegates, particularly among Democrats. She blames the reforms and the candidacy of George McGovern for this dearth of party officials, which she believes destroyed the party's chances of winning that November. Of course, the prediction turned out to be true, as McGovern lost in a landslide in 1972. However, Kirkpatrick's assessment of cause is more problematic.

In 1976 Jimmy Carter, a relatively unknown outsider who had served one term as governor of Georgia and before that as a state senator in Georgia, won the Democratic nomination and went on to defeat an incumbent president, Gerald Ford. At the convention, Carter had defeated several better known and

Figure 7-5. *Delegates Who Have Held Public Office, 1980–2008*

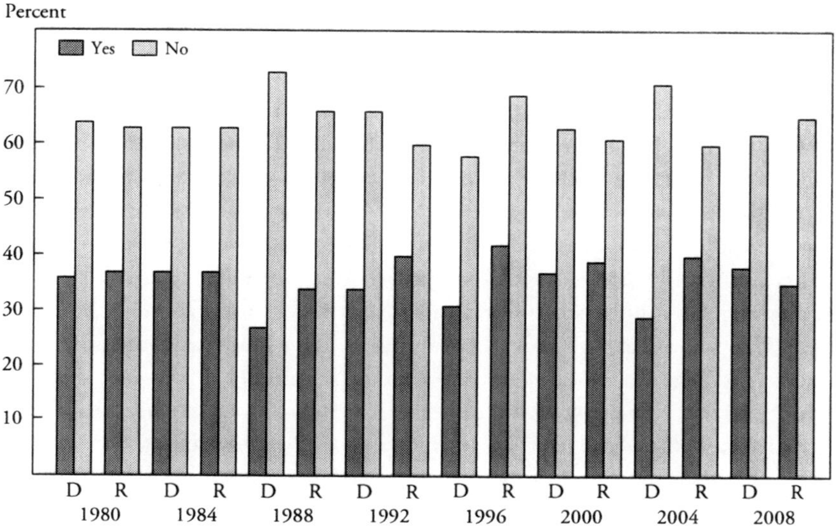

Percent

Source: Author surveys.

more national figures for the Democratic nomination. His improbable victories seemed to many observers to be dependent on his skillful use of the new
rules of the game, particularly the McGovern-Fraser Commission reforms.
Some veteran Democratic Party leaders were skeptical of rules that opened up
the party to newcomers like McGovern and Carter. Following Kirkpatrick's
reasoning, critics thought that these new rules hampered Democrats' com-
petitiveness in the general election. In addition, practical politicians and some
scholars, most notably Nelson Polsby (1983), argued that Carter's nomination
campaign, where he emphasized his outsider status and his independence
from the party, actually made him a weaker and less effective president. So
the question of how many elected officials attend the conventions, the scope
of their role there, and their later relationship with the president has been a
central one for a long time.

William Crotty studied the numbers of elected officials participating in
the national conventions between 1956 and 1968 and compared them to
the postreform conventions of 1972–76. He finds that the numbers and
percentages of governors, senators, and House members in the postreform
era declined precipitously in both 1972 and 1976, undoubtedly reflecting
the new rules discouraging ex officio delegates (quoted in DiClerico and

Uslander, 1984, 30–31). The Democratic leadership persevered in this ban for two more election cycles in spite of this criticism and all the dire predictions (Crotty, 1982, 68).

In preparation for the 1980 convention, Democrats appointed a new reform commission, the Winograd Commission, which made recommendations for adjustments that they hoped would make Democrats more competitive. The commission allowed up to 10 percent of delegates to be high-level public officials and party officials. However, these officials, too, had to declare their presidential preferences early and had to reflect the proportional representation distribution. This change proved to be ineffectual in substantially increasing the numbers of public and party officials for 1980. So the Democrats appointed a new reform commission. The Hunt Commission instituted the idea of superdelegates, or a set-aside number of delegate slots, up to 20 percent, to be guaranteed to high-level public and party officials. (They are officially known as *party leader* and *elected official* positions, but they are mostly known by the more popular term *superdelegates*.) After 1984, superdelegates tend to range from 15 to 18 percent of total delegate slots. Many observers thought this plan an attempt by the Hunt Commission and the Democratic National Committee to reinvigorate the role of top party leaders in the choice of the party's presidential nominees (Kamarck, 2009, 155–57).

This plan was designed to eliminate the need for a governor, a senator or representative, or even a member of the Democratic National Committee to run in the delegate selection phase of the primaries or to fight through several stages of caucuses, county conventions, and state conventions, the selection route for ordinary delegates. One of the motivations was that some believed that superdelegates would tend to favor the front-runners and that they could best choose the most competitive candidate. Democrats hoped that exempting superdelegates from the normal rounds of competition at the primary and caucus level would ensure that they would be inclined to support the party ticket in November. Extending the logic even further, Democrats also wanted to have the public officials, and certainly members of Congress, invested in the party's ticket and platform, and if they won the presidency, perhaps it would make cooperation on public policy positions more likely across the executive and legislative branches. It was an attempt to bridge some of the gaps endemic to the separation-of-powers system.

All these possibilities were embedded in the Democratic Party's rules for selection of national convention delegates, but they went mostly unnoticed in the contests that followed, until 2008, when the Obama versus Clinton race ran on and on in the spring of that year. At first the superdelegates who announced public positions favored Clinton, since she was the early frontrunner. Then slowly, as Obama won more and more primaries and caucuses, the tide turned and the superdelegates came to favor Obama. In late May they helped to put him over the top. In 2012 there were also predictions that the support of a Republican version of superdelegates would be required to finally put Mitt Romney over the top, and although they helped him, superdelegates did not prove to be pivotal for Romney.

Figure 7-5 shows that Republicans had a higher percentage of public officials at the conventions than did Democrats in all cases except 1984 and 2008. Republicans do not have superdelegates in the way Democrats do, but they do provide for some of their high-level public and party officials to hold at-large designation. At least since the beginning of the reform era in 1970, Republican conventions have been dominated by the party establishment—those who hold and wield public and party power. Perhaps that is one of the reasons that Republicans typically nominate the recognized establishment candidate.

Republican delegations are selected largely unencumbered by the complex national party rules that control and guide the Democratic Party's selection of national convention delegations. The result is that state and local rules and procedures and informal practices usually prevail, and state and local Republican officials still retain more prerogatives and can guarantee themselves access much more readily than Democratic officials can. This is another indicator that becoming a delegate to the Republican Party's national convention is somewhat of a game for party and political insiders, and delegate status is related to other sources of political power.

Delegates and Election Reform

It is often said that incumbents in public office are satisfied with the status quo and in particular with the electoral system in which they were selected, since that system and its rules worked well for them. They played the game successfully under the prevailing rules and have no interest in changing them. This argument seems to have some prima facie legitimacy, as many elite actors seem committed to the status quo. Nevertheless, in party politics in the last quarter of the twentieth century, that was not always the prevailing sentiment among party elites.

As we have seen, Democrats in the 1968–84 era established reforms that revolutionized the way the nation selects presidential candidates. Several of those reforms undermined the powerful and privileged place that prior elites held in the inner councils of the party, and the reform movement generally enhanced the potential for greater circulation by party elites. Republicans have not been as revolutionary on the procedural front, as befits the more conservative party, but they have been impacted very substantially by Democrats' changing the rules of the nominations game. In addition, Republicans have initiated their own procedural changes on occasion, usually under the leadership of the Republican National Committee, and they have had a vigorous internal party debate over ways the Republican Party may need to change in order to continue to be competitive.

For example, there has been a long-running internal party debate over how to broaden and diversify the appeal of the Republican Party. Often this debate has been centered on how to appeal to new groups, particularly minorities like African Americans and Hispanics. The naming of Senator Mel Martinez of Florida to chair the Republican National Committee during the last years of the Bush administration was such an attempt. The naming of the former lieutenant governor of Maryland, Michael Steele, to be the RNC chair early in 2009 was made on the premise that he would appeal to the African American community, and he promised to diversify the party as a part of his own platform. The fact that Steele then encountered many difficulties and engendered much subsequent political controversy within the party, and only lasted one term, indicates how difficult it is to change the party's image, much less its internal power distribution, via high-profile personnel appointments like chair of the RNC.

So in general, while Republicans have not been as aggressive about procedural changes in their rules as the Democrats have, they have been aggressive in surveying the political environment and considering ways they may need to change in order to continue to be competitive, especially in the nomination and election of their presidential candidates. In this study we explore this issue across time by analyzing the answers of respondents from both parties to the question of whether delegates would support specific changes in the presidential nominating process or whether they advocated the status quo. It is quite evident from the results that a significant group of delegates from both parties were willing to contemplate a significant change in the way their presidential nominees are selected (figure 7-6).

The preference for "No change" attracted 34 percent of Republican delegates in 1992 and 30 percent in 2004. Notably, both were years when the Republicans had an incumbent, George H. W. Bush and George W. Bush, running for reelection, so in these instances political circumstances may have enhanced the delegates' feelings of satisfaction with the status quo. Otherwise there was some support in both parties for a national primary. The range was from 14 percent to 26 percent for the period between 1992 and 2008. Support for a national primary was greater in 1980 and 1984; however, the

Figure 7-6. *Delegate Preference for Primary Election Reform, 1980–2008*[a]

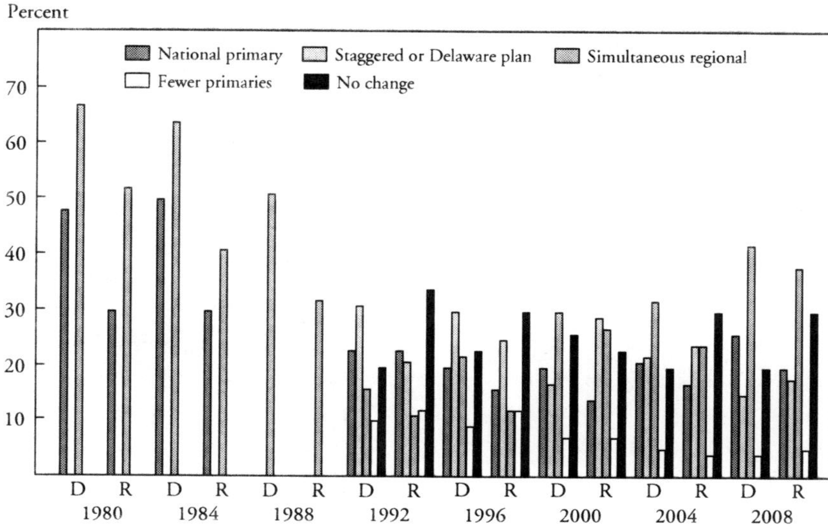

Percent

Source: Author surveys.

a. The options offered changed somewhat between 1988 and 1992, producing a notable shift in responses between those two years.

options we offered those years were more limited, and this result may be somewhat an artifact of the way the questions were worded and the fact that we allowed the delegates to support multiple options. The support for a national primary was somewhat stronger among Democrats than among Republicans during this entire era, no matter how the question was phrased.

Preference for primary election reform is one subject on which party elites are clearly out of step with the national electorate. Public opinion polls show that a national primary is consistently supported by a majority of the American people. Primaries have become an intrinsic part of the American political culture, and their use and popularity have grown since the Progressive Party advocated for them at the turn of the twentieth century. State primaries now dominate the presidential nominations process and ordinarily determine rather quickly who the nominee of both parties will be (although for Democrats 2008 was something of an anomaly on that score). To most Americans the evolution of the presidential nominations system into a national primary is widely supported, whether or not they understand all its ramifications and complications. Party elites in both parties, perhaps not surprisingly, are much more cautious about this procedural change.

Elites of both parties are much more willing to consider some form of regional primary, as figure 7-6 indicates. Unfortunately, since the popular labels and the political discourse changed, we did not always adopt exactly the same labels for the various regional primary options across all of these years, so the longitudinal data are incompatible for the era before 1988 and after 1992. A limitation of doing longitudinal research is that the terms of the debate are always evolving. But overlooking these qualifications, it still appears that a healthy percent of delegates support some form of regional primaries. A small minority, generally under 10 percent, also endorses some steps (unspecified) to reduce the overall number of primaries. One can presume that this option may have evoked an image of greater use of caucuses in preference to primaries, which would have been sensible for these party insiders. This option could also be an indicator of support for regional primaries, since most regional plans would reduce the number of days on which primaries would be held to three or four, spread across the spring calendar.

Conclusion

Taken as a whole, these longitudinal results certainly indicate that the party activists who are selected to the national conventions largely consist of people who have an open mind about the procedural requirements of the nominations process. This is not a picture of clear and overwhelming support for the status quo among those who have benefitted most from the prevailing system. This openness to the consideration of alternatives is true of the elites of both parties during the turbulent era of the late twentieth and early twenty-first centuries in American party politics. A theme of this book is that openness, flexibility, and strategic opportunism are the key reasons that the two major parties, which are now well over 150 years old in their current identity, have persisted for so long. They have warded off third-party challenges and responded to the changing political environment with enough innovation and political entrepreneurship to continue the dominance of the two-party system.

Debate over procedures and over future direction will likely continue in both parties in the next decades of the twenty-first century. Both parties set up rules commissions to study the selection process for 2012, pointing to the accuracy of that prediction. Not much is ever finally settled, and few debates are even finally over in American politics. There were many critics of the 2008 presidential nominations process, and there was much to criticize. A year like 2008—which saw the longest, the most frontloaded, the most expensive season; the most unsettled rules; and the most contentious debate over national versus state party prerogative (as in the case of Florida and Michigan's primary dates)—was likely to lead to quests for ways to address these issues. Many of those same issues and conflicts resurfaced in 2012 and will have an impact again on 2016. The results for the Iowa caucuses were in contention for two weeks in 2012, and there was much conflict over the accuracy of the vote count (Barabak, 2014). The results for the Maine caucuses were even more problematic, and the winner was disputed. Both events show the problems in letting state parties conduct caucuses, under widely varying rules and sometimes sketchy provisions for quality control over the count. These two state problems led the Republicans to consider modifications in their rules controlling the early contests for 2016.

Party elites will continue to try to settle the procedural and substantive issues in such a way as to maximize the advantage to their party in the electoral competition. In so doing, they also maximize the ability of the two-party system to continue its dominance in the American electoral system. They also define the two parties by their values and their actions. In a related vein, Nolan McCarty, Keith Poole, and Howard Rosenthal, in their book *Polarized America* (2006, 192), make the same point: "First, if there is sufficient uncertainty about voter preferences, the distinct ideological preferences of politicians and the activist bases of each party will produce divergence in platforms. In such situations, rational parties make tradeoffs between satisfying ideological preferences and choosing more moderate policies in order to win elections. Consequently, the position of each party will partially reflect the views of its activist base."

That is why it is important to document the views and values of the activist base. In addition, the dilemma of which values prevail, the ideological values or pragmatic priorities, constantly faces these party leaders. The maximizing of one will often conflict with the other, and how to do that balancing act and under what circumstances to compromise is a constant question that party activists face. The record of the past four decades is that the elites of both parties have managed that balancing act reasonably adeptly, and both have reason to be pleased with their record. A sort of strategic opportunism has been the hallmark of both parties. In individual years, however, and in the nomination of particular candidates, they have failed and have suffered the electoral consequences.

Internal struggles and conflict over which objectives and values to maximize continue to divide and animate the activist class of both parties. This brings us to the factions and coalitions that mark the internal struggles and drive the group dynamics of each party. While each party is dedicated to the cause of winning power and opposing the agenda of the opposite party, each party is also on occasion deeply divided by internal factions, and party coalitions must be built to get anything done. This is the subject we consider in the next chapter.

8

The Candidate and Party Factions

I t has been recognized at least since Jeane Kirkpatrick's study (1976) of the 1972 conventions that candidates and their staffs play an increasingly important role in the organizing and conduct of the national conventions and especially in attracting state and local party activists to their banner as convention delegates. Indeed, one could go all the way back to 1960 and John F. Kennedy's very personal campaign organization and appeal to the party activists of that day to see the roots of this phenomenon in modern presidential politics (White, 1962). A primary, of course, is essentially candidate centered rather than party centered. It is also increasingly issue oriented and faction driven.

Sometimes the party's leaders will get involved in the primary in support of their favored candidate and the one they think will run best in November. Occasionally this strategy works; sometimes it fails. After a bruising primary battle, no matter who wins it, the party has to pull itself together and try to put on the best campaign possible for the November election. This was the challenge faced by Democrats in June 2008, when Barack Obama finally prevailed over Hillary Clinton in their epic primary fight of that year. Mitt Romney, in 2012, faced a similar challenge: to win over the supporters of his former rivals. Factional fights had to end, and the party coalition had to be reassembled.

After the primary is over, the campaign becomes largely a contest between the two major parties and their standard-bearers. Party organizations and the images that voters have of them become very important in the general election. There is much evidence that the choices in the general election are seen through a partisan prism, even though certainly the candidates and their images also remain crucial to the parties' prospects in the fall (Pomper and Weiner, 2002, 185–200). The ultimate voter choice thus comes down to a combination of partisanship, candidate image, and the issues, and this has been the case since the 1952 election (Campbell and others, 1960). What has changed, at the margins at least, is the relative importance of these three explanatory factors.

Candidate-centered campaigning was perfected by John Kennedy and expanded by Ronald Reagan, and now the political science literature is replete with descriptions of the candidate-centered politics of the modern political era (Wattenberg, 1991). As with most campaign politics, presidential campaigns led the way. Especially during the primary and caucus season, candidates' personal organizations raise money, hire consultants and staff, and develop campaign themes and positions. One of the candidate organization's major obligations is to, early on, recruit the most popular party activists as committed delegates for their candidate. A putative candidate who does not take these early steps may, ultimately, not enter the fray. For example, in 2011 the lack of organizational and fund-raising activity for Sarah Palin and Mike Huckabee seemed to indicate that both would ultimately decide against making the race for the 2012 Republican nomination, which they did.

One of the early markers of how seriously a presidential campaign will be taken by those in the media and by knowledgeable observers is the list of delegates who have filed as pledged to that candidate in the states and congressional districts. Those aspiring delegates with well-recognized names are also those most likely to be recruited by campaigns early in the primary contests. It is very much a two-way street between the interests of presidential candidates and their supporters. It is a game that rewards strategic planning, and the rational presidential campaign will devote great care and resources to those early decisions, which are imperative for a successful national campaign. Just understanding the vagaries of the primary calendar alone is a significant challenge, and the candidate who hires a staff that knows the calendar's demands, and how to prepare for those demands, is better prepared for the primary wars. For example, in 2008 it was widely believed that the Hillary Clinton campaign totally counted on a big win in the primaries held on February 5, or Super Tuesday. When Clinton instead got a split decision that day and had to share the media spotlight with Obama, the Clinton staff was unprepared to take her campaign to the next stage of the nominations process (Kamarck, 2009, 43–47).

On the Republican side in 2012, former senator Rick Santorum was hampered in his competition with Mitt Romney by his campaign's failure to file delegate slates in key states like Virginia and Illinois, and his early lack of resources hurt his later momentum. This ability to make strategic long-range plans, and then to execute them no matter what exigencies arise, is the mark of a truly professional, and likely successful, presidential campaign. One of the requirements for such a strategic plan is to be able to envision the geographic, interest group, and demographic dynamics that drive modern American voting behavior at the mass level. In short, one must ask if the candidate is predominantly identified with one of the ideological wings of the party or identified with the more moderate faction. Is the candidate identified with party insiders, or is he or she predominantly considered an outsider, or long-shot, candidate? Is the candidate associated with a narrow faction or locked into a particular region, or does he or she have the potential for a national following? Is the candidate mostly known for advocacy of a single issue, or does he or she have broad-based appeal? Does the candidate appear to have the image, the record, and the gravitas to be a serious contender? This chapter considers these candidate-based components of the presidential campaigns of 1976, 1980, 1984, 1988, 2004, and 2008.

Presidential Campaign, 1976

In 1976 Jimmy Carter faced a variety of better-known candidates, most of them fixtures in Washington. The initial field included Senator Henry Jackson from Washington State, Representative Morris Udall of Arizona, Senator Frank Church of Idaho, Governor Jerry Brown of California, and Governor George Wallace of Georgia. Hubert Humphrey publicly toyed with making the race again, but he ultimately decided against it because of concerns about his health (Witcover, 1977, 316). Carter and Jackson were considered the moderate candidates, and Wallace was certainly the conservative. This left Udall, Church, and Brown as the liberals. From the perspective of recent politics, after the two parties have been so dramatically sorted across the ideological spectrum, it would seem that the Democratic nominee would most likely be a liberal (Levendusky, 2009). However, back in 1976 there were lots of moderates and conservatives still active in the Democratic Party, just as there were liberals and moderates in the Republican Party. The sorting process had begun by then, but it certainly was not complete. The question we used to get at the delegates' initial preferences for the nomination was, "Regardless of your

Figure 8-1. *Delegate Support for 1976 Democratic Candidates, by Ideology*

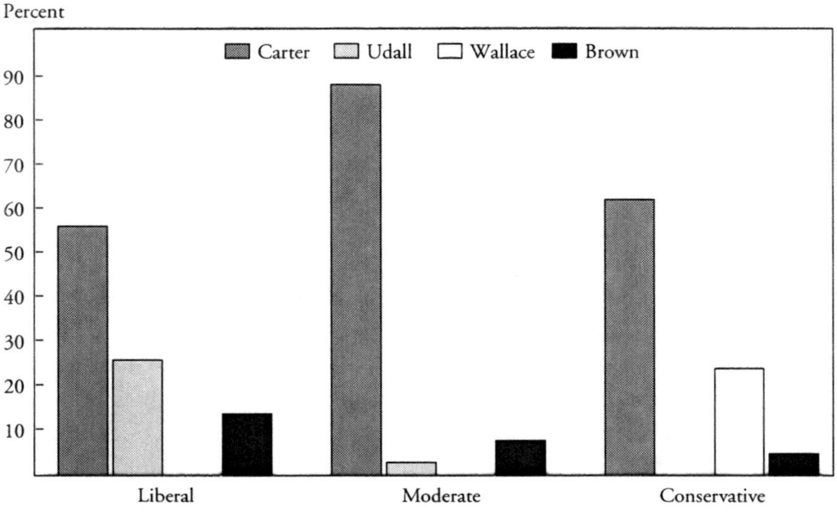

Percent

Source: Author surveys.

official position at the time of your selection, *which candidate did you personally favor* for the nomination?" We then cross-tabulated this question with an ideological self-identification question. Figure 8-1 gives the results.

It is evident from this figure that Carter enjoyed a good strategic position, from the ideological perspective. That is, he had significant support from all ideological components. Clearly, Carter was not the overwhelming favorite among liberals; however, his support among that crucial group was solid. Otherwise, he probably could not have prevailed in the nominations struggle, given the pivotal role of liberals in Democratic national conventions. Among moderates, Carter was the prohibitive favorite, at 88 percent. Not surprisingly, George Wallace did his best among the very small group of Democratic delegates who considered themselves conservative. However, even here, Jimmy Carter came in first.

Carter thus was able to demonstrate significant strength across the ideological gamut in 1976, and this broad appeal was undoubtedly a key to his success in gaining the nomination. This appeal also contributed to his victory over Gerald Ford in the general election. By 1976 the conservative end of the spectrum was fading in numbers and influence among Democratic Party elites. That was the last year in which they had any significant presence at the Democratic national convention. They were like their Republican counterparts on

Figure 8-2. *Delegate Support for 1980 Democratic Candidates, by Ideology*

Percent

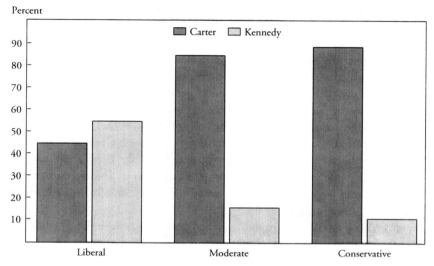

Source: Author surveys.

the liberal end of the continuum, who were rapidly fading from influence in the Republican Party. Both parties were well on their way to being sorted according to ideology, which took place at an accelerating pace during the 1980s (Levendusky, 2009). The nomination contests of 1980 and the presidential election of that year contributed significantly to the advancement of that sorting process (Hetherington and Weiler, 2009; Levendusky, 2009).

Presidential Campaign, 1980

From the recent record it is evident that when there is a real intraparty nomination contest of the variety experienced by both parties in 2008, delegates' support of candidates is affected by demographics, ethnicity, race, and party faction. Rarely, if ever, is a random choice made. Ideological, issue, and commitment factors are involved in the choices made by these groups as to the candidates they support in the nominations season. In addition, a division of the delegates according to which candidate they initially supported for president is a good way to map the component parts of a coalition. Figure 8-2 provides such a map for the Democrats in 1980.

While most of the criticism of Carter during his 1977–80 term came from Republicans and conservatives, criticism of Carter was also common among

Democrats, especially those from the more liberal wing of the party. During his term in the White House, Carter generally tried to govern from the center of the political spectrum, and in so doing, he frequently angered or disappointed some liberal components of the Democratic Party, especially the more liberal Democratic members of Congress. (Modern parallels with President Obama's problems in dealing with Congress in his first term, while also trying to keep the liberal base of the party mollified, are striking.) In light of that history, we start this exploration with the hypothesis that Jimmy Carter would be more widely supported by moderate and conservative Democratic activists and Senator Ted Kennedy of Massachusetts would be supported disproportionately by liberal activists, since he was a leader of the liberals in Congress and had been widely expected to run for president ever since the assassinations of his brothers, President John F. Kennedy in 1963 and Attorney General Robert F. Kennedy in 1968.

Although there is some support for that hypothesis, the support is mostly limited to Democratic delegates at the most extreme end of the continuum—that is, those who term themselves left liberal to radical (these data are not shown in figure 8-1).[1] That group was marked as 90 percent supporting Kennedy and only 10 percent supporting Carter. The division within the merely liberal group was much closer, with 49 percent supporting Carter and 51 percent supporting Kennedy. If we collapse the two liberal categories together, as in figure 8-2, the liberals break 55 to 45 percent in favor of Kennedy. This ideological division is even more evident among moderate delegates, 85 percent of whom supported Carter, with 16 percent supporting Kennedy.

If it had been a purely liberal convention in 1980, or even one with fewer moderates, Carter may not have prevailed in his long-running contest with Ted Kennedy. There were not many conservatives remaining among the Democratic Party's activists in 1980; however, 89 percent of the conservative delegates supported Carter, while only 11 percent backed Kennedy. This was probably the last time a sizable group of conservative activists played any significant role in choosing the Democratic Party's nominee. Overall, it is clear that ideology did play a role in the Kennedy challenge to Carter in 1980, but Carter's strength not only among liberals but also, and especially, among moderates was key to his victory over Kennedy.

1. We used the terms *left liberal to radical* and *conservative or right wing* for the extreme options in the first surveys. We changed in 1984 to the more standard American National Election Studies terms, *very liberal* and *very conservative*.

Figure 8-3. *Delegate Support for 1980 Republican Candidates, by Ideology*

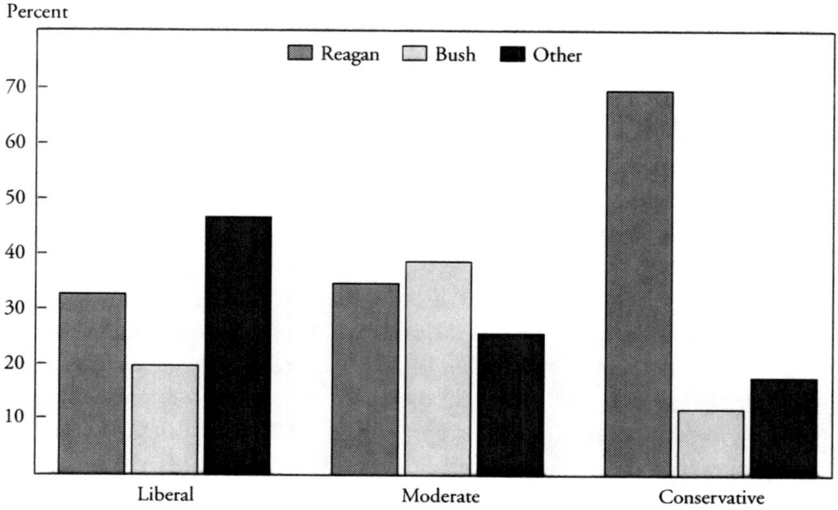

Percent

Source: Author surveys.

Figure 8-3 examines the ideological fault line within the Republican Party made evident by the 1980 nominations battle. This race featured Ronald Reagan making his third run for the presidency. George H. W. Bush was his most prominent opponent. This convention showed a significant ideological dimension to the support given to the candidates, with a clear correlation between ideology and candidate choice. Fully 70 percent of the conservative delegates supported Reagan, leaving only 12 percent who supported George H. W. Bush and 18 percent who supported other Republican candidates. The ideological differences in candidate support were even greater among that relatively small group who called themselves right-wing Republicans in our survey. Of that group 78 percent supported Reagan, the remaining 22 percent supported other Republican candidates, and none supported Bush (data not shown). It was reported at the time that the conservatives did not consider Bush to be one of their own and did not trust him to be sufficiently dedicated to the causes they cared about. Indeed, Bush's reputation placed him in the more moderate and business-friendly confines of the Republican Party, as befitted his Connecticut roots in the eastern establishment wing of Republicanism.

As figure 8-3 indicates, Bush was the initial favorite of 39 percent of moderates, and Reagan had the support of 35 percent of that category. Only the very small group of liberal delegates provided an exception to expectations, with 33 percent supporting Reagan and only 20 percent supporting Bush; however, almost half (47 percent) supported other Republican candidates (probably Representative John Anderson). The self-identified ideological positions of the moderate and conservative delegates in 1980 certainly support those popular perceptions of where the candidates were arrayed on the political spectrum by those who made the nomination. Bush simply did not do very well among conservatives, and by then conservatives of one stripe or another were controlling the Republican Party. That lack of support proved to be an insurmountable obstacle for Bush in 1980.

To the extent that these delegates also represented the grass roots of the political parties at the state and local levels, these data document the fact that Reagan and Bush came from two different wings of the Republican Party. In offering the vice presidency to Bush, Reagan also engaged in the widely recognized practice of ticket balancing, in this case, seeking ideological balance. By reaching out to the more moderate elements of the Republican Party, Reagan was helping to make his ticket more competitive for the general election. This tradition of ticket balancing is still practiced and may include geography, age, and job experience. Age, experience, and geography are undoubtedly three of the characteristics that recommended Senator Joe Biden to Barack Obama in 2008. Age, experience in Washington, and budgetary issue positions all seem to be relevant factors in the selection of Representative Paul Ryan by Mitt Romney in 2012. Ideology was clearly important in composing the Republican ticket in 1980, and it succeeded in helping Reagan to transcend the ideological fault lines in the party.

Presidential Campaign, 1984

Ideological divisions among the 1984 Democratic delegates are evident in figure 8-4. Walter Mondale, the eventual nominee, was a traditional liberal. His background was in the progressive Democratic-Farmer-Labor Party of Minnesota, and his mentor and closest political ally was another traditional liberal, Hubert Humphrey. Mondale was backed by a combination of forces from the old New Deal coalition of the Roosevelt era, especially labor unions and civil rights groups, for which he had been a strong advocate both during his time in the Senate and in the Carter White House. At the same time, he had stiff competition, particularly from Jesse Jackson, for the vote of the most prominent civil rights advocates.

As expected, Mondale did well among those who called themselves liberals, winning their vote by a margin of 48 percent to 39 percent for Senator

Figure 8-4. *Delegate Support for 1984 Democratic Candidates, by Ideology*

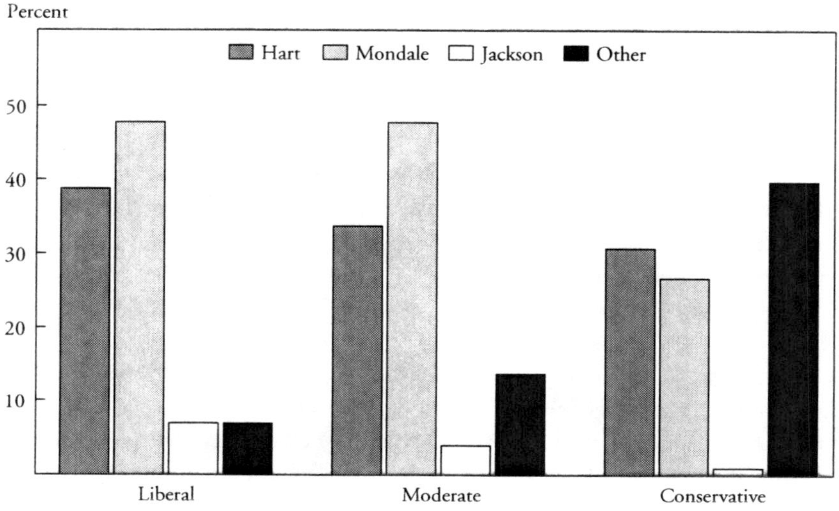

Percent

Source: Author surveys.

Gary Hart from Colorado and 7 percent for Jackson (when the two labels of liberal and very liberal are combined). Mondale was also the favorite among a plurality (48 percent) of moderates. Only among conservatives did Hart beat Mondale and then by only a narrow margin. Liberals should have been Jackson's best supporters, and while they did provide the bulk of his support, he was effectively challenged by Hart and Mondale for the support of the liberal groups that were the base of party activists by 1984. It is notable that 40 percent of the conservative group favored some other Democrat that year; however, their ranks were too thin to make much difference.

The key to Mondale's victory on the ideological front was his strong support among moderates, who numbered half of the delegates at the Democratic convention in 1984. They gave Mondale 48 percent of their vote. The prevailing idea at the time was that Hart was running to the right of Mondale and was more popular with moderate voters in the primaries and with the more moderate delegates. Our research here indicates that, on the contrary, Mondale showed more strength with both moderates and liberals, and his strength across all the ideological categories was probably key to his victory in the convention. In that sense, Mondale's nomination in 1984 was comparable to Carter's nomination in 1976 in that both showed significant strength across the ideological factions comprising the Democratic Party at that time.

There was no effective challenge to Reagan's nomination in 1984, so we do not report on that contest.

Presidential Campaign, 1988

As discussed earlier, 1988 was an open-seat contest. Ronald Reagan was retiring after two terms, and his vice president, George H. W. Bush, wanted to take his place. Bush was challenged by a variety of other Republicans seeking the nomination. These included Senator Robert Dole from Kansas, former Delaware governor Pierre DuPont, General Al Haig, who had served in the Reagan administration as secretary of state, and the television evangelist Marion G. "Pat" Robertson.

The fight for the Democratic nomination opened with no dominant front-runner, although Michael Dukakis, the governor of Massachusetts, had the most money and the most support. Dukakis was challenged by Representative Richard Gephardt of Missouri, then the majority leader; Al Gore, a moderate senator from Tennessee; Paul Simon, a respected liberal senator from Illinois; Gary Hart, making his second run; Jesse Jackson, a veteran civil rights leader, also making his second run; and Bruce Babbitt, former governor of Arizona and a liberal environmentalist. Dukakis and Bush ultimately prevailed, becoming the nominees of their parties, but not before a series of spirited contests in the primaries and caucuses. Figures 8-5 and 8-6 show who the delegates initially supported, cross-tabbed with ideology.

As figure 8-5 shows, Dukakis received 47 percent of liberal delegates' initial preferences. Jackson received 16 percent of liberal support, second to Dukakis. Jackson was widely perceived to be the most liberal candidate in the field that year, and this view is supported by the results from the "very liberal" group of delegates. Jackson received 50 percent of that group's support, initially exactly matching the Dukakis results (data not shown). More important, Dukakis did better among moderates than any other Democratic candidate, receiving 43 percent of their early support. Dukakis also received initial support from 32 percent of delegates who called themselves conservatives. The rest of the candidates received only scattered support in any of the ideological categories. Dukakis was simply dominant in the crucial liberal and moderate categories. Dukakis's candidacy in 1988 looked very much like Mondale's in 1984 in that both candidates showed considerable initial strength among the ideologies that control the party's nomination, that is, the very liberal to the moderate categories, which is where most of the Democratic delegates reside.

Figure 8-5. *Delegate Support for 1988 Democratic Candidates, by Ideology*

Percent

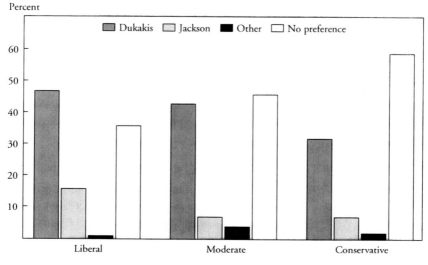

Source: Author surveys.

Figure 8-6. *Delegate Support for 1988 Republican Candidates, by Ideology*

Percent

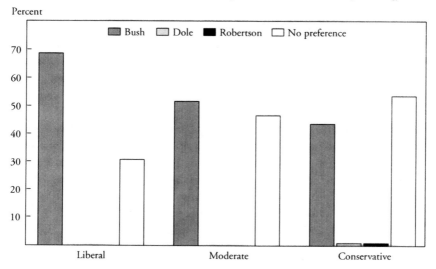

Source: Author surveys.

For both Dukakis and Mondale, their support was distributed evenly ideologically, rather than being concentrated in one wing of the party. This is a basic precept that strategic planners of a presidential campaign would do well to emulate. The same may be said for George H. W. Bush in his 1988 quest for the Republican nomination. Initially, he was opposed by candidates who claimed to be conservatives of some stripe. Each of Bush's challengers suggested that Bush was insufficiently conservative in his heart and that he had been a late convert to the Reagan cause since Bush had initially challenged Reagan vigorously for the nomination in 1980. By 1988, however, Bush had been a constant cheerleader for Reagan as his vice president for eight years. The data in the figure indicate that Bush won over at least a number of his critics on the right, receiving early support from 44 percent of conservative delegates. However, 54 percent initially supported someone else or failed to answer the question. These results from the all-important conservative side of the spectrum in 1988 may indicate some of the reason the Republican ticket featured Robert Dole and Kemp in 1996. We did not ask the question of initial support in comparable form in 1992 through 2000.

Presidential Campaign, 2004

We turn here to an analysis of the results for 2004 on the Democrats' side and the spirited fight they waged that year for the opportunity to challenge George W. Bush. The question used in 2004 and 2008 was worded slightly differently: "What candidate did you originally prefer in the presidential race?" While the wording is somewhat different, we think the intent of the question is the same and the results comparable to those obtained in the earlier years.

Since George W. Bush had no effective challenge in the Republican nominations season, the question seemed moot, and we do not report the Republican results for 2004. The Democrats, by contrast, were deeply divided over who their nominee would be, as there was no prohibitive favorite. The leading candidates included Senator John Kerry, Senator John Edwards, Howard Dean, former governor of Vermont, and General Wesley Clark, former NATO commander in Europe. Dean was the initial front-runner and led most of the polls in late fall of 2003. However, his candidacy faltered in January and February of 2004, and he was replaced as front-runner by Kerry, who cinched the nomination early.

It is difficult to ideologically characterize the candidates for the Democratic nomination in 2004, because they were fundamentally all liberals with the possible exception of Clark, who ran as a moderate as befits a former military

Figure 8-7. *Delegate Support for 2004 Democratic Candidates, by Ideology*

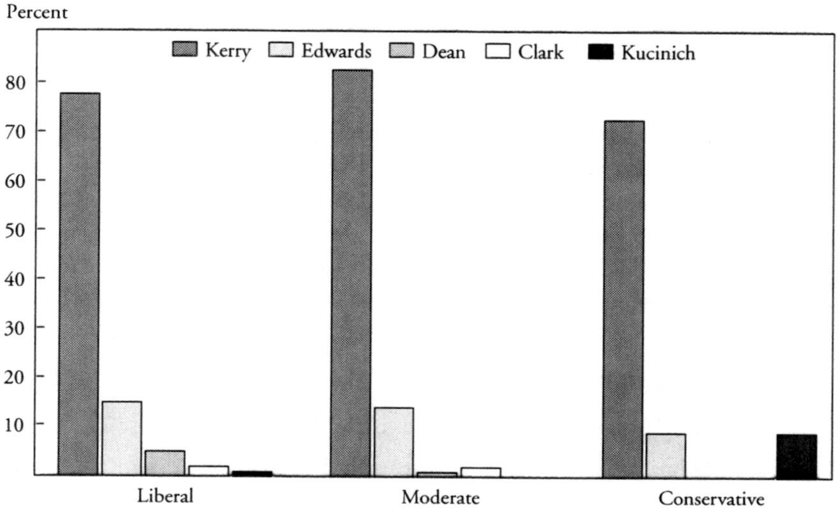

Percent

Source: Author surveys.

man. Dean became the darling of the newly emerging Internet faction of the Democratic activist base as well as of those deeply opposed to the war in Iraq. He garnered the most excitement from those who would have considered themselves the party's outsiders and those who would likely have been the most progressive or liberal components of the activist base of the party. For these reasons we simply adopted the null hypothesis that there would likely be very few significant differences between the ideological commitments of the various delegates supporting the 2004 Democratic candidates. Figure 8-7 gives these results.

The story of 2004 for the Democrats is Kerry's strength among all the ideological factions. He dominated the liberal category, claiming more than three-fourths (78 percent) of their support. His position was even more dominant in the moderate category, with 83 percent of their support. There were not many conservatives at the Boston convention of 2004, but Kerry got almost three-fourths of their initial support as well. The reader should keep in mind that this questionnaire was distributed the week after the national convention was held, so there may be some halo effect for the winner here, but we asked the delegates for the candidate they had initially supported personally, not who they voted for in the end, and a number of them responded with a name other than Kerry.

These results indicate that some enthusiasts for unsuccessful candidates fail to switch sides to support the final nominee and thus are not ultimately selected to be national convention delegates. However, the support that John Kerry ultimately received among Democratic Party delegates in 2004 is impressive indeed. The Democrats may have lost in 2004, but it was a close race in the fall, and part of the success that Kerry achieved may be attributed to his overwhelming support from party activists, no matter what their ideological predispositions were. The Democratic base largely united in 2004 in their effort to oust Bush, which was one of the keys to their making it a very close race in the fall. They fell short, but the closeness of the race made the party's activist base even more determined to defeat the Republicans in 2008.

Presidential Campaign, 2008

Twenty-eight years after the epic battle between Jimmy Carter and Edward Kennedy, the Democrats had another divisive fight over who their nominee would be for the presidency. The 2008 nomination contests were equally contentious and internally divisive, at least up through the convention; however, the 2008 contest turned out dramatically different. The fight in 1980 exposed the deep factional divisions within the Democratic coalition. Those wounds were not entirely healed by the November election, contributing to Jimmy Carter's defeat by Ronald Reagan in the general election. Democratic defections to Reagan far exceeded the Republican crossover voters for Carter in 1980. By contrast, although the Clinton versus Obama contest was also hard fought, and there were bitter feelings on both sides, the divisions were partially healed by the national convention, and by November Clinton supporters were mostly committed to a victory by Obama. In fact, 89 percent of all Democratic identifiers supported Obama and 90 percent of all Republican identifiers supported McCain, indicating just how polarized the electorate was by 2008—but also indicating how united both parties were (Stanley and Niemi, 2009–10, 114–15).

It is difficult to project whether the delegates' ideological dispositions would be systematically related to support of Obama or Clinton. Both were known to be liberal senators, and their voting records supported that designation. Both were historic pathbreakers for their demographic group. Each took issue stances during the campaign that were only marginally more liberal or more moderate than the other's. Some analysts indicate that Clinton's support came somewhat disproportionately from blue-collar, white, working-class Democrats who predominated in several of the primary states she won, while Obama appealed more to well-educated and affluent segments of the

Figure 8-8. *Delegate Support for 2008 Democratic Candidates, by Ideology*

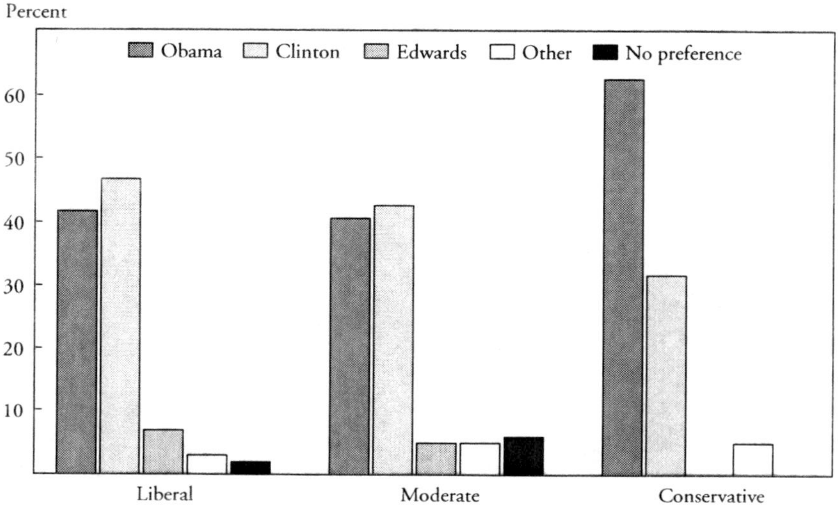

Percent

Source: Author surveys.

Democratic Party's modern base. If so, some systematic ideological differences might arise between the supporters of each side. On the other hand, many commentators remark that there was little substantive policy distance between the two candidates. There did not appear to be a clear overlay between the recognizable factions within the Democratic Party and their support for either candidate. Thus we projected the null hypothesis for the correlation between the ideology of the delegates and the candidate they said they initially supported in the campaign for the presidency (figure 8-8).

This failure of candidate supporters to overlay the current ideological fault lines within the party probably helped make the process of party reunification more feasible for the fall campaign. In other words, from a strategic viewpoint and for the sake of party unity it is best for candidate support lines not to be coterminous with, or neatly overlay, the preexistent ideological fault lines within the party. Thus the prospects for achieving party unity among Democrats in the fall of 2008 were better than they were in 1980, because the factions were not as well defined. Obama was able to achieve ideological unity within the party for the general election of 2008 to a degree that eluded Carter in 1980.

The situation in the Republican Party was quite different (figure 8-9). Before the primary season got under way in 2008, many conservative Republicans had deep reservations about John McCain. He had opposed their

Figure 8-9. *Delegate Support for 2008 Republican Candidates, by Ideology*

Percent

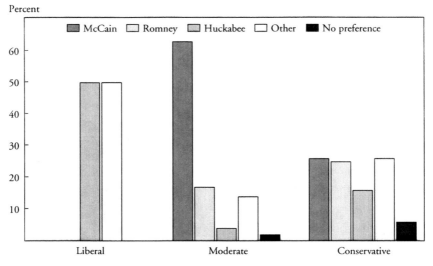

Source: Author surveys.

champion, George W. Bush, in 2000. He had sponsored legislation, especially the McCain-Feingold campaign finance law, that they abhorred. Many of these conservatives strongly opposed McCain's nomination, most notably radio talk-show host Rush Limbaugh and Focus on the Family leader James Dobson. However, in 2004 McCain strongly supported George W. Bush's reelection and campaigned vigorously for him. After Bush was reelected, McCain took steps to mend his relationship with conservatives and especially with evangelical church leaders, who are so crucial to the Republican nomination, including delivering a well-publicized speech at Jerry Falwell's Liberty University. Many observers saw these moves to the right as McCain's attempt to ingratiate himself with that core constituency in anticipation of his run in 2008. However, there were lingering doubts among the most conservative factions of the Republican Party.

However, the main problem for the conservative core was that it did not have an agreed-upon champion to rally around, and its support was divided among several Republican candidates. As many suspected, the Republican delegates who termed themselves moderate predominantly favored McCain. Almost two-thirds of that group (63 percent) said their initial choice of a candidate was John McCain, leaving slightly over one-third scattered across the other viable Republican candidates, with Mitt Romney garnering the second-highest support (17 percent) from that group. The problem for moderates is that they are outnumbered by those who term themselves either conservative or very conservative. In the conservative group, McCain still scored best, with 26 percent; however, Romney was favored by 25 percent, and Mike Huckabee was favored by 16 percent. Certainly, it was a challenge for McCain to reunite his own party base in the fall, and that may be part of the explanation for his choice of Sarah Palin as his running mate, since her strongest appeal was among the most conservative elements of the Republican coalition. Her selection is almost certainly a part of the reason the Republicans went down to defeat in the general election of 2008.

Ideological divisions played a role in the Republican Party's run-up to the 2012 nominations, with all the candidates claiming the conservative mantle. There were divisions among libertarian, social conservative, and economic conservative factions and their favorite candidates. Romney appeared to have problems with the most conservative base early on, and he was challenged for the conservative mantle, at various stages of the race, by Newt Gingrich, Rick Santorum, Rick Perry, and Herman Cain. However, conservatives could never coalesce around any alternative to Romney, so he ultimately prevailed. By November the Republicans had closed ranks behind Romney—or perhaps behind defeating Obama.

Party-line voting in 2012 was 92 percent for Democrats and 93 percent for Republicans, setting a record in recent presidential elections (Stanley and Niemi, 2013–14, 117). The 2012 conventions simply continued the string of polarized presidential elections, which include 2008, 2004, and 2000 and extend back to the 1990s.

Conclusion

From a strategic perspective, candidates most likely to win the nomination have broad-based support from party activists and from others with a mix of ideologies. It is best strategically if candidate support is not concentrated in major and recognizable party factions. Winners usually are not those who have put together what Paul T. David and his associates long ago termed a "factional victory" (David, Goldman, and Bain, 1964, 309). Instead, it is important for Democratic candidates that their support encompasses liberal and moderate members of the activist base. For Republicans, support can be centered in very conservative and conservative activists, who are the dominant wing of the party; however, it is also useful to include at least some of the much smaller moderate faction.

For either party it is difficult, if not now impossible, to start from an exclusively moderate base before the nominating season and to reach toward one of the party's wings to win the nomination. A candidate from either party with a predominantly moderate strategic identification is unlikely to survive the early days of the primary season. Candidates need to appeal to their party's committed and enthusiastic activist base to win the nomination, even though the party base is now very polarized, having sorted itself out rather clearly across the ideological divide. Candidates also need to appeal to the moderates in the party (and to various shades of independents) to have a realistic chance in November. That dilemma is always evident in planning the primary season strategy, as opposed to the strategy for the general election.

All of this is, of course, relevant to the question of who has the best potential for a victory in November. That is the most important strategic question the party's activist base (as well as its primary voters) must answer. After all, if a candidate cannot bridge the internal gaps and mollify the factions within his or her own party by the end of convention season, the chances of assembling a winning coalition for the national vote in the general election are slim. Neither side commands the allegiance of a majority of the American people. Conservatives consistently outnumber liberals by about two to one; however, conservatives are ordinarily in the high thirtieth to low fortieth percentile of all Americans, and liberals are close to or slightly above the twentieth percentile (Jones, 2014a, 2014b). This is why Republican candidates can afford to label themselves conservative almost without exception and why Democrats usually call themselves progressives, or some euphemism, rather than liberal. The aspiring presidential candidate for either party still must appeal to the middle of the spectrum, even though that middle is not as large as it once was. And he or she still must have the votes of independents.

In summary, a candidate must adopt a strategy that appeals to and energizes the core of the party while eschewing rhetoric and issue positions that brand him or her as radical. It is not an either/or choice between mobilizing the base and appealing to independents and moderates; it is a strategy driven by an inclusive, both/and, logic.

An old saying among practical politicians asserts that building winning coalitions is about addition and multiplication and not subtraction and division. The survey results shown in this chapter lend credence to that aphorism.

9

Summary and Conclusions

In this chapter I sum up the findings and draw some conclusions about the American presidential nominations system and the party activists who are so central to the party organizations. In addition, this chapter offers some proposals for possible changes, as the parties and the American government face the challenges of the coming decades.

The essence of this study is the documentation of how political parties have evolved in the last quarter of the twentieth century and what the party organization base looks like for Democrats and Republicans at the middle of the second decade of the twenty-first century. The 1970–2000 electoral era saw the creation of what is essentially a new American party system, and it is a highly polarized system. The period studied here is a historic and volatile one in American politics. The two parties had to scramble for survival, and many commentators thought one or both might not survive. It was also the age of party reform, when the changes initiated by the McGovern-Fraser Commission in particular and by the political environment in general led to profound changes in the way the nation selects its president. This is the era when a polarized political party system evolved from the older system, in which the ideological composition of the two major parties was much more diverse than it is now.

This was also the period when the American party system changed from a pragmatic model to an ideological and policy-oriented model. The latter model resembles the responsible party model in important ways, although with a peculiarly American flavor (White and Mileur, 1992; Green and Herrnson,

2002; Stonecash, 2010). This eclectic new party system incorporates parts of other familiar models also, for example the Republicans' pioneering emphasis on developing service party functions; however, the current party system has developed in a uniquely American way. The most important change is that the United States has become an ideologically polarized nation, as is often noted even in the popular media of today, and the era under study here includes the exact time period when that polarization took place (McCarty, Poole, and Rosenthal, 2006; Stonecash, 2010). At the end of the 1960s, that polarization had already started; its roots go back to the New Deal coalition's diverse and inherently unstable composition and, later, to Harry Truman's policies. However, that was a time when there were still numerous liberal to moderate Republicans and even more conservative Democrats. The historic misalignment of the South, based in the old Civil War divisions and allegiances, was mostly to blame for that previous ideological mashup, when a lot of different ideological perspectives were found in both parties. Ideology, religious beliefs, and party identification were cross-cutting cleavages in American society in the previous era, instead of largely being coterminous, as they are today. Harry Truman's civil rights advocacy and Lyndon Johnson's Civil Rights Act of 1964, Voting Rights Act of 1965, and his liberal Great Society legislative agenda forced Democrats to take a stand on the important matters of race, protections for minorities, and help for the powerless and downtrodden in a way that accelerated the revolution in party alignments.

In sum, the nation adopted during this era some of the major tenets of the responsible party school of thought, which was first articulated by the Committee on Political Parties of the American Political Science Association (1950). The United States has certainly not achieved the full-blown model realized in some Western European nations, because this country has a separation-of-powers system with a strong, independent presidential form of government, rather than a parliamentary system in which the chief executive and the government emerge out of the legislative body. Each political branch has its own constituency and electoral timetable. Those basic constitutional provisions of American government will always make it impossible to realize all the requirements of a fully developed responsible party model. However, the United States has, in other ways, achieved a nearly complete ideological realignment of the two parties, in which most conservatives have been "sorted" into the Republican Party and most liberals into the Democratic Party (Levendusky, 2009). The ideological realignment of the parties is well advanced at the elite level, though there is some remaining "misidentification" at the mass level. The research reported here, especially in chapters 5 and 6, documents the extent of the sorting process at both the mass and elite levels during the period of profound change captured in our longitudinal studies. Although I cannot definitively address the causal sequence, I have made the simplifying assumption that elites are much more influential in the sorting process than mass voters, who, in fact, more likely follow the elites. This assumption is in line with the theoretical position taken by other scholars who have studied this phenomenon (McCarty, Poole, and Rosenthal, 2006; Zaller, 1992).

Our research effort was originally influenced by the classic study of convention delegates done by Herbert McClosky and his associates (McClosky, Hoffman, and O'Hara, 1960). Their study adopted the presumption that the McClosky distribution was likely when liberals and conservatives anchor each end of the ideological continuum, with the moderates in the middle, and with the party elites being the outliers. In general, this is the pattern demonstrated in chapters 5 and 6, although this distribution is also affected by, for example, who the presidential candidate was. For example, at the Democratic Party's convention in 1972, liberals were much more dominant among party activists than among the rank and file. That level of liberal dominance was not achieved again in the twentieth century, and among Democrats liberals still share power with moderates. In contrast, conservatives do not share power with many self-identified moderates in the grassroots organizational levels of the Republican Party. Republican elites are often very close to the Republican base in their embrace of the conservative ideological banner. This lends credence to our claim that, on both ideology and issue stances as well as in demographics, the Democratic Party is the more diverse party. Their consistency allows Republicans in Congress, in the White House, and in most state governments to be more focused on their policy themes and more pure in their pursuit of their conservative agenda than the Democrats, especially with regard to taxes and budgets. The internal dissention they do face is tempered by their unity on the symbolic appeal of being conservatives and by an almost universal aversion to taxes and to an expansive view of the role of government, except with regard to national defense.

Chapter 7 examines nominating convention delegates, their personal backgrounds and party histories. Some of the findings support the classic Pareto concept of circulation of elites, which posits that new people and new ideas are needed to keep an organization vital, allowing new social groups access to positions of power. If organizations are going to change, they must have new participants who move toward the inside into leadership positions, and the channels of recruitment must be open to new groups. We found the circulation of elites true for both parties, Democrats more than Republicans. These new groups consist of more women, more young people, and more African Americans than the established groups ever have had.

Democrats have been more aggressive at the national party level in the effort to recruit new people and to bring previously excluded groups into positions of power. They have relied for this on the power of the national party and especially on the party's jurisdiction over delegate selection and the convention rules. Republicans have done this also, but their efforts are much more dependent on the initiative of state and local parties. Only in the development and control of the nominations calendar has the Republican Party been as aggressive as Democrats in exerting national party control. Perhaps this hands-off approach is fitting for the conservative party, which places a higher value on states' rights than their competitors do. This means that the Republican Party is much more homogeneous in both demographic and ideological terms than the Democratic Party is.

Chapter 8 examines the factional composition of the two parties as it impinges on the nominations process. Both parties have serious internal divisions and fault lines. This has always been the case; however, the factions are now much different from those of the 1960s. For Democrats, the ideological divisions are between liberals and moderates. For Republicans, although there are divisions between conservatives and moderates, conservatives are so dominant that further division within their ranks is the important line of demarcation. In almost every presidential year we examined, there were differences between the ideological wings of the two parties and the candidates they supported at the beginning of the primary season. The interesting finding is that some candidates, those who were the strongest and ultimately prevailed, were supported almost equally by the differing ideological camps, while those supported by only one wing of the party were not as competitive, or were factional candidates, and thus more likely to be denied the nomination. We explored the reasons that a candidate who wins the nomination by appealing to the base in the winter and early spring of election year is able, in the fall, to move to the ideological middle without losing the party's base.

Party elites and party identifiers count the most during the primary season and the run-up to the national conventions. They perform the incredibly important function of gatekeepers, winnowing a plethora of candidates down to the two who will compete, one of whom will be the next president. Then the spotlight shifts to the mass public and especially to the various brands of political independents, although the party base must also be brought along, mobilized and mollified during the fall campaign. This is a demanding tightrope performance, which only a few candidates can accomplish. Again, the strategic planning of the candidates must be grounded in rational thought and action, and it must be complemented and supported by similar rational strategic thinking by the elite of the party. Finding success in the nominations phase of the campaign is difficult, demanding, and draining, as the prolonged contest between Obama and Clinton in 2008 and the drama between Mitt Romney and his foes in 2012 demonstrated. The strategic and spatial implications of the Downsian model are unmistakable for those who are familiar with the classic literature on the placement of the candidates and the voters on the ideological continuum (Downs, 1957).

This study started by adopting the theoretical model of rational decision-making as the undergirding perspective. We posited that elite-level actors are especially well equipped to meet the demanding information-gathering and ideological coherence requirements of that model. We also relaxed the demands of that model by recognizing that candidates often are forced to make "satisficing decisions," which allow them to muddle through the demands of a national campaign. We posit that political activists strive toward the rational model, especially in an era when the party label and the ideological symbol are so pervasive in the media and when reference groups and communities of interest seem to be increasingly homogeneous and selected for their ideological compatibility and reinforcement of their belief systems.

We posited from the outset that party leaders want their parties to survive and prosper, in an era when many predicted that the nation's long-standing commitment to the two major parties was receding and that one or both parties would not survive the challenges of the 1970s and 1980s. But survive they did, and this book documents the era during which that survival was ensured. And they not only survived, they prospered, becoming stronger, better funded, more enthusiastically supported, more securely networked with compatible interest groups, and more institutionalized than at any other period in their history. Their brand names are clearer and more coherent than at any other time in history. This is due in no small part to the party leaders studied here. They made the strategic choices, the hard and close calls, to keep their party competitive. They responded to the external pressures. They juggled the competing demands from the external environment and the problems created by the divisive internal factions. The two parties are not the same organizations as they were in the 1960s, but there is significant symbolic and institutional continuity with their past. The national organizations are quite recognizable by their signature values, by the major interests they represent, and by their policy commitments. So the two parties, while strengthened and transformed, have not fundamentally changed in their basic organizational outline and name brand identity and in the functions these assets provide for the system.

Party Model Implications

What has developed is a uniquely American edition of the responsible party model. The U.S. Constitution requires a separation-of-powers and checks-and-balances system of government, and that institutional arrangement trumps everything else. James Madison carefully constructed the system as an institutional guarantee against any kind of dictatorship or tyranny developing. This structural separation, and the different constituencies and electoral calendars of the two political branches, the executive and Congress, make it very difficult to achieve the majorities necessary to mount a coherent policy approach to the nation's major problems and to pass significant legislation through all of the salient choke points in the legislative labyrinth. In the more than 220 years since the implementation of the Constitution, the government usually has been able to meet the nation's basic internal and external challenges in part because the two major parties provided the glue that held the system together. The parties usually found ways to work together when necessary, to fashion legislative compromises, and to develop policy solutions. This has happened in periods of both unified and divided government.

In some rare instances one party has controlled both branches of government, which occasioned bursts of major policy innovation and historic advancement in a coherent direction. Franklin Roosevelt's New Deal, at least up through 1936, and Lyndon Johnson's Great Society from 1964 through 1966 are the most widely recognized cases in point. One could also argue that the same recognition should go to the first two years of Ronald Reagan's first administration as a similarly productive time, although that was a situation of divided government, with the Democrats controlling the House. Ad hoc majorities had to be formed on a bipartisan basis, and the major changes wrought were in a conservative rather than a liberal direction, because of the pivotal role of the conservative coalition in Congress. Today, because of Senate rules, particularly the filibuster rule—which makes sixty votes a requirement for passage on many issues—it usually takes a supermajority for one party to drive the policymaking process. Thus in normal legislative seasons, compromise is required for the legislative and executive branches to reach agreement. When either side will not compromise, the system does not work very well. This has been the case recently.

In the decades since the 1960s the two parties have become more and more divided into ideologically different and often warring camps, and the nation has become more polarized. This commitment to ideological fervor may well have been very good for the parties and the development of internal party cohesion and esprit de corps; however, that division has not worked to the advantage of the overall political system. The polarization of the parties has been analyzed by many scholars and has been covered in some detail in the earlier chapters of this book (Coffey, 2011; Stonecash, 2010; Abramowitz, 2010a, 2011; McCarty, Poole, and Rosenthal, 2006; Fiorina, Abrams, and Pope, 2005). Liberals have sorted into the Democratic Party and conservatives have sorted into the Republican Party, and the overlap in the middle has become smaller and smaller (Levendusky, 2009). This sorting and its policy implications have been especially notable in Congress, where Republicans and Democrats are now more polarized ideologically and more isolated from each other than at probably any other time in American history. Even the Supreme Court is deeply divided along partisan and ideological fault lines. With respect to the changed role of parties in Congress, two leading scholars, David Rohde and John Aldrich (2010, 249), define the new more polarized and more internally homogeneous and unified parties as "conditional party government."

> We have sought to account for the increase in the strength of political parties in Congress over the last four decades through the application of the theory of conditional party government. The theory contends that observed increases in the homogeneity of policy preferences within congressional parties, and the increases in policy conflicts between the parties, are rooted in electoral changes. In turn, the increased intraparty homogeneity and interparty conflict led members of Congress to be willing to delegate strong powers to their party leaders, in order that those leaders as agents of the members could secure political advantages for their respective parties.

Intraparty homogeneity and interparty conflict are hallmarks of the presidential wing of the party and are the most important considerations when the nominations and general election phase of the electoral cycle are reached. Whether this new party system is called conditional party government or some other term, the implications of the new system for making policy and for governing the nation are still unclear and evolving. So far, in the new era, the prospects for either party having the ability to govern are not particularly promising. The two parties now have so much that divides them, are committed to such different visions and views of the role of government in society, have such different mind-sets about the relevant facts on which policy should be based, and represent such different groups and interests that it has become very difficult and often impossible for them to reach any kind of common ground and to find a modus vivendi that will allow them to govern coherently. Indeed, it often appears that the two parties occupy some alternative universe and that their definitions of reality have become almost diametrically different. The fight over global warming and climate change and the causes is a case in point.

The challenge to the president's ability to govern has grown to be more demanding during this era. In fact, it is reasonable now to wonder if any president can govern under these circumstances. Certainly, much of this challenge emanates from and is centered in Congress, particularly during an era marked by divided government. The opposition of Congress can have a profound effect on the executive branch as well, which presents an even more fundamental challenge. For example, during President Obama's first term, Republicans used the filibuster, or the threat of the filibuster, an unprecedented number of times to ensure that legislation that they opposed never reached a vote. This meant that it effectively took sixty votes to invoke cloture and to move legislation to the floor of the Senate to even get to hold a vote (Burden, 2011; Binder, 2011). Getting loyal personnel in place to head the bureaus has also proved daunting. Individual Republican senators used their special privileges to block nominations they opposed by putting a personal hold on the nomination and stopping Obama's nominations. Elizabeth Warren's 2011 nomination to head the Consumer Financial Protection Bureau is a significant case in point. At first President Obama gave her the job through executive appointment. As Republican opposition to her continuation in that capacity, and to the implementation of the Dodd-Frank bill to increase regulations of financial institutions, grew, she withdrew her name from consideration and went home to Massachusetts to run for the U.S. Senate. Obama then turned to Richard Cordray, who had been attorney general of Ohio, to head the bureau. Again, Republicans promised a filibuster and refused to allow Cordray's nomination to be voted on in the Senate. After some delay and strategic retreat, Obama made a recess appointment of Cordray to that position, while Congress was out of town—but technically in pro forma session (Nakamura and Sommez, 2012). Republicans blasted the move as illegal and promised another fight (Cooper and Cushman, 2012). Well over a year later, Obama officially appointed Cordray to the position, but it was over strong Republican opposition. Thus it is that the battle for policy implementation continues long past the moment when Congress and the president pass a law. An extreme case in point is the intense opposition by Republicans in Congress to the 2010 Affordable Care Act four years after its enactment.

There is no doubt but that the development of more ideologically cohesive party systems has allowed both parties to grow. Likewise the partisan media, especially as centered in the cable networks with their high-profile ideological stars, have enhanced the attachments of their partisan audiences to their own interests, framing the issues and even their basic definition of reality. The result is often polarization of public opinion, which encourages policy stalemate in the most crucial issue areas, such as health care, the environment, civil rights, gun control, the size and mission of the military, and most notably, taxes and the budget. Job approval of the president, whether it be for Clinton, Bush, or Obama, is directly tied to partisanship, as are citizens' positions on such basic questions as diverse as the invasion of Iraq, stem cell research, abortion, the bailout of the banks, and support for the automotive industry. This division is especially clear on tax policy and questions related to the budget, the deficit, and the national debt. Even the labels combatants use, for example "estate tax" (Democrats) or the "death tax" (Republicans), consistently divide the partisans. Sometimes such policy stalemates lead to government shutdowns, as happened in the summer of 2011. That debacle and the resulting Standard and Poor's downgrade of the U.S. credit rating demonstrate the determination of the parties to maintain their positions even to the detriment of the economic security of the nation.

The fight over the budget and the debt ceiling, as well as the Affordable Care Act, was then repeated in the fall of 2013, when the nation was again taken to the brink of financial destabilization by governmental gridlock. This gridlock led to the shutdown of the U.S. government for sixteen days in October, when over 800,000 "nonessential" government employees were laid off and many services and agencies were closed or severely curtailed. The possibility of default on the sovereign debt of the United States and the resultant chaos in domestic and world markets led to threat of recession.

As a result, the American people in contemporary polls have delivered their most critical verdict on the job that Congress is doing. Congress's approval ratings fell to the historic low of only 13 percent nationwide (Gallup polls, October 4 to October 12, and November 14, 2011). Gallup reported that "congressional job approval for 2011 is on track to be the lowest annual rating in Gallup's history" (November 14, 2011). In December 2011 Gallup reported that only 11 percent of Americans approved of the way Congress was doing its job and that the average approval rate for the year was 17 percent, the lowest since Gallup had been asking the question (starting in 1974; see Newport,

2011). Another pollster, Scott Rasmussen (2011), reported at the end of 2011 that almost a majority of Americans (48 percent) believed that most members of Congress are corrupt. In 2012 and 2013 public opinion polls continued to provide bad news for Congress. There may be good grounds for the low ratings given to Congress in the polls. Separate research by J. Tobin Grant and Nathan J. Kelly (2008) provides empirical evidence supporting popular disenchantment, reporting that the Congress ushered in by the 2010 elections was the least productive since the 1880s.

The only possible resolution seemed to be, back in 2012, a mandate for one or the other party to emerge from the elections. However, that did not happen; the government remained divided, with the Senate and the White House under the control of Democrats and the House under the control of Republicans. In any case, policy mandates provided by elections, in the American system, are vague and transitory at best. Such mandates depend on how the president and his allies in Congress choose to define them and what they decide to do with them. The interpretation of a mandate is in itself controversial and partisan. Instead, elections provide the president with the opportunity to take over the executive branch and try to govern. Republicans in Congress, especially the House, continued to vigorously resist Obama's policy agenda after his 2012 victory, and gridlock continued.

After the 2012 elections the polls showed the public to have an even lower opinion of Congress than in earlier years, with its job approval sinking to new lows. The negative views of Congress were exacerbated by the government shutdown, which began on October 1, 2013, and lasted for sixteen days. An *ABC News/Washington Post* poll taken in mid-October shows approval of the job Congress was doing at only 12 percent, compared to 85 percent who disapproved. This was a record low for the forty years the poll had been taken. In addition, a large percentage claimed that they would vote to throw all incumbents, including their own member, out of office; of course, whether they would follow through on this resolve in the 2014 midterms was not at all certain (Falcone, 2013; Balz and Clement, 2013). Gallup reported in November 12, 2013, that approval for Congress had sunk to a new record low of 9 percent.

All of this ideological gridlock and policy stalemate happened because of the political parties, especially the party in government, aided and abetted by their own narrow electoral interests and the groups that support them. Party leaders organize the government in both political branches and then hold so tightly to their most active members' views that there are few grounds for compromise. Individual members of Congress are usually so committed to their announced ideological positions, so wedded to their constituents and interest groups, so frightened of casting a vote that will stir up a primary opponent, and so beholden to their campaign funding sources that they are unable to make concessions and compromise. Legislation depends on compromise, yet compromise has become anathema to the true believers in both parties. This is what you get with separation of powers overlaid with ideology and partisanship taken to its logical and extreme conclusion.

So the United States has its own unique version of the responsible party model, or perhaps the conditional party model, superimposed on the separation-of-powers system. At this point in U.S. history, this edifice does not seem to work so well. The parties as organizations have survived and prospered magnificently. The national and state party organizations are healthier and more robust than ever. But public opinion on how well the political system is working, on whether the nation is heading in the right direction, and on whether Congress is doing its job is at near record lows. The percentage who approved the way President Obama was doing his job hovered in the mid-forties just a year before the start of the 2012 campaign. It inched up to just above 50 percent after his reelection, only to decline to the high forties during the 2013 government shutdown fight. During his second term his percent approval was in the mid- to high forties and only occasionally broke through the majority barrier. Obama's overall ratings were similar to those of George W. Bush during his two terms in office (Gallup, October 21, 2013). Both experienced similar judgments, in opposite directions, from a deeply polarized American electorate.

Job approval for Congress was, as noted, much worse. Ironically, many scholars in the past, like the notable scholars who formed the Schattschneider Commission in the 1950s, and like Woodrow Wilson before that, were strong advocates for various forms of the responsible party model or for party government (Green and Herrnson, 2002; White and Mileur, 1992). Now that one American mutant version of the model is in place, the problems with applying it in this context are more evident. Congress, which has never been popular as an institution, is consistently held in disdain. The famous "right track" versus "wrong track" measures have been off track in a negative direction for several electoral cycles, and the numbers seem to decline each year no matter what the government does. Presidential job approval ratings, whether for President Obama or President Bush, reflect deep partisan divisions. It seems that no president, no matter how high he starts, can avoid scathing criticism and decline in support, especially from independents and the other party's base.

The result is institutional stalemate on major policy questions related to the economy, to infrastructure development, to entitlement funding, to health care, to gun control, and to global climate change (Schmidt, 2014). On many issues—global climate change, for example—there is not even a shared definition of reality. Even on small, everyday matters related to the routine questions ordinarily before Congress—for example, the approval of nominations—the pace is lethargic or nonexistent, as meetings are bogged down in partisan wrangling and stalemate.

Most important, the art of compromise, so critical to the legislative process, is regarded with disdain by some members of Congress and by many of the people and groups they represent. The Tea Party movement, especially, holds compromise in public contempt. Some in the Occupy Wall Street movement, which seemed to spring up spontaneously in the fall of 2011, showed similar impatience with the realities of the American political process as defined by the Constitution, especially the separation-of-powers provisions. The present political parties seem to be responsible to only the most activist and extreme elements of their base and to the interest groups and the very wealthy individuals who fund campaigns through their unlimited donations to political action committees. These super PACs came into their own in the 2012 election cycle and proved that big-money contributors had made a major comeback in American presidential politics. Somewhere in this mix, the idea of responsibility to a larger national interest and to the common good has been lost.

What Should Be Done?

This rather grim picture raises the question of how to create a government in which problems can be defined, workable solutions developed, a working majority assembled, and legislation drafted that addresses the problems. My answer to the toxic political situation starts with an activist and empowered chief executive. The president drives the political agenda and heads the vast executive branch. He, far more than any other officer, is the face of the government for the American people and for people throughout the world. The president is elected to lead, and even in the face of the many obstacles put up by the separation-of-powers system, he is the key figure in the government. If a presidential candidate wins the presidential election, he or she should be given the opportunity and tools to try to govern. To be sure, this will require the support of the president's party in Congress, but that support should also include some members of the other party, especially if that party's interests and concerns have been met at least part way in the drafting of the legislation.

This requires an activist president, who has an agenda and the will to lead. Possession of these qualities marks the more successful presidents (Neustadt,

1960). Of course, getting the entire executive branch to bend to the president's will and committed to his agenda is always a challenge. The question is, How can this go forward? How is the United States to make the changes necessary to realize this goal, of vigor in the executive coupled with action by the legislative branch? Absent debate and compromise, the result is gridlock and a dysfunctional government.

Some observers advocate a wholesale switch to the parliamentary system, in which the election brings in a party with a mandate to form a government and then to govern (Powell, 1996). While all parliamentary votes are not party-line votes, the big issues and the most important policy questions of the day are usually settled by the government's declaring them to be party questions, and thus the members of parliament of the majority party or ruling coalition are expected to follow the prime minister and the party's dictates. Failure to do so by enough members can result in the fall of the government and the calling of new elections. Legislative stalemate of the kind seen routinely in the United States at least theoretically should not be a problem, although I recognize that this is a somewhat simplified and idealized version of how parliamentary parties function in the real world.

The parliamentary option may have some abstract appeal and is worth studying from a comparative perspective; however, it is not at all likely to be adopted in the United States. Such a change would require a wholesale reconstruction of the most basic edifice of American government, probably a new constitutional convention, and a level of success in surmounting conflict and change that is probably impossible to accomplish. Our political culture is deeply imbued with the separation-of-powers and checks-and-balances concepts, and the American people are not about to accept that radical of a departure from what has always been considered a fundamental feature of the American Constitution.

Thus I am more inclined to search for less drastic changes to advocate, since the United States has to use eighteenth-century government institutions to face twenty-first-century challenges. One possibility that should be explored at the mass level has to do with civic education. I am convinced from many years in the classroom that the educational system in this country is failing in its basic duty to teach civics and citizenship. Public and private school educators are simply not helping young people understand the basic features of American government and civic culture. Numerous studies document the vast ignorance of most Americans, and especially of young people, about the fundamentals of their government. The most recent was released by the National Task Force on Civic Learning and Democratic Engagement

(2012, 6–7). The study was commissioned by the Department of Education (Berrett, 2012). The following are the report's "Indicators of Anemic U.S. Civic Health":

—Only 24 percent of graduating high school seniors scored at the proficient or advanced level in civics in 2010, fewer than in 2006 or 1998.

—Less than one-half of twelfth graders reported studying international topics as part of civic education.

—Half of U.S. states no longer require civics education for high school graduation.

—Among 14,000 college seniors tested in 2006 and 2007, the average score on a civic literacy exam was just over 50 percent, an F.

Civic education, formerly taught in school, is now mostly gleaned in a haphazard fashion from television news, cable comedy shows, and commentators who are more entertainers than journalists or educators. The civic culture is also purveyed online by thousands of bloggers, Facebook commenters, and Tweeters, where the only credential needed is access to the Internet. Opinions are often strong and even outrageous and expressed in colorful and provocative language. That is where many young Americans find community and learn their basic political values. Thus I believe that basic civic education, which was one of the founding objectives of the profession of political science, should be renewed and elevated in stature in the schools of America. Ultimately, offering civic education to all students is the most effective route to changing the political culture. I am a proponent of rational decisionmaking in all facets of American politics. I believe that a rational public can lead to a more rational republic. Rationality crucially depends on education, and especially civic education.

Beyond that mass objective, however, I am interested in institutional changes that could enable the current system to function better and to make public policy in an atmosphere conducive to addressing the nation's most immediate problems while taking into account the common good and the long-term national interest. One important step would be for the Senate to banish the filibuster. My view stems from my deep commitment to the value of rule by a simple majority. The filibuster now requires sixty votes for the Senate to pass a bill, or even to take up debate, over the objection of the minority. It formerly required sixty-seven votes for cloture; a compromise engineered in 1975 reduced it to sixty. The filibuster is only a rule (rule 22) of the Senate; it is not in the Constitution. Changing the rules of the Senate only requires enough senators, either a majority or 60 percent, depending on what issue is at stake, to change it. It may be much more difficult to change practically and politically, since both parties have used the filibuster, when they were in the minority, to veto legislation they did not support but could not stop with an up or down vote. The filibuster is an anti-majoritarian device of the most pernicious sort. Barry Burden (2011, 6) summarizes the practical argument against the filibuster as follows: "The filibuster was once a costly and rare practice. In recent years, it has become an easy way to stop not just the majority party in the Senate but the entire federal government from advancing new policies."

Many Americans do not understand that it effectively takes sixty votes to move most legislation through the Senate, and they have even less idea how difficult that standard is to achieve. Most of those who are aware of the existence of the filibuster do not understand that it is only a rule rather than a constitutional provision. In an online article regarding the pernicious effect the filibuster has on the ability of the Senate to function, Sarah Binder (2011, 12) makes the following cogent point:

> For those matters in which the House plays no role—namely, judicial and executive branch nominations—the legislative process has barely worked in recent years. Roughly half of judicial nominees are left in limbo each Congress, with the minority often unwilling to allow votes on even noncontroversial or minor nominees. Other times, the minority has voted lockstep against nominees whose credentials seemingly made them strong candidates for the bench. The rise of polarized parties has moved legislative deal making off the Senate floor and has left the chamber often incapable of completing legislative priorities, even sometimes those with bipartisan support.

All of the distrust of Congress and frustration with its inability to deal with the nation's major problems would not disappear overnight if the filibuster were to be repealed, but reverting to a simple majority would ensure that energy in the executive could be matched by energy in the legislative branch and that one party or the other could move its legislative priorities out of the Senate. Then that party could and should be held accountable at the next election. We have a system we like to call democratic, and that means we must adopt rules that ensure majority control rather than rule by an intense and implacable minority (Dahl, 1956). Getting rid of the filibuster would be a step in that direction. The same is true for getting rid of the Senate's rule allowing a single senator to place a hold on nominations and certain legislation, thus preventing a vote from being held. It is an even more pernicious practice, clearly violating the basic tenets of majority rule in the most extreme way. The rule should be repealed in the interests of democracy and in the interest of increasing the public's trust and confidence in Congress.

My other suggestion for fixing Congress is much more difficult to attain, and it would require a constitutional amendment. The reform is to move House terms to four years rather than two. In addition, the terms should be coordinated with presidential terms, so, in effect, midterm House elections, which cause so much upheaval in American government, would be eliminated. (If Senate terms are left at the current six years, this would mean that one-third of Senate terms would continue to end at the president's midterm, which would bring a midterm correction of a sort.)

When the U.S. Constitution was promulgated in 1789, travel was slow and communication was difficult. House members moved to Washington and largely stayed for the duration of their terms. Today, communications are instantaneous, and iPhones and Blackberries are never turned off. Commercial airliners fly into and out of Washington airports in a steady stream. The typical House or Senate session begins on Tuesday and ends on Thursday, when the member is back on a plane heading out to the district or to another political function or fundraiser.

A significant number of recently elected members have not personally moved to Washington, and they make something of a fetish of living in the congressional office buildings, sleeping on office couches, and showering in the gymnasium. They consider these choices marks of their disdain for Washington and devotion to their district. This is not a healthy environment in which to develop and produce thoughtful and rational policy designed to address the nation's problems. These lifestyle and time management decisions contribute to the hostile, polarized, and dysfunctional state of Congress, especially the House, and are directly related to the imperatives of the two-year term and the need for constant campaigning, fundraising, and fence mending at home.

The two-year term for the House of Representatives was an eighteenth-century accommodation to the realities of travel and political necessities as well as a philosophical statement. Many founders wanted the House to be the sensitive barometer of the people's opinions, and having them elected every two years was a way of keeping them directly accountable to the vagaries of public opinion. Indeed, the elections were one of the very few practical ways of gauging public opinion in that era. Today we have many ways of testing and demonstrating public opinion, including public opinion polling, which allows leaders to keep their fingers on the pulse of the people. In addition, there is the steady feedback provided by the mass media, with their twenty-four-hour news cycle and the constant commentary of the pundits and their guests. More recently there is the ubiquitous companionship provided by the Internet, where electronic communities meet daily to share news and commentary in ways that the people of the eighteenth century could never have imagined. We do not need the midterm elections to provide a constant stream of criticism, feedback, and evaluation of the governmental elites.

I am certainly not the first to suggest this innovation. Lyndon Johnson, a veteran of the House and Senate, suggested the same thing in his farewell address to Congress in 1969. Johnson's proposal died with his departure from Washington; however, the problems he was trying to address have only gotten worse in the intervening decades.

Eliminating one election cycle, held every two years, out of the electoral calendar would ensure that one party could have control of the House for four years, allowing the president to pursue an agenda over a long enough period for the people and the political elites to judge how viable the agenda is. A president who enjoys a working majority in Congress would be positioned to get his or her policies enacted and implemented. At present a newly elected president has about eighteen months to unveil the legislative agenda, present it to Congress, defend it in the media and before the court of public opinion, and enact it before everything grinds to a halt while the country holds yet another national election.

It is not surprising, for example, that the last two presidents, George W. Bush and Barack Obama, spent so much early time and attention and spent so much political capital on their highest priority issues, reforming Social Security in 2005 for Bush and passing a national health care reform plan for Obama in 2009–10. They both knew that their window of opportunity for winning approval from Congress and the American people would close as the midterm elections approached. Both saw their partisan majorities collapse in these elections. After barnstorming around the country in 2005 in a campaign to garner support for his Social Security plan, Bush saw it fail entirely in Congress. He was done in by the implacable opposition of the Democrats and by the tepid support of his own partisans, many of whom were concerned only about the upcoming midterm elections. While Obama was able, in 2010, to enact his national health care plan, or a much-compromised version of it, he then faced the fact that the plan could not be completely implemented until after the 2012 election. In fact, several key provisions were not scheduled to take effect until after the elections, and people did not see much improvement in their lives resulting from the 2010 law. This delay then helped to prolong the conflict into 2013 and 2014.

Even if the president got a divided government out of the presidential election cycle or out of the Senate midterm elections, he or she would arguably still have a better opportunity to work on coalition building and winning over partisan and ideological opponents if House members knew they had a four-year rather than a two-year term to develop their own records and to see how the president's policies were working out. The president is obligated to try to build a working majority in Congress. Under divided government it is especially necessary. If the president is not saddled with the arcane and archaic filibuster rule and the veto power of one senator, he or she might have a fighting chance to build such coalitions on each crucial vote. A president presiding over a divided government would be tested by trying to discover how to assemble that winning coalition, probably including taking into consideration the views of the more moderate members of the other party, and reaching a modus vivendi with the opposition. That would not be an easy assignment, but it would be clear who is in charge in the White House for four years and what must be done to address the nation's persistent problems. If that goal is not achieved, then again, commensurate with the requirements of the responsible party model, the American people would have somewhat clearer means for judging who was in charge and who succeeded or failed.

The better alternative, however, would be that the president wins and helps to maintain or bring in a majority of his own party, who are at least somewhat committed to the same basic principles and loyal to the same ideological point on the philosophical compass and to the same interest groups. Then the country would get some of the benefits of responsible party government, or at least a better form of the conditional party government that is possible under the separation-of-powers system.

The major objective of this redesign of American government is for the president to be able to assemble a workable majority and advance his or her program: in a word, to be allowed to govern. That objective is not currently being met, and the polls show that the American people are constantly disenchanted with and distrustful of the same government their own votes, taken in mass if not as individuals, created. The two parties spend their time trying to checkmate the other, and the opposition in Congress announces that its highest priority is the defeat of the president in the next election. The time line is always just the next two years, which in essence is the next eighteen months, before the next election. These electoral time lines need to be loosened and elongated. This proposal would put America on a four-year electoral cycle, led by an invigorated president.

Party Reform Possibilities

This book is focused on party reform and an examination of the results produced by the last reform era. Much has been accomplished, and many elements of the system have been transformed in order to ensure the survival of each party's basic identity and fundamental values. The party activists included in this study are the architects and supporters of those changes. Other changes can and should be made to ensure the adaptability of the party system and to encourage more rationality in the way both individual and collective decisions are made.

In the first decade of the twenty-first century, the calendar and the window for holding presidential primaries and caucuses were dominant and divisive issues for both parties. This competition to be at the head of the line set off a new wave of tactical maneuvers by the states in the run-up to 2012, which was remarkably similar to the scenario of 2008. Even the sanctions threatened were the same: the Republican National Committee threatened to take half the delegate votes away from Florida or any other state that violated the starting-date rule; the Democratic National Committee threatened to take away all the delegates from those states. The final compromise (placing Iowa on January 3, 2012, just two days after New Year's Day, and New Hampshire on January 10, followed by South Carolina on January 21, Florida on January 31, and Nevada on February 4) was not significantly different from the solution reached by both parties in 2008. Although both parties in 2008 also threatened punishment for the renegade states of Florida and Michigan, the final results did not greatly injure the delegations from those states in the conventions. Naturally, this ultimately timid and overtly political outcome did little to deter the same states and others in their planning for 2012. Once again there was uncertainty in the rules of the game, which lasted well into the fall of 2011; that uncertainty had a bigger impact on Republicans than Democrats, who were sure to nominate President Obama once more.

My position is that, as with any game, rules should be agreed upon and settled before the game starts. Recent history teaches that the parties cannot rely on individual states to fix the problem. States, especially state legislatures and governors, look out for their own parochial interests and have little to no regard for the national interest. It takes a national party law, or even the intervention of Congress, to settle disputes. That is why I favor national party rules: both parties should settle on what the window will be and then must enforce it. If the ultimate sanction is the loss of all or a significant part of a state delegation's seats and votes at the conventions, then that is the price the national party should exact. It will only take one year for state parties to get the message, if sanctions are effectively employed. Many critics thought the McGovern-Fraser rules could never be promulgated over state objections, but the story of this book is that they were adopted, institutionalized, and made to stick.

Of course, this decision will also need the backing of the party's presidential candidates, and they should be challenged to give such assent. If the presidential nomination race is already settled by the time the convention starts, as it almost inevitably will be, presidential candidates will back their national party law, and delegates from the states in compliance will applaud the candidate who has the courage to stand with them against the renegades. Again, the 1970 McGovern-Fraser reforms record suggests that only one such historic example will be necessary to create the precedent. In short, I favor a preset window for the primaries for both parties and then sticking to it, no exceptions allowed.

For all of the reasons cited above and others, I also favor the institution of regional primaries to take the place of the hodgepodge of state laws and informal customs and national party laws that currently control the calendar. For decades now, two states, New Hampshire and Iowa, have enjoyed privileged positions. In 2008 Nevada and South Carolina were added to that list of privileged early contests approved by the national parties. This was an attempt to introduce a bit more diversity to the starting four: Nevada has a fairly high proportion of Hispanic voters, unions are strong in Las Vegas, and African American voters make up a significant minority of the South Carolina population. Naturally, this move upset other states, and some—like Florida and Michigan—tried to do something about it by moving to the front of the calendar. Other states joined the parade in 2012. The result is a patchwork of states that hold caucuses and primaries on completely idiosyncratic dates for their own parochial reasons. Which candidates are favored in which early states is totally the luck of the draw, coupled with some calculated effort on the part of candidates to game the system. Obama's unexpected victory in Iowa in 2008 may have worked out to be in the national interest, but it did not appear that way to Senator Hillary Clinton and her supporters at the time.

The narrow (eight-vote) Mitt Romney "victory" over Rick Santorum and the rest of the field in Iowa in 2012 was widely reported, and he got a major boost from apparently winning that very close election; however, a more careful tabulation of the Iowa votes cast doubt on whether he had won the most votes after all. The Republican Party of Iowa, on January 19, finally certified its statewide caucus vote totals and gave a narrow thirty-four-vote margin to Santorum. Nevertheless, the story line for two weeks had been that Romney won the first two contests in 2012. Caucus results for the Republicans in Nevada and Maine were even more confused and contentious and led to demands for the states to take over what was essentially a party affair. All of these are examples of early victories in marginal states brought about by emotion, arbitrary media interpretation, and spin.

Rotating regional primaries on a strict calendar would be a better way. Regional primaries would ensure that the initial contests, and then each new contest in the sequence, would introduce a much higher level of diversity in the electorate than currently exists when officially New Hampshire and Iowa get to go first, South Carolina and Nevada go next, followed by a haphazard collection of self-starters in the next tier of Super Tuesday states. One or two small states should not be able to start a stampede. Preventing the out-sized influence of small and idiosyncratic states would be served by regional primaries. Taken as a whole, the states of the Northeast are far more diverse, and far more representative of the nation, than the state of New Hampshire alone. The same could be said of the composition of the electorate of Iowa compared to the total electorate in the Midwest. Under a regional primary plan, far more voters would be involved in the first contests and they would be far more representative of the nation as a whole than is currently the case. There is no way to guarantee that idiosyncratic and irrational outcomes may not occur; however, they would be less likely than is true now.

I hypothesize also that the candidates who survive a regional primary are more likely to appeal to a broader audience, perhaps to be more moderate, more inclined to compromise, and less doctrinaire than candidates who win under today's parochial formula. Even if the winning candidates are predominantly known as liberals or conservatives and appeal to the party's activist base, as they probably will, they may also be pragmatists who understand the importance of the art of compromise. Regional primaries or caucuses that include a relatively large and diverse population would be more representative of the nation as a whole than the current system.

There are several viable rotating regional primary plans (Jackson, 2008a, 2008b). I prefer the one advanced by the National Association of Secretaries of State (Kamarck, 2009). In essence, this plan would divide the nation into four geographical regions. A random procedure would then determine which region would hold its primaries or caucuses on which date in a two-to-four-month period. The primary calendar would rotate each presidential election until each region had its turn at the front of the calendar, and then the rotation would start again. Most advocates believe that this rule could be adopted by the two major parties acting in concert, and there is ample Supreme Court doctrine supporting the prerogatives of the national parties to back that view. Others believe that the measure should be made into federal law through congressional action. Still others maintain that such a change could only be mandated by an amendment to the Constitution.

However the nation arrives at a consensus, the use of rotating regional primaries would bring the following benefits. The calendar would be agreed upon in advance. Each region would get its place at the head of the line. Each region would be treated equally. For candidates, campaigning in one region at a time would be more efficient and less expensive than in the current system. Staff resources could be focused on one region at a time, and media costs could be less.

Critics point out, accurately, that the candidates could still be advantaged or disadvantaged by the luck of the draw. That is, a candidate from one region is likely to enjoy some advantages if their home region is selected to go first. There is something to that claim; however, the same is true today, in that home-state candidates usually enjoy some advantages in their own states and regions, and if those happen to come near the front of the calendar, the home-court advantage can accrue to them. Southern candidates usually are thought to have the advantage in southern states, for example. But the media and commentators are perfectly capable now of discounting regional victories and of raising the bar higher if the candidate is supposed to have a regional advantage.

Edmund Muskie was supposed to win New Hampshire handily in 1972 because he was from the neighboring state of Maine. When he got only 46 percent of the vote, it was deemed "disappointing," even though he far outstripped the second-place George McGovern, who got only 37 percent. McGovern was credited with a "better than expected" performance and dubbed the frontrunner (Ragsdale, 1988, 49). In 1992 Tom Harkin won his home state of Iowa's caucuses, but because of his favorite-son status there, most of the other major candidates had stayed away, and this victory was his only success in that race. He quickly faded when Bill Clinton garnered the most publicity out of his second-place finish in New Hampshire the next week. In short, the vagaries of geography are almost always random in the system we have now, and there is no reason to expect that they would get any worse in the rotating regional primary system. It could even improve on the present system when several states share a single election day.

The other major criticism of the regional primary system is that it would be very expensive, because candidates would need to make significant advertising buys in all the major media markets in every region. Thus they would need to raise more and more money as the battle dragged on. However, the cost of a successful campaign for the presidency is already astronomical, and the longer it goes on, the more expensive it is. Hillary Clinton, for example, was not prepared to go all the way through the last primary in May 2008. In spite of her long years in politics and the networks she and her husband had cultivated, she wound up having to loan her campaign $5 million in personal funds to continue to compete. In 2012 Santorum literally ran out of money two weeks before the primary in his home state of Pennsylvania. One rule of thumb about money is that the candidates spend all the money they can get their hands on as long as they think they are viable. Thus no matter what the rules are, there is probably only a finite amount of money available to each candidate, and it is time bound and inelastic. Usually supporters will ante up enough to keep their candidate in the game only while he or she has a realistic chance to win the nomination. That finite amount is not likely to be larger under a regional primary system than under the current system, and the resources available will continue to be sequential and time bound.

I believe that the rotating regional primary plan is more rational, more systematic, and more predictable than the current system. It also holds the possibility of addressing some of the most pernicious effects of the present ideologically polarized system. The present system is only institutionalized and rationalized because the national parties have stepped in and rationalized it since the reform era began. That is one of the legacies of this important era. However, it is time to take another and somewhat more ambitious step along that route to reform.

Even if that step is not taken, however, it has to be acknowledged that the two parties have come a long way toward developing a nationalized system of party rules. Those rules have led to the institutionalization of the national parties. That is no small accomplishment for parties that were not long ago thought to be on the brink of extinction.

Concluding Thoughts on Compromise

The polarization of American politics and the two-party system has been much studied in the academic and popular press. The empirical sections of this book document some important contours of that polarization at both the elite and mass levels. The policy gridlock in Washington is often attributed to that polarization.

For all the importance of those developments, though, a case can be made that there is still room for something different to grow out of the current ideological gridlock that seems to grip the federal government and many state governments. The national government, especially Congress, is in grave trouble in the eyes of the American public. Presidents often find themselves in greater and greater political difficulty as their term wears on, and if they get a second term, they frequently have to face a restive public and a hostile Congress very soon after reelection. I am convinced by years of study of the party activists that many of them, and certainly the ordinary voters they represent, would endorse and support a different approach, one in which ideology has a role in the political discourse and in the campaign but is not the final word in the making of public policy. However, it will take leadership and courage from the party in the government and those who run for office, especially those who run for president, to achieve those ends.

Approximately 60–70 percent of the mass public identify as either liberal or conservative, leaving 30–40 percent in the middle, depending on when the poll is taken (Jones, 2014b). But I contend that, leaving bloggers and listeners to talk radio aside, the average person is more interested in results than ideology. Political leadership in Congress and the White House must be willing to fashion public policies that are empirically based. This entails a study of the policymaking literature and the intellectual curiosity to want to know the evidence for or against any particular policy or program. Such respect for the evidence should take precedence over fidelity to ideology. Members of Congress should take the time to study and understand the policies in their areas of expertise, relying on their staffs, committee staffs, the Congressional Research Service, and other members with expertise to learn enough to cast an informed and rational vote on the important issues. They should adopt Mayor Richard J. Daley's dictum that, in the long run, "Good government is good politics." This will restore the people's faith in Congress.

The argument here is that the presidential nominations and the election system have helped to produce a new kind of party activist and a new party organization base. Activists are more ideological and more partisan than activists in the old pragmatic party system, and they have been sorted and realigned along ideological and partisan lines. This polarization has been reinforced by party polarization.

The confluence of all these trends—reinforcing one another as they do, and reinforced by new trends in the mass media and among more partisan interest groups, especially a newly mobilized religious community, coupled with major demographic trends that are changing America—has left us with concurrent and overlapping social and political cleavages rather than the cross-cutting cleavages of the old system. These developments have hardened into the partisan and legislative gridlock of today, where the government finds it difficult and occasionally impossible to perform its basic functions. An ineffectual and seemingly incompetent government feeds popular cynicism and distrust. The president, especially, finds it difficult to govern in these circumstances. But stalemate need not be a permanent condition. There is potential for change with a different approach.

A significant proportion of the political party activists encountered in this study claims a specific ideological identification; however, these activists also fit the familiar professional model more than the amateur model of activism. They are more interested in winning the next election than in winning their argument. Most of them are flexible in their beliefs when it comes to winning elections and ensuring the success and survival of their party. Democrats gave up the white South and Republicans gave up African American voters and are close to abandoning Hispanic voters in service to their strategic vision of what their party must do to respond to the larger social movements and ensure its long-term survival. Even on perhaps the most ideological and values-oriented issue of all, the pro-life versus pro-choice battle, our data show that party activists are surprisingly pragmatic and quite diverse in their views. The prevailing policy position in the wake of *Roe* v. *Wade* is a messy mixture of respect for a woman's right to choose in the first trimester coupled with increasing restrictions as the pregnancy advances. More state-imposed restrictions are added if the woman is a minor.

A significant majority of the American public is similarly ambivalent about the thorny problem of immigration. Americans want to secure the borders and control illegal entry, but they are also somewhat sympathetic to immigrants personally, especially the young. This attitude has led to the surprising endorsement by such Republican presidential hopefuls as Rick Perry, Newt Gingrich, and Mike Huckabee of elements of the Dream Act. Other very conservative political elites with ties to agricultural and business interests that need the help of undocumented workers supported President Bush's proposal for temporary worker permits. Many Republicans also support a path to citizenship for those who have been here for many years and for the children who were brought to the United States at a very young age. President Obama's decision in June 2012 to allow these undocumented young people to remain for up to two years without threat of deportation was not consistent with his earlier position; however, while it caused criticism, it did not create much of an uproar and was met with only a muted critique from his opponent, Mitt Romney.

None of this is very pure ideologically, but the parties have accommodated to it, and majoritarian public opinion supports this ambiguity. It is a form of political and pragmatic compromise. In this era of extreme polarization, we must find a path back to a system where compromise is not only possible but respected as one of the requirements of a separation-of-powers system. Polarization is the inevitable result of Americans sorting themselves into different and increasingly hostile camps, which can lead to government paralysis. Self-inflicted economic and political damage is not a rational outcome. Political leaders must recognize this, and those activists and mass voters who support and enable them must demand less gridlock and more action to confront today's problems. Government must be the route to collective decisionmaking. Political elites have to act rationally individually so the system can produce rational aggregate results. Voters, too, must study the issues and the records of the candidates and cast the most informed and rational votes possible. Voters are central not only to the general election but also to the nominations process. They can do better and so can those who represent them.

A

About the Book Sources

This study is based on several primary data sources. The first, and most important, is the author's surveys of Democratic and Republican national convention delegates from 1976 through 2008. That work is described below.

The second is official and unofficial studies of the delegates, the conventions, and the rules drawn from party records, starting with the McGovern-Fraser report, *Mandate for Reform,* 1970. These are cited at the relevant places. A particularly invaluable source is the series of polls of the delegates from 1968 through 2008 and summarized in *CBS News/New York Times,* "Overview of the Democratic Delegates, 1968–2008," and *CBS News/New York Times,* "Overview of the Republican Delegates, 1968–2008." These data were used by permission. They are also reproduced and summarized conveniently in Harold W. Stanley and Richard G. Niemi in their useful series entitled *Vital Statistics on American Politics* and released periodically. The most recent included here is the 2013–14 edition. Tables 1-23 and 1-28 are especially relevant. The data reproduced in chapter 5 used this source, with permission. The advantage these data have is that they are comprehensive and go back to the pre-reform year of 1968.

The third source of data is the work of other scholars who have published studies of convention delegates. Those studies, like the author's, are drawn from surveys of the delegates. The classic work is *The Politics of National Party Conventions,* by Paul T. David, Ralph M. Goldman, and Richard C. Bain. This work was invaluable in setting the basic markers for the pre-reform era. In addition, Jeane Kirkpatrick's study of the 1972 delegates, published in 1976, was also helpful in documenting the first conventions after the McGovern-Fraser reforms. Finally, the data on party identifiers are drawn from the University of Michigan Survey Research Center's American National Election Studies. Each iteration of the author's own surveys was conducted in the same manner. That is, the sample frame was drawn from the official list of names and addresses of each party's national convention delegates and was obtained from the Democratic National Committee or the Republican National Committee or from party sources at the conventions. While there is considerable variation by year and party, essentially each list is organized alphabetically, by state, includes names and addresses, and is published each election year.

We used those lists to draw a systematic random sample each time. The list was entered at a random starting point, and a skip interval was established sufficient for reaching a target of 1,000 initial contacts for each delegation. The Democrats ranged from approximately 3,000 to 4,000 delegates during this period, and the Republicans numbered around 2,000 delegates each year. We started with a sample of approximately 1,000 names. This meant establishing a skip interval, taking every second name for the Republicans and every third name or every fourth name for the Democrats. (For delegation size for each party for this period, see Stanley and Niemi, 2009–10, table 1-27.)

When the survey list was established, the delegates were mailed a questionnaire with a cover letter from the study directors. Since 1992 that cover letter was signed by John S. Jackson from the Paul Simon Public Policy Institute at Southern Illinois University Carbondale and by John C. Green at the Ray C. Bliss Institute at the University of Akron. This cosigning lent an aura of bipartisanship, given the identification of the founders of the two institutes involved. Our general division of labor was that the questionnaires were assembled and mailed from the Paul Simon Institute and returned to the Ray C. Bliss Institute, where the data were coded and assembled. The first wave of the questionnaires was mailed in the week immediately after the party's national convention ended. A second wave for nonresponses was usually mailed in mid-October. Generally the study ended on the day of the national election, although in a few instances stragglers received soon after the national election were included in the final database. The leadership of John C. Green and the staff of the Ray C. Bliss Institute are gratefully acknowledged.

The return rates were generally very good judging by other mailed questionnaire responses. Most years the rates for both parties were in the 40–50 percent range. A few years we dipped into the 30–40 percent range for one or the other party. Each specific year's response rate has been published in previous publications. For example, in 2004 we achieved a response rate of 40 percent for the Democrats and 33 percent for the Republicans. (See Jackson and Green, 2011, 58). In the early years of this study the return rates tended to be in the 40–50 percent range. Usable returns numbered between 300 and 500 for each party. (See author's publications listed in the references for specific return rates for the earlier studies.) It has become difficult to get a high response rate in more recent years. In the earlier years a comparison of the demographic characteristics of the respondents to known characteristics of the full delegate universe showed no significant differences, and the data were not weighted. More recent years show some discrepancies in some demographic groups, especially for low rates of returns for African American delegates some years, and the data had to be weighted to make up for those differences. Overall we are convinced that we have a representative sample of the universe of delegate opinions each year.

In a longitudinal study, question wording is a crucial issue. Where it was relevant and possible we adopted the question wording verbatim from the American National Election Studies. In a few cases, other national surveys, such as the Gallup poll, were used as the source of the questions. In a number of instances we developed the wording for the questions as we needed them. As far as possible we used the same question wording from one year to the next. Questions across the parties were only modified to reflect that party's identification or other occasional idiosyncratic qualities. However, times change, and the standard usage of some words and labels change, and we tried to make modifications when that happened. So some of the longitudinal wording of the questions is not entirely compatible. We have flagged those changes on the tables where appropriate. For example, our question on abortion, or pro-choice versus pro-life, has certainly evolved as the debate has evolved. This problem is probably most troublesome on the issues related to the projected party reforms reported in chapter 7. Overall, however, the basic terms of the debate have remained remarkably stable, increasing the reliability of these results. These are political elites, after all, and they are accustomed to the language and terminology of politics, which is what we tried to capture in these studies.

References

Abramowitz, Alan I. 2010a. "Ideological Realignment among Voters." In Jeffrey Stonecash, ed., *New Directions in American Political Parties*. New York: Routledge.

———. 2010b. "How Large a Wave? Using the Generic Ballot to Forecast the 2010 Midterm Elections." *PS Political Science & Politics* 43, no. 4: 631–32.

———. 2011. *The Disappearing Center: Engaged Citizens, Polarization, and American Democracy*. Yale University Press.

Aldrich, John H. 1995. *Why Parties?* University of Chicago Press.

Almond, Gabriel A. 1960. "Introduction: A Functional Approach to Comparative Politics." In Gabriel A. Almond and James S. Coleman, eds., *The Politics of the Developing Areas*. Princeton University Press.

Almond, Gabriel A., and Sidney Verba. 1963. *The Civic Culture*. Princeton University Press.

American National Election Studies. Various years. Center for Political Studies, University of Michigan (www.electionstudies.org/).

Baer, Denise L., and David Bositis. 1988. *Elite Cadres and Party Coalitions*. New York: Greenwood.

Balz, Dan, and Scott Clement. 2013. "Major Damage to GOP after Shutdown, and Broad Dissatisfaction with Government" (http://washingtonpost.com/politics/poll-major-damage-to-gop-after-shutdown).

Balz, Dan, and Haynes Johnson. 2009. *The Battle for America 2008*. New York: Viking.

Balz, Dan, and James Silberman. 2013. *Collision 2012: Obama vs. Romney and the Future of Elections in America*. New York: Penguin.

Balz, Dan, and others. 2010. *Landmark: The Inside Story of America's New Health Care Law and What It Means to You*. New York: Public Affairs Press.

Barabak, Mark Z. 2014. "GOP Wonders If Iowa Is Too Important in the Presidential Race." McClatchy News, March 10.

Bartels, Larry M. 2000. "Partisanship in Voting Behavior, 1952–1996." *American Journal of Political Science* 44: 35–50.

Bentley, Arthur. 1908. *The Process of Government.* University of Chicago Press.

Berelson, Benard R., Paul F. Lazarsfeld, and William N. McPhee. 1954. *Voting.* University of Chicago Press.

Berrett, Dan. 2012. "Democracy Faces a 'Crucible Moment,' Says Report, but Colleges Can Help." *Chronicle of Higher Education* (www.aacu.org/civic_learning/crucible/).

Binder, Sarah. 2011. "Through the Looking Glass, Darkly: What Has Become of the Senate?" *The Forum* 9, no. 4, article 2 (www.bepress.com/forum/vol9/iss4?art2).

Black, Earl, and Merle Black. 1987. *Politics and Society in the South.* Harvard University Press.

———. 1992. *The Vital South: How Presidents Are Elected.* Harvard University Press.

Broder, David. 1972. *The Party's Over.* New York: Harper and Row.

Burden, Barry C. 2011. "Polarization, Obstruction, and Governing in the Senate." *The Forum* 9, no. 4, article 4 (www.bepress.com/forum/vol9/iss4/art4).

Burnham, Walter Dean. 1970. *Critical Elections and the Mainsprings of American Democracy.* New York: Norton.

Campbell, Angus, and others. 1960. *The American Voter.* New York: Wiley.

Carmines, Edward, and James Stimson. 1989. *Issue Evolution: Race and the Transformation of American Politics.* Princeton University Press.

Carsey, Thomas M., and Geoffrey Layman. 2006. "Changing Sides or Changing Minds? Party Identification and Policy Preferences in the American Electorate." *American Journal of Political Science* 50 (April): 464–77.

CBS News/New York Times. 2008a. "Overview of the Democratic Delegates, 1968–2008," August 24 (www.cbsnews.com).

———. 2008b. "Overview of the Republican Delegates, 1968–2008," August 31 (www.cbsnews.com).

Ceaser, James W. 1979. *Presidential Selection: Theory and Development.* Princeton University Press.

Ceaser, James W., Andrew E. Busch, and John J. Pitney Jr. 2009. *Epic Journey: The 2008 Elections and American Politics.* Lanham, Md.: Rowman and Littlefield.

Cigler, Allan J., and Burdett A. Loomis. 2002. *Interest Group Politics.* 6th ed. Washington: CQ Press.

Clark, Peter B., and James Q. Wilson. 1961. "Incentive Systems: A Theory of Organizations." *Administrative Science Quarterly* 6, no. 2: 129–66.

Clinton, William Jefferson. 2004. *My Life.* New York: Knopf.

Coffey, Daniel J. 2011. "More than a Dime's Worth: Using State Party Platforms to Assess the Degree of American Party Polarization." *PS Political Science & Politics* 44, no. 2: 331–36.

Commission on Party Structure and Delegate Selection. 1970. "Mandate for Reform." Washington: Democratic National Committee.

Committee on Political Parties of the American Political Science Association. 1950. *Toward a More Responsible Two-Party System*. New York: Rinehart.

Converse, Philip. 1964. "The Nature of Belief Systems in Mass Publics." In David Apter, ed., *Ideology and Discontent*. New York: Free Press.

Cooper, Helene, and John H. Cushman Jr. 2012. "Defying Republicans, Obama to Name Cordray as Consumer Agency Chief." *New York Times,* January 4, p. 1.

Cotter, Cornelius P., and Bernard Hennessy. 1964. *Politics without Power: The National Party Committees*. New York: Atherton.

CQ. 1975. *Guide to U.S. Elections*. Washington: CQ Press.

———. 2001. *National Party Conventions: 1831–2008*. Washington: CQ Press.

Craig, Barbara Hinkson, and David M. O'Brien. 1993. *Abortion and American Politics*. Chatham, N.J.: Chatham House.

Crotty, William. 1982. "Two Cheers for the Presidential Primaries." In Thomas E. Cronin, ed., *Rethinking the Presidency*. Boston: Little, Brown.

———. 1984. *American Parties in Decline*. 2nd ed. Boston: Little, Brown.

———. 2001. "Policy Coherence in Political Parties: The Elections of 1984, 1988, and 1992." In Jeffrey Cohen, Richard Fleisher, and Paul Kantor, eds., *American Political Parties: Decline or Resurgence?* Washington: CQ Press.

Crotty, William, and John S. Jackson. 1985. *Presidential Primaries and Nominations*. Washington: CQ Press.

Crotty, William, John S. Jackson, and Melissa Miller. 1999. "Political Activists over Time: Working Elites in the Party System." In Birol A. Yesilada, ed., *Comparative Parties and Party Elites over Time*. University of Michigan Press.

Dahl, Robert A. 1956. *A Preface to Democratic Theory*. University of Chicago Press.

David, Paul T., Ralph M. Goldman, and Richard C. Bain. 1964. *Politics of National Party Conventions*. New York: Vintage.

Delegates and Organizations Committtee. 1971. "The GOP and Reform Report." Washington: Republican National Committee.

Dennis, Jack. 1976. "Trends in Support for the American Party System." *British Journal of Political Science* 5: 187–230.

DiClerico, Robert E., and Eric Uslander. 1984. *Few Are Chosen: Problems in Presidential Selection*. New York: McGraw-Hill.

Downs, Anthony. 1957. *An Economic Theory of Democracy*. New York: Harper and Row.

Dupree, Jamie. 2014. "GOP Moving Ahead with 2016 Primary Challenges." *Atlanta Journal-Constitution,* January 22 (www.ajc.com/wedlogs/jamie-dupree/2014/january/22/gop-moving).

Duverger, Maurice. 1967. *Political Parties: Their Organization and Activity in the Modern State*. New York: Wiley.

Dye, Thomas R., and Susan A. MacManus. 2012. *Politics in States and Communities*. 14th ed. Upper Saddle River, N.J.: Pearson.

Easton, David, and Jack Dennis. 1969. *Children in the Political System.* New York: McGraw-Hill.

Edwards, George C. 2007. *Governing by Campaigning: The Politics of the Bush Presidency.* New York: Pearson Longman.

Eldersveld, Samuel J. 1964. *Political Parties: A Behavioral Analysis.* Chicago: Rand McNally.

Eldersveld, Samuel J., and Hanes Walton Jr. 2000. *Political Parties in American Society.* 2nd ed. Boston: Bedford/St. Martin's.

Eilperin, Juliet. 2006. *Fight Club Politics: How Partisanship Is Poisoning the House of Representatives.* Lanham, Md.: Rowman and Littlefield.

Epstein, Leon. 1979. *Party Politics in Western Democracies.* New Brunswick, N.J.: Transaction.

Eulau, Heinz, and Kenneth Prewitt. 1973. *Labyrinths of Democracy: Adaptations, Linkages, Representation, and Policies in Urban Politics.* Indianapolis: Bobbs-Merrill.

Falcone, Michael. 2013. "How Low Can Congress Go?" *ABC News,* October 22 (http://abcnews.go.com/blogs/politics/2013/10/how-low-can-congress-go-the-note).

Fiorina, Morris P., with Samuel J. Abrams and Jeremy C. Pope. 2005. *Culture War? The Myth of a Polarized America.* New York: Pearson Longman.

Flanigan, William, and Nancy H. Zingale. 2006. *Political Behavior of the American Electorate.* 11th ed. Washington: CQ Press.

Fleisher, Richard, and Jon R. Bond. 2001. "Evidence of Increasing Polarization among Ordinary Citizens?" In Jeffrey Cohen, Richard Fleisher, and Paul Kantor, eds., *American Political Parties: Decline or Resurgence?* Washington: CQ Press.

Gelman, Andrew. 2008. *Red State, Blue State, Rich State, Poor State: Why Americans Vote the Way They Do.* Princeton University Press.

Gibson, James L., Cornelius P. Cotter, John F. Bibby, and Robert J. Huckshorn. 1985. "Whither the Local Parties?" *American Journal of Political Science* 29: 139–60.

Gingrich, Newt. 1994. *Contract with America.* New York: Times Books.

Grant, J. Tobin, and Nathan J. Kelly. 2008. "Legislative Productivity of the U.S. Congress, 1789–2004." *Political Analysis* 16, no. 3: 303–23.

Green, John C., and Daniel J. Coffey. 2007. *The State of the Parties: The Changing Role of Contemporary American Politics.* 5th ed. Lanham, Md.: Rowman and Littlefield.

Green, John C., and Paul S. Herrnson. 2002. *Responsible Partisanship? The Evolution of American Political Parties since 1950.* University Press of Kansas.

Green, Donald, Bradley Palmquist, and Eric Schickler, 2002. *Partisan Hearts & Minds: Political Parties and the Social Identities of Voters.* Yale University Press.

Greenberg, Stanley B. 2004. *The Two Americas: Our Current Political Deadlock and How to Break It.* New York: St. Martin's.

Hadley, Charles D., and Lewis Bowman, eds. 1998. *Party Activists in Southern Politics.* University of Tennessee Press.

Hamby, Alonzo L. 1995. *Man of the People: A Life of Harry S. Truman.* Oxford University Press.

Harris, John F. 2005. *The Survivor: Bill Clinton in the White House.* New York: Random House.

Herrnson, Paul. 1988. *Party Campaigning in the 1980s.* Harvard University Press.

Hershey, Marjorie Randon. 1984. *Running for Office: The Political Education of Campaigners.* Chatham, N.J.: Chatham House.

Hetherington, Marc J. 2001. "Resurgent Mass Partisanship." *American Political Science Review* 95: 619–31.

Hetherington, Marc J., and Jonathan D. Weiler. 2009. *Authoritarianism and Polarization in American Politics.* Cambridge University Press.

Hofstadter, Richard. 1996. *The Paranoid Style in American Politics and Other Essays.* Harvard University Press. [first published 1964]

Huckshorn, Robert J., and John F. Bibby. 1983. "National Party Rules and Delegate Selection in the Republican Party." *Political Science* 16 (Fall): 656–66.

Jackson, John S. 2008a. "The 2008 Presidential Nominations Process, a Marathon and a Sprint: An Analysis of What Happened and Why." Occasional Paper 11. Paul Simon Public Policy Institute, Southern Illinois University.

———. 2008b. "Presidential Nominations and Regional Primaries: An Analysis of Proposals for Reform." Occasional Paper 9. Paul Simon Public Policy Institute, Southern Illinois University.

Jackson, John S., Nathan S. Bigelow, and John C. Green. 2007. "The State of the Party Elites: National Convention Delegates, 1992–2004." In John C. Green and Daniel J. Coffey, eds., *The State of the Parties.* 5th ed. Lanham, Md.: Rowman and Littlefield.

Jackson, John S., Barbara L. Brown, and David Bositis. 1982. "Herbert McClosky and Friends Revisited." *American Politics Research* 10 (April): 158–80.

Jackson, John S., and William Crotty. 2001. *The Politics of Presidential Selection.* New York: Longman.

Jackson, John S., and John C. Green. 2011. "The State of the Party Elites: National Convention Delegates, 1992–2008." In John C. Green and Daniel J. Coffey, eds., *The State of the Parties.* 6th ed. Lanham, Md.: Rowman and Littlefield.

Jacobson, Gary C. 2004. *A Divider, Not a Uniter: George W. Bush and the American People.* New York: Pearson Longman.

Jamieson, Kathleen Hall, and Paul Waldman. 2003. *The Press Effect: Politicians, Journalists, and the Stories that Shape the Political World.* Oxford University Press.

Jennings, M. Kent, and Gregory B. Markus. 1984. "Partisan Orientations over the Long Haul: Results from the Three-Wave Political Socialization Panel Study." *American Political Science Review* 78: 1000–18.

Jennings, M. Kent, and Richard G. Niemi. 1968. "The Transmission of Political Values from Parent to Child." *American Political Science Review* 62: 169–84.

Johnson, Loch K., and Harlan Hahn. 1973. "Delegate Turnover at National Party Conventions, 1944–68." In Donald R. Matthews, ed., *Perspectives on Presidential Selection.* Brookings Institution Press.

Jones, Jeffrey. 2014a. "Record High 42% of Americans Identify as Independents." Gallup poll, January 8 (www.gallup.com/poll/166763/record-high-americans.aspx?utm_alert&ut).

———. 2014b. "Liberal Self-Identification Edges up to New High in 2013." Gallup poll, January 10 (www.gallup.com/poll/166787/liberal-self-identification-edges-new-high-new-high-2013.aspx?utm_source).

Judis, John B., and Ruy Teixeira. 2002. *The Emerging Democratic Majority*. New York: Scribner.

Kamarck, Elaine C. 2009. *Primary Politics: How Presidential Candidates Have Shaped the Modern Nominating System*. Brookings Institution Press.

Kessel, John H. 1968. *The Goldwater Coalition: Republican Strategies in 1964*. Indianapolis: Bobbs-Merrill.

Key, V. O., Jr. 1958. *Politics, Parties and Pressure Groups*. 4th ed. New York: Thomas Y. Crowell.

Kingdon, John W. 1999. *America the Unusual*. New York: Worth.

Kirkpatrick, Jeane. 1976. *The New Presidential Elite: Men and Women in National Politics*. New York: Russell Sage/Twentieth-Century Fund.

———. 1978. *Dismantling the Parties: Reflections on Party Reform*. Washington: American Enterprise Institute.

Kohut, Andrew, John C. Green, Scott Keeter, and Robert C. Toth, 2000. *The Diminishing Divide: Religion's Changing Role in American Politics*. Brookings Institution Press.

Leiserson, Avery. 1958. *Parties and Politics: An Institutional and Behavioral Approach*. New York: Knopf.

Levendusky, Matthew. 2009. *The Partisan Sort: How Liberals Became Democrats and Conservatives Became Republicans*. University of Chicago Press.

Lindbloom, Charles E. 1959. "The Science of Muddling Through." *Public Administrative Review* 19 (Spring): 79–88.

Maggiotto, Michael A., and Gary D. Wekkin. 2000. *Partisan Linkages in Southern Politics: Elites, Voters, and Identifiers*. University of Tennessee Press.

Maisel, Sandy, ed. 1994. *The Parties Respond: Changes in the American Party System*. Boulder, Colo.: Westview.

Malbin, Michael J., ed. 2006. *The Election after Reform*. Lanham, Md.: Rowman and Littlefield.

Mayer, William G. 2009. "Superdelegates: Reforming the Reforms Revisited." In Steven S. Smith and Melanie J. Springer, eds., *Reforming the Presidential Nomination Process*. Brookings Institution Press.

McCarty, Nolan, Keith T. Poole, and Howard Rosenthal. 2006. *Polarized America: The Dance of Ideology and Unequal Riches*. MIT Press.

McClosky, Herbert, Paul J. Hoffman, and Rosemary O'Hara. 1960. "Issue Conflict and Consensus among Party Leaders and Followers." *American Political Science Review* 56 (June): 406–29.

McCullough, David. 1992. *Truman*. New York: Simon and Schuster.

McGinniss, Joe. 1969. *The Selling of the President: 1968.* New York: Washington Square Press.

McMullen, Jody, and Barbara Norrander. 2000. "The Gender Gap in Presidential Nominations." In William Mayer, ed., *In Pursuit of the White House 2000.* New York: Chatham House.

Milbrath, Lester W., and M. L. Goel. 1977. *Political Behavior.* Chicago: Rand McNally.

Miller, Warren. 1988. *Without Consent: Mass-Elite Linkages in Presidential Politics.* University Press of Kentucky.

Miller, Warren E., and M. Kent Jennings. 1986. *Parties in Transition: A Longitudinal Study of Party Elites and Party Supporters.* New York: Russell Sage.

Miller, Warren E., and Donald Stokes. 1963. "Constituency Influence in Congress." *American Political Science Review* 57 (March): 45–56.

Monroe, Kristen Renwick. 1991. "The Theory of Rational Action." In William Crotty, ed., *Political Science: Looking to the Future: The Theory and Practice of Political Science.* Vol. 1. Northwestern University Press.

Myrdal, Gunnar. 1944. *An American Dilemma: The Negro Problem and Modern Democracy.* New York: Harper.

Nakamura, David, and Felicia Sommez. 2012. "Richard Cordray Appointed by Obama to Head Consumer Watchdog Bureau." *Washington Post,* January 4 (www.washingtonpost.com/politics'rachard-cordray-appointed).

National Task Force on Civic Learning and Democratic Engagement. 2012. "A Crucible Moment: College Learning and Democratic Engagement." Washington: Association of American Colleges and Universities (www.aacu.org/civic_learning/crucible/index).

Neal, Steve. 2002. *Harry and Ike: The Partnership that Remade the Postwar World.* New York: Scribner.

Nelson, Candice J. 2011. *Grant Park: The Democratization of Presidential Elections, 1968–2008.* Brookings Institution Press.

Neustadt, Richard. 1960. *Presidential Power: The Politics of Leadership.* New York: Wiley.

Newport, Frank. 2011. "Congress Ends 2011 with Record-Low 11% Approval." Gallup poll, December 22 (www.gallup.com/poll/151628/Congress-Ends-2011-Record-Low).

Pareto, Vilfredo. 1935. *The Mind and Society: A Treatise on General Sociology.* Vol. 3. Translated by Andrew Bongirno and Arthur Livingston. New York: Dover.

Phillips, Kevin. 1969. *The Emerging Republican Majority.* N.Y.: Arlington House

Pika, Joseph A., and John Anthony Maltese. 2002. *The Politics of the Presidency.* 5th ed. Washington: CQ Press.

Pitkin, Hannah F. 1987. *The Concept of Representation.* University of California Press.

Polsby, Nelson, 1983. *The Consequences of Reform.* Oxford University Press.

Pomper, Gerald M. 1980. *Party Renewal in America.* New York: Praeger.

———. 1996. "Alive! The Political Parties after the 1980–1992 Presidential Elections." In Harvey L. Schantz, ed., *American Presidential Elections.* State University of New York Press.

————. 2001. "Party Responsibility and the Future of American Democracy." In Jeffrey Cohen, Richard Fleisher, and Paul Kantor, eds., *American Political Parties: Decline or Resurgence?* Washington: CQ Press.

Pomper, Gerald M., and Susan S. Lederman. 1980. *Elections in America.* New York: Longman.

Pomper, Gerald M., and Marc D. Weiner. 2002. "Toward a More Responsible Two-Party Voter." In John C. Green and Paul S. Herrnson, eds., *Responsible Partisanship?* University Press of Kansas.

Popkin, Samuel L. 1991. *The Reasoning Voter: Communication and Persuasion in Presidential Campaigns.* University of Chicago Press.

Powell, Lee Riley. 1996. *J. William Fulbright and His Time.* Memphis: Guild Bindery Press.

Prewitt, Kenneth. 1970. *The Recruitment of Political Leaders: A Study of Citizen-Politicians.* Indianapolis: Bobbs-Merrill.

Putnam, Robert D., and David E. Campbell. 2010. *American Grace.* New York: Simon and Schuster.

Ragsdale, Lyn. 1988. *Vital Statistics on the Presidency.* Washington: CQ Press.

————. 1975. *Curing the Mischief of Faction.* University of California Press.

Ranney, Austin. 1975. *Curing the Mischief of Faction.* University of California Press.

Rapoport, Ronald B., and Walter J. Stone. 2005. *Three's a Crowd: The Dynamic of Third Parties, Ross Perot, and Republican Resurgence.* University of Michigan Press.

Rasmussen, Scott. 2011. "New High: 48% Say Most Members of Congress Are Corrupt." Rasmussen polls, December 31 (www.rasmussenreports.com/public_content/politics/general_politics).

Reiter, Howard L. 1985. *Selecting the President: The Nominating Process in Transition.* University of Pennsylvania Press.

Rohde, David, and John Aldrich. 2010. "Consequences of Electoral and Institutional Change: The Evolution of Conditional Party Government in the U.S. House of Representatives." In Jeffrey Stonecash, ed., *New Directions in American Political Parties.* New York: Routledge.

Rossiter, Clinton. 1960. *The American Presidency.* Rev. ed. New York: Harcourt Brace.

Sabato, Larry J. 2009. "Picking Presidential Nominees." In Steven S. Smith and Melanie J. Springer, eds., *Reforming the Presidential Nomination Process.* Brookings Institution Press.

Sabato, Larry J., and Bruce Larson. 2002. *The Party's Just Begun: Shaping Political Parties for America's Future.* 2nd ed. New York: Longman.

Savage, Sean. 1991. *Roosevelt the Party Leader, 1932–1945.* University Press of Kentucky.

Schattschneider, E. E. 1942. *Party Government.* New York: Holt, Rinehart, and Winston.

————. 1960. *The Semi-Sovereign People.* New York: Holt, Rinehart, and Winston.

Schlesinger, Joseph A. 1966. *Ambition and Politics: Political Careers in the United States.* Chicago: Rand McNally.

———. 1991. *Political Parties and the Winning of Office.* University of Michigan Press.

Schmidt, Michael S. 2014. "Obama, Aggravated by Gridlock, Stresses Results in Midterms." *New York Times,* May 9 (http://nyti.ms/SK7Crq).

Shafer, Byron E. 1988. *Bifurcated Politics: Evolution and Reform in the National Party Convention.* Harvard University Press.

———. 1991. *The End of Realignment? Interpreting American Electoral Eras.* University Press of Wisconsin.

Silk, Mark, and Andrew Walsh. 2008. *One Nation, Divisible: How Regional Religious Differences Shape American Politics.* Lanham, Md.: Rowman and Littlefield Publishers.

Simon, Herbert A. 1957. *Administrative Behavior.* 2nd ed. New York: Macmillan.

———. 1982. *Models of Bounded Rationality.* Vol. 1. MIT Press.

———. 2000. "Public Administration in Today's World of Organizations and Markets." *PS Political Science & Politics* (December): 749–56.

Simon, Paul. 1989. *Winners and Losers.* New York: Continuum.

Simon, Roger. 2013. *Reckoning: Campaign 2012 and the Battle for the Soul of America.* Los Angeles: Sumner Books.

Skinner, Richard M. 2008–09. "George W. Bush and the Partisan Presidency." *Political Science Quarterly* 123 (Winter): 605–23.

Smith, Steven S., and Melanie J. Springer, eds. 2009. *Reforming the Presidential Nomination Process.* Brookings Institution Press.

Sorauf, Frank. 1992. *Inside Campaign Finance.* Yale University Press.

Sorauf, Frank, and Paul A. Beck. 1988. *Party Politics in America.* 6th ed. Harper Collins.

Southwell, Priscilla L. 2012. "A Backroom without the Smoke? Superdelegates and the 2008 Democratic Nomination Process." *Party Politics* 18, no. 2: 267–83.

Stanley, Harold W., and Richard G. Niemi. 1992, 2000, 2006, 2007, 2008, 2009–10, 2013–14. *Vital Statistics on American Politics.* Washington: CQ Press.

Stockman, David. 1984. *The Triumph of Politics: Why the Reagan Revolution Failed.* New York: Harper and Row.

Stonecash, Jeffrey, ed. 2010. *New Directions in American Political Parties.* New York: Routledge.

Theiss-Morse, Michael W. Wagner, William H. Flanigan, and Nancy H. Zingale. 2011. *Political Behavior in Midterm Elections.* Washington: CQ Press.

Truman, David. 1951. *The Governmental Process.* 2nd ed. New York: Knopf.

Verba, Sidney, and Norman Nie. 1972. *Participation in America.* New York: Harper and Row.

Wattenberg, Martin P. 1991. *The Rise of Candidate-Centered Politics.* Harvard University Press.

White, John Kenneth. 2003. *The Values Divide.* Chatham, N.J.: Chatham House.

White, John Kenneth, and Jerome M. Mileur, eds. 1992. *Challenges to Party Government.* Southern Illinois University Press.

White, John Kenneth, and Dan Shea. 2001. *New Party Politics: From Jefferson and Hamilton to the Information Age.* Boston: Bedford/St. Martin's.

White, Theodore H. 1962. *The Making of the President 1960.* New York: Pocket Books.

Wilcox, Clyde. 2000. *Onward Christian Soldiers? The Religious Right in American Politics.* 2nd ed. Boulder, Colo.: Westview.

Wildavsky, Aaron. 1965. "The Goldwater Phenomenon: Purists, Politicians, and the Two-Party System." *Review of Politics* 27: 386–413.

Wilson, James Q. 1962. *The Amateur Democrat: Club Politics in Three Cities.* University of Chicago Press.

Witcover, Jules. 1977. *Marathon: The Pursuit of the Presidency: 1972–1976.* New York: Viking.

Zald, Meyer. 1970. *The Political Economy of the YMCA.* University of Chicago Press.

Zald, Meyer, and Patricia Denton. 1963. "From Evangelism to General Services: The Transformation of the YMCA." *Administrative Science Quarterly* 8 (September): 214–34.

Zaller, John R. 1992. *The Nature and Origins of Mass Opinion.* Cambridge University Press.

Index

Clinton, William J. ("Bill"): DLC and, 94; elections of, 28, 36, 45, 80–81, 123, 124, 210; image of, 117; national health insurance and, 101, 136; philosophies and policies of, 124; recruitment of party activists by, 160; size and scope of federal government and, 99

Clinton (William J.) administration, 106–07

Clyburn, James ("Jim;" D-S.C.), 53

Cold war, 5, 105, 106

Commission on Party Structure and Delegate Selection (1970; McGovern-Fraser Commission), 3, 7, 19, 47, 49–53, 54, 56, 57, 60–61, 68, 189, 208

Commission on Presidential Nomination Timing and Scheduling (2004), 53

Commissions: Fowler Commission (1984–88), 53; Hunt Commission (1980–84), 53, 55, 164; McCaskill-Clyburn Commission, 53–54; Mikulski Commission (1972–76), 53, 70; Schattschneider Commission (1950s), 199; Winograd Commission (1976–80), 53, 71–72, 164

Committee on Political Parties (APSA), 190

Congress: ability to govern, 196; approval rating of, 197–98; compromise and, 200, 211–14; congressional elections, 23, 33–34; elections of 1964 and, 33; elections of 2010 and, 37; midterm elections and, 35; national health insurance and, 103; partisan polarization in, 17, 37; political parties and, 8; powers delegated to, 5; president and, 37, 205; public opinion of, 97; Republican Party and, 44

Congressional caucus, 6

Conservatives and conservatism, 120–45, 174–88, 190–91. *See also* Polarization and partisanship; Political parties; *individual conservatives by name*

Constitution (U.S.): articles of, 5; checks and balances and, 194, 201; selection and election of presidents and, 6; separation of powers and, 194, 201; Twenty-sixth Amendment to, 69

Contract with America (1994), 98–99, 113

Conventions: advent of national convention system, 33; bargaining in, 162; brokered conventions, 59, 64–66, 162; candidates and, 6; Commission on Party Structure and Delegate Selection and, 52–53; federal subsidies for, 53; ideological tenor of, 96; party bosses and, 162; party elites and, 192; reforms and rules, 22, 48–53, 64–65, 162–64; role of, 52–53; segregation of, 74; selection of presidential nominees, 52; strategic planning and, 71; winners in, 187–88; winner-take-all rules, 52, 57, 58–59. *See also* Elections; Primaries and caucuses; Public policy issues

Conventions—delegates: abortion and, 110; allocation of, 58; at-large designation of, 165; attaining the position, 152; campaign focus on, 57–58; circulation of elites, 191–92; cognitive and social skills of, 83–84, 148–49; convention delegate selection process, 66t, 67–68, 152–53, 154, 172; court rulings for, 65; delegates at their first convention, 149–55; demographic representation and, 68; effect of rules changes for ethnic minorities, 74–79; effect of rules changes for women and superdelegates, 70–74, 76, 164; effect of rules changes for youth, 79–81; election reform and, 165–68; ideology of, 92, 93t, 118t, 119t; increased diversity among, 89–90; local and state parties and, 2; naming of party nominees and, 2; occupations, education, and

2/12/16

CPSIA information can be obtained at www.ICGtesting.com
Printed in the USA
LVOW07s1524020216

473347LV00002B/594/P